Communication Ethics in an Age of Diversity

Communication Ethics in an Age of Diversity

Edited by
Josina M. Makau and Ronald C. Arnett

University of Illinois Press
Urbana and Chicago

This book is printed on acid-free paper.

Library of Congress Cataloging-in-Publication Data

Communication ethics in an age of diversity / edited by Josina M. Makau and
  Ronald C. Arnett.
      p.   cm.
    Includes bibliographical references and index.
    ISBN 0-252-02269-6 (acid-free paper). — ISBN 0-252-06571-9 (pbk. : acid-
free paper)
    1. Communication—Moral and ethical aspects. 2. Pluralism (Social sciences).
I. Makau, Josina M.   II. Arnett, Ronald C., 1952– .
  P94.C572   1997
  174—dc20   96-4496
                                                                CIP

Contents

Preface

JOSINA M. MAKAU AND RONALD C. ARNETT

Little more than a decade ago, James Jaksa, co-director of the Western Michigan University Center for the Study of Ethics in Society, worked with colleagues from around the nation to form an organizational base for those dedicated to the study of communication ethics. This volume commemorates the tenth anniversary of the resulting formation of the Speech Communication Association's Commission on Communication Ethics. Three National Ethics Conferences, a syllabus clearing house, a widely distributed newsletter, numerous convention programs, and this volume attest to the organization's high level of activity since its inception.

The chapters in this volume focus on issues of particular importance to the commission's membership. As the authors of each of the chapters note, ethical communication theory, practice, and pedagogy do not occur in a vacuum. How we communicate with one another is influenced significantly by numerous social, political, economic, and other cultural factors. Similarly, culture is shaped in large part by the nature and quality of our communication interactions. Massive changes in national and international demographics have redefined cultural boundaries. The resulting racial, ethnic, religious, and sexual diversity brings with it both promise and challenges unique to this age. At the same time, major social changes brought about by technological interventions call upon us to reconsider long-standing assumptions about how, when, and with whom we interact. In less than three decades the world has been transformed by the infiltration of computers, FAX machines, satellite dishes, and other technology. These changes have called forward a new era in social and critical thought. Scholars and practitioners in all disciplines are called upon to acknowledge and question long-standing foundational assumptions about relationships between symbols, culture, knowledge acquisition, production, and use.

The authors in this volume provide insights of value to anyone engaged in this difficult process of inquiry. They consider implications to a diversity of communication contexts—from personal friendships to communication over the Internet, from intimate classroom dialogues to mass-mediated communication. Together, the communication ethicists represented in this volume seek to help develop constructive responses to the challenges unique to this age.

The overall goal of this series of essays is to help frame the communicative ethics needed to guide interaction and actions in the emerging age of diversity. Recognizing the complexities associated with diverse contexts, the book provides a forum for exploring issues related to each of the following: race, ethnicity, gender, and sexual orientation. The volume examines related pedagogical and free speech issues, media practices, issues related to the emerging Internet, and communication associated with high-risk technologies. The volume invites readers to consider perspectives on ethnicity research and to explore the nature and functions of friendship and community building.

Each essay is written by a major communication scholar whose expertise relates directly to the selected set of issues. The essays identify significant ethical concerns, make clear the significance of these concerns for the broader cultural context, and offer guidance for ethical responses to the challenges posed by the context in question.

The volume is divided into three parts. Part 1, "Dialogue in the Midst of Diversity," explores the impact of diversity on interpersonal communication, community building, and pedagogy. This section invites readers to consider not only the complexities accompanying the recognition of our world's rich diversity, but also the promise inherent in that diversity.

Wood's essay explores implications of difference and commonality on the development of friendships. She encourages readers to embrace the tension between diversity and commonality. Borrowing from recent insights in the field, her essay offers an ethical framework for relational communication. Arnett outlines the dialectical tension of exclusion and inclusion that guides a sense of community. His essay suggests specific means for building community in public discourse that honors diversity. Finally, Makau's essay explores relationships between diversity, communication ethics, and responsible pedagogy. She argues that problems commonly associated with diversity actually find their roots in incompetent and unethical communication practices. She suggests strategies for developing responsible and responsive pedagogy.

Part 2, "Culture, Diversity, and Ethics," examines issues associated with race and ethnicity, gender differences, and sexual orientation. This section underscores the importance of acknowledging and understanding the notion of a situated self. Peoples' experiences are influenced significantly by their standing within the broader community. At the same time, experiences shape meaning within and outside one's culture(s). Recognizing that norms and practices are influenced significantly by communally defined practices in turn calls upon scholars, educators, and practitioners to take seriously the impact of viewing individuals as situated beings within a specific historical era impacted by such cultural constructs as race, ethnicity, and sexual orientation. The authors explore the extraordinary complexity of this interplay.

Tanno traces uses of the term "ethnic" to illustrate the profound impact of language use on people's beliefs, perceptions, and actions. She proposes guidelines for ethical language use in research within and across ethnic boundaries. Paige Pointer and Young address issues of race and ethnicity. They raise challenging questions for mainstream approaches to communication ethics. Their analysis suggests, among other things, the presence of systemic bias and widespread deception. They propose an alternative frame designed to facilitate constructive incorporation of diversity issues into ethical communication practice and pedagogy. Stewart invites consideration of similar views in her discussion of cross-gender communication. Her essay includes a set of guidelines for ethical communication between masculine and feminine cultures. Chesebro's chapter pursues a communication ethic for same-sex relations. Noting that society has the potential to foster or inhibit communication ethics, Chesebro offers insights intended to facilitate ethical interaction.

Part 3, "Technology, Diversity, and Responsibility," explores the ethical implications of technologically mediated communication. Johannesen examines the complex relationships between freedom and responsibility in contemporary communication contexts. His exploration of issues associated with rap music lyrics, the distribution of pornography, and the problem of hate speech reveals the need to reconsider guidelines for ethically responsible exercise of free speech. Christians's essay assesses the technological structure of mass media in terms of global diversity. He argues that moral purpose is ravaged by the spirit of "the machine" and calls for a reordering of media systems around communitarian ethics. Jaksa and Pritchard seek to develop standards of communication for those whose products place consumers at risk. They apply the concept of informed consent from medical ethics to communication ethics in the distribution and sale of high-risk products. Finally, Kramer and Kramarae address complex ethical issues associated with the emerging Internet. They note that many have identified this new communication medium as a solution to social and educational problems. Computer communications potentially eliminate inequities associated with race, gender, ethnicity, age, physical abilities, and so on. In this sense, the Internet promises to become a great equalizer. Kramer and Kramarae discuss how well current approaches to Internet ethics have helped systems realize this potential.

Using the problem of sexism as a case study, they explore the potential and challenges of Internet systems and communications. In particular, they consider four conceptual themes dominating these early days of the Internet—anarchy, frontier, community, and democracy—and look at the ways they have shaped the beliefs, ideology, and ethics of the Internet. They reveal serious shortcomings with each of these themes, arguing for an alternate approach that utilizes feminist discussions.

Covering different foci and starting points and representing sometimes sharply differing perspectives, these essays nevertheless draw several remarkably similar conclusions. Throughout the volume, the authors conclude that communication ethics in an age of diversity requires the will and ability to listen carefully, to pursue and practice mutual respect, invite reciprocity and inclusiveness, and to live openly and responsibly with the dialectical tensions inherent in commonality and difference. These findings challenge us to carefully consider recent deliberations about the nature and function of communicative ethics. On the one hand, the essays support strongly the kind of work Habermas and others have done encouraging moves away from instrumental to communicative action. On the other hand, however, they challenge ethicists to consider narrative and cognitivist approaches to communicative ethics. Despite their many differences, most of the authors in this volume appear to call for a revisioning of much communication theory, practice, and pedagogy.

Particularly noteworthy in this regard is the evidence of postmodern influences on the majority of the essays. Many of the authors challenge enlightenment approaches to ethical issues, calling for the abandonment of abstract universalism. Most acknowledge the role society plays in shaping ethical ideological frameworks. Emotions receive acknowledgment and serious attention in many of the chapters. The chapters also share a recognition that fruitful scholarship on communication ethics integrates theory and *praxis*. The authors reject modernist tendencies to denigrate applied research.

Significantly, however, most of the authors in this volume affirm the enlightenment's critique of privatized truth. Most of the authors also reject the postmodern tendency to abandon the quest to find meaningful ways to deliberate across differences about ethical issues. The chapters in this volume are written with the hope of contributing to this critical but difficult search.

Readers will find in this volume not only theoretical insight, but specific proposals for ethical theory, practice, and pedagogy. The result is a richly nuanced, provocative volume designed to invite continued dialogue. Only through such interaction can we hope to meet the challenges and fulfill the promise associated with the emerging age of diversity.

PART I

Dialogue in the Midst of Diversity

Introduction

The chapters in this opening section of *Communication Ethics in an Age of Diversity* explore how we might invite and celebrate diversity. This section focuses on the implementation and action of communication ethics—building paths for diversity through relationship development, community formation, and pedagogy. As Aristotle suggested, ethics needs to move to the arena of action. The test of any practical philosophy, including a communication ethics, is exemplified in everyday praxis.

The praxis of an academic includes both professional and personal contexts and interactions. Our professional and personal lives offer opportunities for relationship development and for the invitations of human communication. Our approaches to relationship and community building both influence and are affected by our understanding of communication ethics. These elements of professional and personal practice reflect our commitment to nourishing diversity.

Julia T. Wood's "Diversity in Dialogue: Commonalities and Differences between Friends," reminds us that embracing differences in friendship is not only key to nourishing diversity, but to the nurturance of any relationship. It is not only commonality that propels friendships, but difference. Varied "standpoints" point us to new insight; the diversity that surrounds us permits the richness of different standpoints to guide and direct action with a more collective vision. In essence, diversity in friendship helps human beings see more of the horizon of the world.

Ronald C. Arnett's "Communication and Community in an Age of Diversity" examines the limits of a conception of community that embraces Sartre's notion of "bad faith," reconsidering optimistic calls for inclusion without change or sacrifice on the part of new and traditional members. Arnett suggests that inclusion and exclusion both define community. He begins to explore how such a view of community can coexist with a commitment to diversity. Public guidelines for community inclusion become key, and the question of attainability of meeting those guidelines, regardless of racial, ethnic, religious, class, affectional orientation, or gender stance is central to a view of community with a public face and a genuine commitment to diversity. Community in a public context committed to diversity reflects an ethic of communicative action; "doing" moves one in or outside a community.

Action that is diversity sensitive calls for friendships that see the limits of commonality and the contributions of diversity; such communities offer public access because of what one can accomplish and contribute, not because of biology, religion, or socioeconomic status. Diversity of ethnic, racial, religious, class, affectional orientation, and gender perspectives opens us to a broader array of possibilities, permitting difference to enhance and commonality to be found in the realm of action and achievement.

Josina M. Makau's essay, "Embracing Diversity in the Classroom," explores similar issues. She challenges mainstream conceptions of diversity, noting that the concept encompasses a broad range of possible meanings. Her definition calls for a celebration of both the individual and the community, of group location and each person's authentic self. She stresses the importance of developing the ability and desire to engage in ethical dialogic interaction across differences.

Engendering the will and capacity for ethical dialogic interaction requires, however, responsible and responsive pedagogy. Such education is designed to prepare students for ethical participation in communication processes linking persons of diversity in meaningful and just relationships of community.

1   Diversity in Dialogue: Commonalities and Differences between Friends

Julia T. Wood

Historically, the United States has been thought of as a melting pot in which diverse people are assimilated into a uniform substance. Yet, other metaphors are possible. The Reverend Jesse Jackson, for instance, describes the United States as a family quilt that derives its beauty from the distinctiveness of its peoples. Flora Davis (1991) sees the country as a salad bowl whose character depends on differences among ingredients. Reflecting radically divergent attitudes toward diversity and commonality, a melting pot privileges homogeneity and seeks to nullify differences, whereas a salad or family quilt exceeds, yet does not erase, the uniqueness of constituent parts.

Metaphors such as these also express stances toward differences in friendships, which is the concern of this chapter. In it I trace themes of difference and commonality among people, leading me to propose that embracing, rather than resolving, the tension between diversity and commonality is most likely to cultivate personal growth and relationship satisfaction. Underlying my perspective is dialectical theory (Baxter 1988, 1990), which holds that human relationships are marked by tension between contradictory impulses that coexist in an ongoing and productive tension.

My personal interest in this topic is fueled by two important friendships in my life. For many years my friend Louise and I have shared the comings and goings of our days by talking about pleasures and problems, rough spots and moments of joy. Bill, another friend, gives me advice and sometimes hands-on help with computer programming, and he introduces me to new music. I edit his manuscripts and join him for local concerts. Yet because Bill neither seeks nor savors personal conversation, I've felt less close to him. Lately, however, that feeling has attenuated as I've learned that my unacknowledged assumptions about "the right way" to be a friend hindered me from appreciating and exploring different ways people express caring and commitment.

Although Bill and Louise enact closeness differently, they are similar in their commitment to friendship. Because commonalities typically coexist with differences, I launch this chapter by identifying widely shared orientations toward friendship. Next, I explore how disparate social standpoints craft distinctive perspectives on friendship, which may provoke tensions if they are not understood. Finally, I weave together themes of similarities and differences to suggest how, as individuals and as a society, we might ideally engage the dialectic of diversity and commonality.

Commonalities in Human Friendships

This volume's focus on diversity could tempt us to overlook commonalities in diverse peoples' orientations to friendship. Yet similarities among humans form a backdrop for noticing differences that arise out of race, class, gender, affectional preference, and other dimensions of identity. By first considering commonalities we create a context for discussing differences in human friendship.

Common Needs and Goals

Certain interpersonal needs seem common, at least among Westerners. Regardless of race, affectional orientation, gender, and class, humans seek personal affirmation, support, and acceptance from friends, family members, and romantic partners (Sherrod 1989).

Shared interpersonal needs foster common goals for friendships. Even widely held ideas about distinctly gendered objectives—women want intimacy, men companionship—seem overstated (Wright 1988). According to Sherrod (1989), both sexes agree that friendships should provide intimacy, acceptance, trust, and help, a finding echoed by others (Berscheid, Snyder, and Omoto 1989; Jones 1991). Monsour concluded that

women and men have "more similarities than differences in the meanings given to intimacy" (1992:289).

Most recently, Duck and Wright (1993) conducted a sophisticated
analysis of research on sex differences in friendship. They discovered that
men and women are quite similar in what they regard as important in
friendships, although they differ somewhat in how they pursue common
goals. For instance, both sexes want to feel close to friends, yet women
favor personal talk as a route to closeness, while doing things together is
the path men tend to select (Inman 1996; Paul and White 1990; Riessman 1990; Wright 1982). So the sexes differ primarily in the means they
emphasize for realizing shared friendship goals.

Common Willingness to Invest

People also seem relatively similar in their willingness to invest time,
effort, energy, and thought in friendships that matter to them. We have
no evidence of significant differences among races, classes, genders, sexual preferences, or ethnicities in tendencies to care about, help, support,
and make sacrifices for friends. Sherrod's (1989) study of women's and
men's friendships, for example, found that both sexes value friendships
highly and identify close friends as an important part of a fulfilling life.
Although people may not always recognize or appreciate diverse ways of
expressing care, alternative styles should not be conflated with differences
in actual involvement and commitment. This suggests that interpretations of difference are a greater source of tension than differences per se,
a theme to which I will return later in this chapter.

Our somewhat surprising starting point for thinking about diversity
is recognizing commonalities in expectations of and commitments to
friendship. Existing research indicates that, differences notwithstanding,
most people share basic interpersonal needs, goals, and desires to invest
in friendships. With this foundation, we are now ready to consider differences that punctuate friendships and to ask what difference differences
make in the rewards and challenges of sustaining close relationships.

The Origins of Diversity in Friendship

Every friendship reflects the unique personalities of those who create
it. Yet, beyond individual idiosyncrasies, variations in friendship styles
reflect participation in dissimilar social groups. All social groups form
distinctive attitudes, values, and ways of interacting that are routinely
inculcated in members. Understanding divergencies in friendship, then,

requires inquiry into the genesis of patterned differences in the perspectives of social groups.

The Genesis of Diversity: Social Standpoints

Societies organize themselves by creating groups with distinct status and privilege, which, in turn, shape members' access to experiences, opportunities, activities, and circumstances. Thus, location within social groups profoundly influences personal identity, what and how we know, values we embrace, and codes of conduct and communication we consider appropriate in sundry situations.

One way to understand different social locations is to think of them as points where people stand within a culture. Typifying this perspective is standpoint theory, which contends that the place we occupy in the social order affects how we understand ourselves and the world and, therefore, how we think, feel, and act. In her influential book, *Whose Science? Whose Knowledge?*, Sandra Harding (1991) synthesized and extended much of the germinal work that gave birth to standpoint theory (Haraway 1988; Hartsock 1983, 1990; Collins 1986; Ruddick 1989; Smith 1987). Calling attention to the epistemological significance of different positions within a society, standpoint theory claims that social groups sculpt members' experiences of the world, themselves, and, therefore, what is known and valued.

A standpoint is a position within an overall organization that is established by material and symbolic circumstances within which a given group exists (see Hennessy 1993). Primary in the construction of social positions is discourse, which upholds (or resists) culturally authorized ways of sense making. Because knowledge of "reality" is inevitably mediated symbolically, the meanings of all phenomena—including ourselves—are constrained by discourses available in a given time and place (Wood 1993d, 1994c). In illuminating different and differentially valued positions constructed by societies, standpoint logic reveals how symbolically encumbered conditions and frameworks enable and foreclose particular activities, interests, and identities for members of various social groups (Harding 1991).

According to standpoint theory, differences among social groups are produced and reproduced by cultural structures and practices that designate criteria such as sex and race for assigning individuals to groups accorded unequal status and opportunity. Within modern Western culture, for instance, privilege is conferred on those who are European American, heterosexual, male, and middle or upper class; subordination and marginalization accompany membership in groups outside of those social categories. Once distinct groups are constructed, a culture prescribes specific roles that involve and exclude particular activities, which further constrain members' perceptions, knowledge, and subjective consciousness. By allowing disparate experiences to distinct groups, a culture inculcates in members the very features originally used to define the group. Through this process societies systematically reproduce themselves.

Gendered Standpoints

Research on gender demonstrates how standpoints generate different understandings of friendship. Within Western culture gender is primary to social organization (Bem 1993; Fox-Genovese 1991; Harding 1991; Janeway 1971; Miller 1986; Okin 1989; Wood 1993c, 1993d, 1994a, 1994b, 1996). Changes in social attitudes and women's and men's roles notwithstanding, sedimented cultural beliefs define women and femininity by deference, care giving, emotionality, responsiveness, and relationships with others; men and masculinity are characterized by assertion, power, control, rationality, and independence. From birth on, parents, teachers, peers, the media, and others inundate males and females with genderizing messages. Boys are encouraged to play outside, be autonomous, seek challenges, assert themselves, and compete to attain and sustain status. Girls, in contrast, are more typically encouraged to play inside and with others, be caring and cooperative, and maintain harmony.

Because genderizing is ubiquitous and incessant, it is unsurprising that most, but not all, members of each sex are socialized into prescribed gender roles. This is why, for instance, Chodorow (1978, 1989) argues that mothering reproduces mothering, and Ruddick (1989) contends that the process of mothering promotes nurturing and an attentiveness to others. On a personal level this instills relational, responsive orientations in individual women and independence in individual men; on a cultural level genderizing reproduces women's social roles as relationship experts and care givers and men's social roles as autonomous actors.

Socializing processes, then, reproduce women and men as distinct social groups by exposing them to different experiences that normalize dissimilar ways of perceiving, valuing, thinking, and acting. Although group membership based on race, class, and affectional preference also shapes individuals' perspectives, gender seems to generate general differences that hold across other aspects of standpoint. Because feminine socialization emphasizes building connections through personal interaction, women generally rely on talk to create and express closeness with friends

(Aries 1987; Johnson 1989, 1996; Wood 1993b, 1993c, 1994a, 1994b). In contrast, masculine socialization underscores independence and instrumentality, which incline men to use activities more than personal communication to build and sustain friendship (Aries 1987; Maltz and Borker 1982; Tannen 1990b; Wood 1993b, 1993c; Wood and Inman 1993).

Standpoint and Communication Cultures

Standpoint theory can be extended to divulge how communication practices of particular social groups embody and create diverse understandings of friendship. Roughly two decades ago scholars began to notice that different social groups develop distinctive communication practices and patterns that reflect their circumstances and shape how they interact and attribute meaning. According to William Labov (1972), who pioneered this line of inquiry, a communication culture exists when a group of people has understandings of goals and strategies of talk that are not shared by those outside the group and when these understandings are routinely inculcated in new members of the culture (e.g., infants).

Since the 1970s, scholars have identified a number of communication cultures including African American, Hispanic, gay, elderly, lesbian, Native American, people with disabilities, and gender (see Samovar and Porter 1993). Within each culture, or social group, members are socialized into common perspectives on why, when, and how to communicate. Although individual variations exist, a group's basic perspective tends to be largely internalized by a majority of members.

Among communication cultures studied so far, gender has received particularly substantial attention. Research reveals that most girls and women use rules for communicating that differ systematically from those followed by most boys and men (Aries 1987; Beck 1988; Johnson 1989; Kramarae 1981; Tannen 1990a, 1990b; Wood 1993a, 1993c, 1994a, 1994b; Wood and Inman 1993). Individuals socialized into the understandings of feminine culture tend to emphasize relationships and processes more than outcomes, respond sensitively and affectively to others, and value cooperation and inclusion. In contrast, individuals socialized in masculine culture generally learn to use communication to achieve outcomes, assert self, and struggle for individual status and power (Coates and Cameron 1989; Maltz and Borker 1982; Tannen 1990a, 1990b; Wood 1993a, 1993c). Distinctive norms of other social groups have been uncovered and shown to exert similar impact on how members use verbal and nonverbal communication in their relationships (Samovar and Porter 1993; Gaines 1995).

Standpoint theory contributes to our understanding of diversity by highlighting how social locations and the conditions, opportunities, and understandings entailed in them shape individuals' thoughts, feelings, and communication. Although not denying individuality, standpoint theory insists that membership in socially defined groups substantially constrains ways of knowing and acting in the world. This implies that how any individual acts and thinks is not purely personal, since each of us is situated within and shaped by broader horizons of cultural life and the disparate experiences made available to different groups.

Social standpoints, including the distinctive communication cultures they generate, shed light on reasons why members of diverse social groups have different understandings about human interaction in general and friendships in particular. Among various social groups there are multiplicitous rules, expectations, and strategies for being friends. By implication, all understandings are socially constructed, which suggests that there is no single right perspective, but a range of standpoints crafted by particular social locations.

Standpoint theory yields pragmatic insight into friendships between people of different social groups. One implication is that an act of friendship from one standpoint may be unfriendly from another. Relatedly, standpoint thinking cautions us not to interpret others from our personal standpoint, which may diverge from theirs. The converse is also true: what we do and what we think it means may not parallel how our friends interpret the meaning of our activities.

In sum, both actions and the meanings with which we invest them arise in large measure from particular locations in cultural life. These positions, or standpoints, engrave rules that specify what friends do and do not do for each other, how they communicate, and what counts as care, support, and so forth. By extension, this implies that our ways of enacting friendship reflect not some transcendent truth, but subjective, interpretive patterns authorized by social contexts in which we and our activities are embedded. Yet, to return to our dialectical framework, differences in how friendship is enacted coexist with similarities in goals and needs, as well as with an overarching presumption that friends should understand and honor each other.

Diversity in Practice: Rules and Readings

If different standpoints promote distinct views of friendship, then there will be few, if any, generic rules regarding the content of friendship prac-

tices. At a higher level of abstraction, however, there are important tran-
scending premises—ones that comprise a conceptual stance toward the
dialectic between commonality and difference. For instance, between any
friends there should be mutual respect (commonality) for particular ways
of expressing closeness (difference), and common commitment to reflecting on one's own and friends' practices. Within such a perspective, friends
realize that dissimilar material, social, and symbolic circumstances give
rise to distinctive rules for enacting friendship and that these can best be
appreciated through a shared perspective that recognizes that diversity is
a source of powerful learning about ourselves and others.

A Sampling Standpoint: Differences in Action

Existing research identifies a number of interesting friendship patterns
that characterize, albeit not infallibly, members of different social groups.
Although exhaustive enumeration of diversities in friendship is impossible, a few specific examples will clarify the kinds of differences standpoints
cultivate.

Assertion   Because North Americans, especially men, are encouraged to
assert themselves, they tend to seek support and assistance forthrightly.
Members of Eastern cultures are socialized to be more unassuming, so
they are unlikely to make explicit requests of friends. Given this, a Thai
man might perceive a friend from Alabama as arrogant and intrusive for
suggesting, "Let's go out to celebrate my job offer." Similarly, a Taiwan-
ese woman might not get the support she wants because she doesn't state
her wishes to a North American friend, who assumes people speak up
for themselves.

Individuality   Standpoint-generated differences are also likely to surface
between African American and European American friends, such as
Wallace and Jim respectively. Perhaps Jim proposes going to a concert over
the weekend and Wallace demurs, saying he wants to go home to help
his mother care for an ailing aunt. Since Jim's standpoint emphasizes
personal autonomy, he may judge Wallace too dependent; alternatively,
he might reason that no twenty-one year-old guy prefers nursing an aunt
to going out with a friend, so Wallace is using that as an excuse to avoid
saying he doesn't want to spend time with Jim. African-American culture, however, is generally much more communal than European American culture (Gaines 1995), so family members customarily take care of
one another. If Jim attempts to convince Wallace to go to the concert,

Wallace might consider him disrespectful of familial ties. Unless Jim and Wallace discover each other's standpoint, each will misinterpret the other and both will be disappointed in the friendship.

Showing Care   Gendered rules of communication often create misunderstandings in friendships between women and men. Seeking comfort, Rochelle tells her friend Derek she has just learned her parents are separating. After listening for a few minutes, he expresses sympathy, then suggests they go to a movie. Because feminine socialization emphasizes communication as a primary way to sustain connections and express support, Rochelle wants him to help her by talking. From her standpoint, suggesting a movie means he doesn't care about her and her concerns.

Yet, Derek *was* supporting her according to masculine rules, which discourage overt, verbal displays of affection (Riessman 1990; Swain 1989; Wood and Inman 1993). A primary way men support friends is by taking their minds off troubles—providing diversions that distract them from worries. Suggesting going to a film, then, is his way of saying, "I care about you and want to do something to make you feel better." Because Rochelle and Derek have very different rules for how to support friends, she misunderstands his offer, feels hurt, and infers he doesn't care about her, and he feels frustrated and confused when she rejects his form of support. Both wind up hurt. To interpret Derek as not caring, however, assumes that feminine rules for expressing affection (personal dialogue) are right and masculine ones (activities) are wrong (Wood and Inman 1993).

Disclosure   Gendered standpoints may also surface in tensions over disclosure between women and men. Fred has not been having any luck in his job interviews, so when Catrina asks how they are going, he tries to dismiss the topic by saying, "So, so—nothing to talk about." Relying on feminine culture's rules for showing interest, Catrina pursues conversation, asking "Have you gotten a call back for a second interview with Hopewell?" Fred interprets this as a breach of friendship since he experiences it as an intrusion on his autonomy. When he withdraws from what he regards as invasive, Catrina feels closed out, which violates her understanding of how friends treat one another.

Involvement   Standpoint-generated differences in involvement with others similarly may collide in friendships between women and men. When Doug sees his friend Jan is upset about one of her other friend's problems, he may tell her "you're too involved—it's not *your* problem." He is following rules of masculine culture, which dictate keeping a distance between self and others and offering instrumental help—advice for instance. Within a feminine standpoint, however, involvement with friends is desirable, so Jan may feel his response indicates he doesn't care about her and, more generally, is an uncaring person.

Feedback   Feedback is another area in which gendered communication patterns invite misunderstandings. Suppose Carl seeks out Melita to get her feedback on how he plans to handle a problem with a co-worker. Throughout his explanation, Melita nods her head and says "yes" and "I see." When he stops talking, she responds, "I think that approach is going to backfire big time." Because masculine culture regards talk as a means to convey information and establish a stand, he interpreted Melita's feedback as indicating she agreed with his ideas, and he now feels she misled him. In a sharp retort, he snarls, "If you think it's such a bad idea, why did you egg me on while I was talking and act like you agreed?" Exasperated, Melita demands, "Why would you think I agreed just because I listened?" She operated by feminine communication rules, which define feedback as a way to signal attention and interest, not attitude.

Commonalities amid Diversity

At first these examples may seem unrelated, yet common to them is a recurring pattern: in each case, the misunderstanding and hurt arise out of friends' judgments about differences, not the differences themselves. What Derek did or didn't do is not what hurt Rochelle, and what she did or didn't do is not what frustrated him. Instead, it is the judgments each adds to the other's behavior. Notice that both Derek and Rochelle (and others in the examples) respond to *their interpretations* of the other's behaviors, not to what the other actually does. This suggests that one cornerstone for friendships between diverse people is distinguishing what is said and done from our interpretations and judgments. The issue of judgment—and how we deal with it—is so critical that it focuses the remainder of this chapter.

The Tendency to Judge Differences

We don't need additional examples of ways in which diversities may complicate friendship to recognize a basic theme: judgments of differences, not differences per se, are a frequent source of misunderstandings and frustration between friends. The problem, then, is not differences themselves, but what we add to them: our interpretations and evaluations. Without even realizing it, we judge others by the perspectives, rules, and values characteristic of our particular standpoints. And imposing our perspective on others may distort their meanings, motives, and actions.

Hierarchical Judgments of Differences

Within Western culture differences are not regarded as neutral—that is, as simply different. Instead, we view them as better or worse, and better is usually our way and worse the other person's way! Communication between friends takes place against an unexamined and largely unconscious backdrop of assumptions about what is good, right, appropriate, and so forth. These unrecognized assumptions may lead us to misconstrue friends' intentions, feelings, and actions. To respect and learn from our differences with others we must first become conscious of the subjective, arbitrary assumptions that inhere in our own standpoints.

Recognizing Our Own Standpoints

Standpoint theory reminds us that tensions in friendships often stem from failure to realize that individuals from diverse social groups operate by different understandings about friendship. When this realization eludes us, we (mis)interpret others by viewing them from our own standpoints. In the examples, friends judged each other inadequate or wrong for acting differently than they would. Typically, we don't realize how ethnocentric our standpoints are; instead, we assume we are operating by universal principles of friendship. This illusion is dangerous, because it encourages us to judge anything that deviates from our rules as inferior. In turn, this arrests our capacity to appreciate diversity and to enlarge our own views. Friends who have dissimilar social standpoints will differ in understandings, values, rules, and actions. This causes tension when we unreflectively impose our rules of friendship on others. Probing the dynamics of judging may enable us to move beyond hierarchical views of difference.

The Anatomy of Judgments

What is involved in judging anything that deviates from our ways as inferior? First, *attribution* is involved. Rochelle attributes meaning and motive to Derek's suggestion that they go out; she decides what intentions underlie his invitation. Derek, too, engages in attribution when he unreflectively assumes Rochelle will interpret his suggestion to go out as a way of showing support. If we look beneath the attributions themselves, we discover another dynamic in the process of judging diversity in friends.

Egocentrism literally means judging with the self as center. It occurs when we perceive situations, events, and actions from our personal perspective and fail to recognize the existence, much less the legitimacy, of alternative perspectives. Neither Derek nor Rochelle recognizes the possibility of different and equally valid rules for expressing care and commitment. Both err in assuming they have a shared perspective, because each makes sense of the world from her or his own standpoint and the ways of perceiving, valuing, knowing, and communicating it encourages. Misunderstandings are virtually inevitable when friends not only judge egocentrically, but fail to realize they do so.

Because distinct standpoints yield particular—not universal—ways of enacting friendship, strains are inevitable between friends who differ in class, race, affectional orientation, gender, or cultural background. Further, both tensions and egocentric judgments are probably unavoidable in human relationships. What we *can avoid* is failing to see opportunities that inhere in moments of tension. Differences and the frustration they generate can foment growth when friends approach them as paths to learning about each other, themselves, and the range of ways humans enact friendship.

Beyond Judgment

Although the human tendency to judge is perhaps inevitable, remaining stuck in judgment is not. Ideally, we should be able to realize we make a judgment, then move beyond it to recognize, first, that judgments reflect our own standpoints, which are not universal, and, second, that we may not understand what something means from the also-specific standpoints of others. Ironically, doing this requires judging judgment itself. We must be able to say "I recognize something seems wrong from my standpoint, and I evaluate my perception as undesirably limiting me and the friendship." Moving beyond judgment opens us to varied experiences, situations, and relationships with other people. Let's now consider orientations toward difference that foster growth in individuals and friendships.

Fashioning an Ethical Framework toward Diversity

The ideas discussed so far suggest four ways to facilitate moving beyond judgment and toward an appreciation of the opportunities inspired by diversity in friendships.

Self-reflection

Prerequisite to growth and change is self-reflection. To learn from diversity we must become conscious of our own friendship rules and realize that they are not the natural, right, or only legitimate ones. Instead, they reflect what is considered normal and appropriate *within the particular standpoint we occupy.* And that is all they reflect.

Ongoing self-reflection nurtures two noteworthy kinds of growth. First, it enlarges insight into our own social groups and the patterns, values, and understandings they promote. Just as visiting other countries enhances awareness of our native land, experiencing differences in friendship clarifies our own rules and assumptions, which remain largely unconscious as long as they encounter no contrasts. Ronald Arnett (1986) extols the value of differences, arguing that they crystallize our own perspective by juxtaposing it with those of others.

Differences between our views and those of others are invitations to reinspect and re-form our own. We gain a critical perspective that allows us to see ourselves and our ways of engaging in friendship from a new horizon. In other words, learning about others' standpoints allows us to expand our own standpoints and to appreciate intersections between ours and those of others. Again, we see here the interplay between difference and commonality as we realize that engaging differences often enhances commonalities.

In addition, discerning our own friendship rules invigorates personal agency by empowering us to contemplate consciously whether we want to continue following codes we were taught or to experiment with alternatives. For most of us, there will be some editing of our rules—keeping ones that we esteem and rewriting others. The key point here is that when we craft our own frameworks through conscious reflection and experimentation with a range of options, they are *personally considered and chosen,* not externally defined by the groups within which we were initially socialized.

Openness to Others

A companion to self-reflection is belief in the inherent value of others, including ways they differ from us. In advocating openness, I am not suggesting mere tolerance since that is patronizing, premised as it is on the presumption that one person has the right to judge the acceptability of others' ways. Neither am I endorsing a radically relativist stance that suspends all judgment and abrogates any basis for choosing among positions. Distinct from radical relativism is a pluralistic perspective, which respects differences in their own terms and contexts, and also honors individuals' right to prefer particular ones.

Genuine openness is an authentic receptivity to learning about others' views, values, and codes of conduct. It requires a commitment to considering others *on their terms,* not just our own. Just as it would be absurd to assess an apple on its juiciness (fair in evaluating an orange, but not an apple), so it is inappropriate to appraise a male's commitment to a friendship by how fully he discloses his feelings (an equitable criterion for feminine, but not masculine modes of expressing closeness). Being truly open allows us to understand others' standpoints so that we may consider our friends within their interpretive contexts.

Receptivity to others and their ways of thinking, communicating, and being friends does not imply that we have to relinquish our own ways or adopt those of others. This would be only a different form of either-or dualistic thinking. Endorsing the value of openness, Martin Buber (1972) illuminated the signal distinction between being open to others and surrendering our own views. It is possible, he argued, simultaneously to affirm the value of your ways and the different ones of your friends. Buber referred to this as the "unity of contraries," which calls on us to appreciate the worth of our own patterns and beliefs and, at the same time, to respect others and their ways of seeing and acting in the world. In other words, you don't have to abandon your own ways of participating in friendship to honor different ways others employ. Openness, however, does not come easily in a culture that has entrenched hierarchical views of differences. Openness may be cultivated by more particular attitudes and values, including a both-and orientation and curiosity.

Embracing a Both-And Orientation   We gain a first insight into how we might nourish greater openness from Susan Campbell (1986). Reflecting on how judgments limit our lives, she wrote, "if we are to have any chance at all of experiencing the world's abundance, we first need to change our thinking about the kind of world we live in. We need to change our habitual way of constructing what we think of as real. Most of us have been conditioned to think in either-or terms, to divide our world up into bits and pieces and parts . . . in-group and out-group" (163). The either-or thinking that Campbell discusses generates much tension in friendships between diverse people. When we assume that our rules and ways of enacting friendship are right and anything that differs is wrong, we set ourselves up to believe that others either show interest, caring, and commitment our way or they aren't being good friends.

Many people regard differences negatively and select people like themselves as friends. Typically, this is not a conscious choice. Instead, we unthinkingly act as if "my ways are right, so why should I have to tolerate different ways?" or "It's too much hassle to learn how to interact with someone different from me." Clearly, learning to understand and be comfortable with people who differ from us requires investments of energy, time, and thought. In addition, engaging in friendships with diverse people compels us to become more aware of our own patterns of thinking and communicating. The dividends from these investments are freedom to participate in a broad range of friendships and enlarged understandings of the multiplicity of ways humans may form and sustain close relationships.

When we refuse to respect the validity of diversity in friendships, we constrain ourselves to what we learned from the groups in which we were originally socialized. This invites three undesirable consequences. First, it obscures the fascinating variety in human experience. Second, it diminishes us as individuals by limiting the fullness of our moral lives. Finally, rigid adherence to the perspective of our original standpoint entrenches barriers between groups and perpetuates divisive social relations in the culture as a whole.

Curiosity   Along with a both-and orientation toward differences, openness is promoted by cultivating curiosity toward differences. This encourages us to explore and energetically consider ways different from our own. Nourishing curiosity toward differences shifts us from thinking "that's wrong" to "that's interesting—what might I learn here?" Curiosity focuses energy on figuring out what is happening more than on defining and evaluating it. If, on the other hand, we get stuck in judging, we are unlikely to recognize, much less explore, alternatives to what we know.

Being curious about different ways of creating and expressing closeness with friends broadens our understanding of human relationships and our own repertoires for enacting friendship. This enhancement cultivates a full life and ongoing moral growth. As Susan Campbell noted, "seeing the world with an expanded view that shows how interconnected we are with our neighbors can help us bring new resources to bear on problems, resources we might never otherwise discover" (1986:264). Thus, moving beyond judgments to explore what differences mean often discloses new possibilities for ourselves and our relationships. Mining opportunities inherent in differences is most likely when we are self-reflective, open, and curious about what we might learn from others and their standpoints on friendship.

The Values of Diversity in Friendship

Dancing with the dialectic of diversity and commonality enhances us in many ways. According to Arnett, differences between friends add novelty and interest to relationships, since interaction may "quickly grow static and boring if each party is continually in agreement with the other" (1986:273). Recently several colleagues and I investigated how intimate partners make sense of differences between them (Wood et al. 1994). Although some partners were apprehensive about differences, most said they "keep the pot boiling," "add life," and "prevent staleness." Several respondents actively encouraged differences to invigorate their relationships.

Friendships also prosper when standpoint thinking inflects interaction. Realizing that our ways of enacting friendship are socially sculpted makes it clear that we need to explain, or *translate* ourselves to friends. Relatedly, recognizing that different social groups generate different standpoints should temper the impulse to impose our meanings onto friends and, instead, prompt us to ask them to translate their comments and actions so that we can understand what they mean and want. When friends translate themselves, they offer each other not just explanations of particular behaviors, but new perspectives on how to be a friend. Further, the enriched understanding yielded by translations allows friends to communicate in ways that honor each other's perspectives. In turn, this enables them to build a shared standpoint within which differences between them coexist in a productive tension that continually reconfigures what is common to them.

Finally, embracing differences in our friendships promotes transformations in social attitudes toward diversity. When friends explore differences and find they are enriched by doing so, they learn to appreciate not just each other, but differences themselves. As this perspective perforates cultural understandings and as friends embody models of growing from differences, others in society may be led to discover opportunities inherent in diversity.

At this moment our culture is infected by aching divisions that are fueled by assumptions that differences must radically separate humans. So Caucasians don't want people of color in their neighborhoods, Protestants exclude Jews from their clubs, men are hostile to women in the workplace, heterosexuals disdain gays and lesbians, and African Americans form separate communities on predominantly white campuses. As long as we see only what separates us and not what connects us, we will be unable to prosper from diversity and unable to create a society hospitable to all who compose it. In short, devaluing differences restricts the possibilities of individual and of collective life.

Because diversity and commonality coexist, disparaging differences simultaneously constricts understanding of what is common among humans—needs, hopes, dreams, fears, goals, and values we share with others. The divisions that currently contaminate cultural life jeopardize our capacities both to realize how much we have in common and to learn from points of difference. Nobody is enriched by divisiveness, denigrating differences, or denying diversity.

Moving beyond devaluing differences begins when individuals forge friendships with diverse others and seize the opportunities difference offers. Not surprisingly, we find that when people who occupy dissimilar social standpoints do interact, divisiveness usually wanes, probably because interaction reveals commonalities and reconfigures differences. As individuals discover that diversity is enriching, their attitudes tend to spread to others, rippling through society in a manner at once subtle and profound.

Standpoint theory suggests attitudes and responsibilities that might inform a moral stance toward diversity between friends. The cornerstone of these is self-reflection, which empowers us to realize that social locations shape our own and others' perspectives on friendship and to explore how we might be enriched by understanding and, if we choose, incorporating others' perspectives into our own.

Standpoint also implies a number of responsibilities people have to themselves and one another. To our friends we should explain our own positioning so that they may situate our actions within the interpretive framework that guides us. In addition, we have a responsibility to foster our own moral growth by learning to understand and appreciate a range of standpoints that exist in our world. We also have a responsibility to sustain the tension inherent in opening ourselves to multiple perspectives and in recognizing diversity and commonality as an intertwined dialectic. I am suggesting not a formula, but an ethical stance toward friendship—one based on respect for the integrity and validity of varied experience in its own right.

Summary

Two themes animate this chapter. One concerns how friends perceive and respond to differences between themselves. Because diverse social groups shape distinct standpoints, individuals learn dissimilar rules for thinking, feeling, and acting in friendships, as well as for interpreting each other's meanings and motives. When friends openly explore their differences, they enhance the possibilities of understanding each other and building a standpoint that simultaneously honors differences and nourishes commonalities.

The second and larger theme of this chapter is that as a society we benefit by learning from diversity. Within Western culture, diversity historically has been devalued and erased. The melting pot metaphor assumes everyone should be blended into a homogeneous substance. That oneness, however, never reflected all people expected to conform to it. Instead, everyone was expected to assimilate into a white, Protestant, middle-class, heterosexual, and male model. Thus, African Americans could succeed if they acted white, women could be professionals if they adopted male standards, and gays and lesbians were accepted if they camouflaged their affectional preferences. The melting pot neither honors nor preserves diversity, but erases it by insisting on a single standard that in reality embodies only one of the multiple standpoints cultivated by society.

At this moment our culture stands at a crossroads in which emerging appreciation of diversity is met with renewed insistence on a single cultural standard. Revived racial and ethnic tensions punctuate campus life; each day's newspaper reports incidents of hate speech and attacks on minority groups; a neo-Nazi movement is growing; and faculty rancorously debate the relative merits of classical education versus expanded curricula that include contributions of historically marginalized groups. Can we learn to value diversity and commonality as coexisting facets of humanity?

Society is not an abstraction removed from individuals; instead, we are society. Consequently, each of us participates in sculpting our culture's attitudes toward diversity. Whether we promote our views by taking a public voice or by how we deal with differences in our friendships, each of us contributes to social attitudes toward differences. Our choices are not wisely construed as accepting either diversity or commonality since neither makes sense bereft of the other. The two continuously interact in an ongoing dialectic that generates change. The more we explore diversity with openness and curiosity, the more we discover what humans share; and the greater our awareness of commonalities the more clearly we discern differences. Personal and social growth depend on our ability to recognize and embrace the rich dialectic of commonality and diversity.

References Cited

Aries, E. 1987. "Gender and Communication." In *Sex and Gender*. Ed. P. Shaver. Pp. 149–76. Newbury Park, Calif.: Sage.

Arnett, R. C. 1986. "The Inevitable Conflict and Confronting in Dialogue." In *Bridges, Not Walls: A Book about Interpersonal Communication*. 4th ed. Ed. J. Stewart. Pp. 272–79. New York: Random House.

Baxter, L. A. 1988. "A Dialectical Perspective on Communication Strategies in Relationship Development." In *Handbook of Personal Relationships*. Ed. S. W. Duck, D. F. Hay, S. E. Hobfoll, W. Iches, and B. Montgomery. Pp. 257–73. London: Wiley.

———. 1990. "Dialectical Contradictions in Relationship Development." *Journal of Social and Personal Relationships* 7:69–88.

Beck, A. T. 1988. *Love Is Never Enough*. New York: Harper and Row.

Bem, S. 1993. *The Lenses of Gender: Transforming the Debate on Sexual Inequality*. New Haven: Yale University Press.

Berscheid, E., M. Snyder, and A. Omoto. 1989. "Issues in Studying Close Relationships." In *Close Relationships*. Ed. C. Hendrick. Pp. 63–91. Newbury Park, Calif.: Sage.

Buber, M. 1972. *Between Man and Man*. New York: Macmillan.

Campbell, S. 1986. "From Either-Or to Both-And Relationships." In *Bridges, Not Walls: A Book about Interpersonal Communication*. 4th ed. Ed. J. Stewart. Pp. 262–71. New York: Random House.

Chodorow, N. J. 1978. *The Reproduction of Mothering: Psychoanalysis and the Sociology of Gender*. Berkeley: University of California Press.

———. 1989. *Feminism and Psychoanalytic Theory*. New Haven: Yale University Press.

Coates, J., and D. Cameron. 1989. *Women in Their Speech Communities: New Perspectives on Language and Sex*. London: Longman.

Collins, P. H. 1986. "Learning from the Outsider Within: The Sociological Significance of Black Feminist Thought." *Social Problems* 33:514–32.

Davis, F. 1991. *Moving the Mountain: The Women's Movement in America since 1960*. New York: Simon and Schuster.

Duck, S., and P. D. Wright. 1993. "Re-examining Gender Differences in Same-Gender Friendships: A Close Look at Two Kinds of Data." *Sex Roles* 28:708–27.

Fox-Genovese, E. 1991. *Feminism without Illusions: A Critique of Individualism*. Chapel Hill: University of North Carolina Press.

Gaines, S., Jr. 1995. "Relationships between Members of Cultural Minorities." In *Understudied Relationships: Off the Beaten Track*. Ed. J. T. Wood and S. W. Duck. Pp. 51–88. Newbury Park, Calif.: Sage.

Haraway, D. 1988. "Situated Knowledges: The Science Question in Feminism and the Privilege of Partial Perspective." *Signs* 14:575–99.

Harding, S. 1991. *Whose Science? Whose Knowledge?: Thinking from Women's Lives.* Ithaca: Cornell University Press.

Hartsock, N. C. M. 1983. "The Feminist Standpoint: Developing the Ground for a Specifically Feminist Historical Materialism." In *Discovering Reality.* Ed. S. Harding and M. B. Hintikka. Pp. 283–310. Boston: Reidel.

———. 1990. "Foucault on Power: A Theory for Women?" In *Feminism/Postmodernism.* Ed. J. Nicholson. Pp. 157–75. New York: Routledge.

Hennessy, R. 1993. *Materialist Feminism and the Politics of Discourse.* New York: Routledge.

Inman, C. C. 1996. "Friendships between Men: Closeness in the Doing." In *Gendered Relationships: A Reader.* Ed. J. T. Wood. Pp. 95–110. Mountain View, Calif.: Mayfield.

Janeway, E. 1971. *Man's World, Woman's Place: A Study in Social Mythology.* New York: Dell.

Johnson, F. L. 1989. "Women's Culture and Communication: An Analytic Perspective." In *Beyond Boundaries: Sex and Gender Diversity in Communication.* Ed. C. Lont and S. Friedley. Pp. 301–16. Fairfax: George Mason University Press.

———. 1996. "Friendships between Women: Closeness in Dialogue." In *Gendered Relationships: A Reader.* Ed. J. T. Wood. Pp. 79–94. Mountain View, Calif.: Mayfield.

Jones, D. C. 1991. "Friendship Satisfaction and Gender: An Examination of Sex Differences in Contributors to Friendship Satisfaction." *Journal of Social and Personal Relationships* 8:167–85.

Kramarae, C. 1981. *Women and Men Speaking: Frameworks for Analysis.* Rowley, Mass.: Newbury House.

Labov, W. 1972. *Sociolinguistic Patterns.* Philadelphia: University of Pennsylvania Press.

Maltz, D. N., and R. Borker. 1982. "A Cultural Approach to Male-Female Miscommunication." In *Language and Social Identity.* Ed. J. J. Gumperz. Pp. 196–216. Cambridge: Cambridge University Press.

Miller, J. B. 1986. *Toward a New Psychology of Women.* 2d ed. Boston: Beacon.

Monsour, M. 1992. "Meanings of Intimacy in Cross- and Same-Sex Friendships." *Journal of Social and Personal Relationships* 9:277–95.

Okin, S. M. 1989. *Justice, Gender, and the Family.* New York: Basic.

Paul, E., and K. White. 1990. "The Development of Mate Relationships in Late Adolescence." *Adolescence* 25:375–400.

Riessman, J. M. 1990. *Divorce Talk: Women and Men Make Sense of Personal Relationships.* New Brunswick: Rutgers University Press.

Ruddick, S. 1989. *Maternal Thinking: Towards a Politics of Peace*. Boston: Beacon.

Samovar, L., and R. Porter. 1993. *Intercultural Communication: A Reader*. 7th ed. Belmont, Calif.: Wadsworth.

Sherrod, D. 1989. "The Influence of Gender on Same-Sex Friendships." In *Close Relationships*. Ed. C. Hendrick. Pp. 164–86. Newbury Park, Calif.: Sage.

Smith, D. 1987. *The Everyday World as Problematic: A Feminist Sociology*. Boston: Northeastern University Press.

Swain, S. 1989. "Covert Intimacy: Closeness in Men's Friendships." In *Gender and Intimate Relationships*. Ed. B. Risman and P. Schwartz. Pp. 71–86. Belmont, Calif.: Wadsworth.

Tannen, D. 1990a. "Gender Differences in Conversational Coherence: Physical Alignment and Topical Cohesion." In *Conversational Organization and Its Development*. Ed. B. Dorval. Pp. 167–206. Norwood, N.J.: Ablex.

———. 1990b. *You Just Don't Understand: Women and Men in Conversation*. New York: William Morrow and Co.

Wood, J. T. 1993a. "Gender and Moral Voice: From Woman's Nature to Standpoint Epistemology." *Women's Studies in Communication* 15:1–24.

———. 1993b. "Gender, Communication, and Culture." In *Intercultural Communication: A Reader*. 7th ed. Ed. L. Samovar and R. Porter. Pp. 155–64. Belmont, Calif.: Wadsworth.

———. 1993c. *Gendered Lives: Communication, Gender, and Culture*. Belmont, Calif.: Wadsworth.

———. 1993d. *Who Cares?: Women, Care, and Culture*. Carbondale: Southern Illinois University Press.

———. 1994a. "Engendered Identities: Shaping Voice and Mind through Gender." In *Intrapersonal Communication: Different Voices, Different Minds*. Ed. D. Vocate. Pp. 145–67. Hillsdale, N.J.: Lawrence Erlbaum and Associates.

———. 1994b. "Engendered Relations: Interaction, Caring, Power, and Responsibility in Close Relationships." In *Understanding Relationship Processes: Social Context and Relationships*. Ed. S. Duck. Pp. 26–54. Beverly Hills: Sage.

———. 1994c. "Saying It Makes It So: The Discursive Construction of Sexual Harassment." In *Discursive Conceptions of Sexual Harassment*. Ed. S. Bingham. Pp. 17–30. Westport, Conn.: Praeger.

———, ed. 1996. *Gendered Relationships: A Reader*. Mountain View, Calif.: Mayfield.

Wood, J. T., and J. R. Cox. 1993. "Rethinking Critical Voice: Materiality and Situated Knowledges." *Western Journal of Communication* 57:278–87.

Wood, J. T., L. Dendy, E. Dordek, M. Germany, and S. Varallo. 1994.

"Dialectic of Difference: A Thematic Analysis of Intimates' Meanings for Differences." In *Interpretive Approaches to Interpersonal Relationships*. Ed. K. Carter and M. Presnell. Pp. 115–36. Albany: State University of New York Press.

Wood, J. T., and C. C. Inman. 1993. "In a Different Mode: Masculine Styles of Communicating Closeness." *Journal of Applied Communication Research* 21:279–95.

Wright, P. 1982. "Men's Friendships, Women's Friendships, and the Alleged Inferiority of the Latter." *Sex Roles* 8:1–20.

———. 1988. "Interpreting Research on Gender Differences in Friendship: A Case for Moderation and a Plea for Caution." *Journal of Social and Personal Relationships* 5:367–73.

2   Communication and Community in an Age of Diversity

Ronald C. Arnett

Here . . . was . . . an incomparable; here was, debased yet uninjured, the living double kernel of humanity: genuine community and genuine leadership. . . . when I saw the rebbe striding through the rows of the waiting, I felt, "leader," and when I saw the Hasidism dance with the Torah, I felt "community." At that time there rose in me a presentiment of the fact that common reverence and common joy of soul are the foundations of genuine human community.
— Martin Buber (1973:39)

Martin Buber's remembrance of community assumes a narrative context of a people, religion, and ethnic connection. The narrative context that sustains Buber's understanding of community speaks only for some, while it simultaneously excludes others from the community. Buber was not naive about community. He understood the oxymoronic character of community; it both includes *and* excludes. Those outside a community endure closure and barriers, even as words of openness to diversity are uttered.

Introduction

As Buber suggested, *community is both inclusive and exclusive.* We need a realistic view of our understanding and practice of community. Ask any student new to a college that advertises, "We care," who simultaneously feels left out, excluded, and the sting of exclusion is manifested. We quickly discover a darker, more painful side of community—a side we are tempted to ignore as we make optimistic proclamations about community. Such a critique is disheartening for anyone, like myself and many of the readers of this essay, who want inclusion, interpersonal warmth, understanding, and cooperative companionship to guide communicative interaction.

I begin this essay with a confession that community is important to me. My clearest statement on the value of community rests with *Communication and Community: Implications of Martin Buber's Dialogue* (1986). This essay, if read too quickly and without knowledge of my larger work, might be viewed as a negative portrayal of community. Such a reading would, however, miss the point. Community is vital to the quality of our lives. But naive paintings of the life of community do more to mislead and nourish cynicism than any critique of community would be able to accomplish. In essence, it is necessary to keep the dialectical tension of both sides of community in the discussion.

Additionally, it is important to address the limits of the term "we," used throughout much of the chapter. Questioning the value of individualism, the constant use of "I" is then problematic. However, on the other hand, the use of the term "we" is not meant to be culturally universal. Like any author, I work from the historical stance of my own life and studies—primarily Western and middle-class—offering comments for conversation with realization that in the mix of diversity what "we" means is often an open question. Such a task may be an implicit agenda for human understanding as we stumble our way to the twenty-first century.

This essay aims to uphold the two sides of community, inclusion and exclusion, suggesting two concerns for the study of communication ethics in an age of increasing diversity. First, as some enjoy the benefits of community, we need to remember that "our" inclusion rests upon the exclusion of someone else, and vice versa. Second, if inclusion and exclusion are to walk hand in hand, how might we honestly and ethically meet such a challenge in the midst of our desire to honor and support both community and diversity? This essay is a modest effort to invite conversation about communicative ethical dilemmas surrounding the notion of community in an age of diversity of religious, ethnic, ideological, racial, political, and geographical differences.

The Two Sides of Community

Understanding the concept of community requires awareness of the historical moment in which the term is used. If one accepts the view of current life in Western culture as most often the pursuit of comfort, it should be of little surprise that much discussion of community is limited in definition and understanding, frequently void of the "other" side of community, exclusion.

Clearly, it is difficult to make sweeping statements about a person, let alone a culture. But fundamental changes have occurred in the United States, as we have moved from lower-middle-class values of hard work and commitment to concerns based more on the upper-middle-class impulses of comfort and self-concern. Lasch, in *The True and Only Heaven* (1991), makes this case well. He laments the loss of a value system that valued sacrifice for others and ideas—leaving us with expressions of self-actualization and concerns about our own survival. Again, such a position is not the universal view of our historical moment. But this perspective can be accepted as, at least, a partially accurate reading of our current time.

Community without Demand

Buber's view of community, central to this essay, is at odds with a "McMoral" sensitivity that expects quick inclusion without paying a price (Arnett 1992). It is tempting for many of us to long for community that is inclusive, grounded in invitation, openness, and welcome, and that creates no tension with our individual standards: "community" on our terms. We want the part (me) to dictate to the whole (the group) without, of course, giving the impression of being centered on the self.

Bellah et al. (1985) discovered that as they interviewed people throughout the United States there was a strong longing for community, but the language used to discuss the notion of community was often individualistic and psychological. They found community individualized in an attempt to escape the demands of "the other."

When we forget that community requires working out the demands that "the other" places upon us and the demands we place on "the other" an innocent form of treachery is invited. As Glenn Tinder (1980) reminds us, "In truth, the idea that human beings are fundamentally good and innocent is surprisingly treacherous. . . . We do not simply experience frustration in searching for community. We come face-to-face with our finitude, our mortality, and our radical imperfection" (9).

Perhaps one of the most profound demands of community is the admission of the dialectical interplay of inclusion and exclusion; otherwise we fall prey to the innocence suggested by Tinder. As we play one role, there is a simultaneous demand that another plays a different part in the dialectical drama of insider and outsider. Inclusion and exclusion are companions; we invite problems when we insist on speaking only of the inclusive side of community. The destructive nature of this one-sided denial is outlined by Wiebe in *Peace Shall Destroy Many* (1978). He details the life of a fictitious Mennonite community in the midst of World War II. The group opposes the violence of war and speaks of a loving community, while interpersonal violence in the name of religion and peace destroys one life after another.

Wiebe underscores the potential for destruction in the practice of community when there is a lack of awareness of the dark side of inclusion—being on the outside. Preserving the "good" of community requires acknowledging the "evil" that often taints the project of community when we insist on an optimistic, one-sided portrayal of life with one another in community. Dietrich Bonhoeffer, known for his dialectical work with community, puts this dual nature of the term in theological language. He suggests, "There is now no community without sin but on the other hand a 'society' is not just a 'sinning community'" (1960:81). In more secular language, community is both good and bad; it is a two-sided coin. We cannot have one side of the coin without the other's implicit presence. Community is a double-edged sword, cutting both in a direction that helps, and simultaneously, in a problematic direction.

Ignoring the demands or the "cost" of community is nourished by what Bonhoeffer called "cheap grace" (1975:45), an attitude of wanting something without effort or work. Such an orientation invites false hope, a painless ideal unlikely to survive the inevitable difficulties that confront a people. Both Buber, a Jewish philosopher and theologian, and Bonhoeffer, a Protestant theologian, point us to the demands of community.

Additionally, Sartre, in his frequent referrals to the notion of "bad faith," points to the importance of understanding both sides of what we claim—the constructive, as well as the destructive. Simply, there are ontological dangers inherent in self-lying. In his discussion of ethical implications in *Being and Nothingness* (1973), he suggests that bad faith acts as an unknowing lie to oneself that forms the unity of one's belief system. Both secular and religious authors call us to lessen "bad faith" and embrace both the light and the dark of a term we often wish to claim only as good—community. They offer us two warnings that undergird this essay: (1) community is demanding—it exacts a price, and (2) community both includes and excludes.

Community as Contradiction

Community, in an age of diversity: is it possible or even desirable? For those included, the answer is usually a resounding, "Yes!" But for those standing outside the group, the cry is more likely a bitter, "No!" Without foregoing the hope of community, this essay incorporates the wisdom of Glenn Tinder (1980): community is often a tragic ideal, embraced by many and inclusive of few. In Tinder's words, "The unattainability of community (not, be it noted, the undesirability of community) seems to me a crucial and neglected truth. It accounts for the dangerous character of the idea" (1980:2).

Taking Tinder's suggestions seriously without abandoning the concept of community altogether, it is possible to outline a view of community that both nourishes its importance and recognizes the often tragic implications of unsubstantiated optimism and utopianism. Our task is to join the hope of community with the reality of its difficulty and demands. Such a view of community is caught within oxymoronic tension suggested by the following terms: idealism/realism, commonality/difference, and optimism/pessimism.

Buber called us to a communicative life that works to find the "unity of contraries" (1966:111). Perhaps this approach to community might assist us as we march increasingly faster into a twenty-first century world of diversity that throws "us" and "them" together, both with and without consent. This understanding of community undergirded Buber's suggestions of fifty years ago for Israeli and Arab unity: "I do not make a basic distinction between what is right morally and what is right politically. Something immoral may be of temporary benefit, but it cannot benefit generations or even one generation. The basic outlook of the prophets was politically realistic. They were not defeatists. In the final analysis there is no contradiction between realistic politics and moral politics. One has to sacrifice temporary benefits for future existence" (Menders-Flohr 1983:266).

The above view of community suggests a communication ethic sensitive to the contrary nature of life, an ethic that in a world of diversity uplifts moral claims concerning the importance of human togetherness while fostering a political realism that acknowledges the inclusive and exclusive nature of human community. Such simultaneously contrary demands make the benefits of community for all elusive. High ideals have the chance of guiding us to a better tomorrow, and additionally, to the cynical realization of life's disparity between theory and praxis.

In summary, the results of the two sides of community reveal those who feel excluded *and* those content with their own inclusion. However, this one-sided view of happiness is actually closer to what Aristotle called pleasure (1985:1095b 17). Going beyond the happiness and disappointment of inclusion and exclusion requires us to examine in good faith the justice and honesty in our communication of the term "community." The latter part of this essay suggests the importance of *public* windows of inclusion as an alternative to community based upon more private and elusive standards. The "common good" requires not just "my" happiness, but honesty in how the term is understood in practical living, and in public invitations for genuine inclusion of "me" and "the other."

The Wish: An Often Unattained Ideal

Robert Bellah et al., in *Habits of the Heart* (1985), remind us of the importance attached to the term "community." Many of us possess a great desire for the intimacy of community and yet rarely discover a genuine sense of community in our own lives. Bellah's thesis is similar to that of M. Scott Peck's in *The Different Drum* (1987): "On my lecture tours across the country the one constant I have found wherever I go—the Northeast, Southeast, Midwest, Southwest, or West Coast—is the lack of—and the thirst for—community. This lack and thirst is particularly heartbreaking in those places where one might expect to find real community . . ." (57). Both Bellah and Peck as contemporary and popular writers on the notion of community suggest that there is a *wish for community that for many goes unfulfilled.*

The wish of community unrestrained by the reality that for many the mere term, community, is a hoax, a nightmare, can become a tragic ideal if used too easily and quickly. A quotation from a colleague reveals this view of community: "Community is great when you are a participating contributor. However, it is a form of living interpersonal hell when you are excluded; you walk outside emotional attachment that is positive and powerful for the 'included' members." Perhaps the wish of community goes unfulfilled for many due to a limited understanding of its multiple nature and complex demands.

Irony and Community

An exemplification of the tension between the hope for community and the danger it offers is reflected in a conversation I had with a person, Henry, who lives in a small town he deeply loves.

Henry's view of community is limited, but not unknown or perhaps even unusual. He implicitly defines community as geographical and tied to agreement and consensus on basic ideas that guide the people in "his" town. Others may tie community to ethnic, religious, racial, or some other identifying features. But in each of the above cases, the notion of agreement on basic ideas and values often undergirds a popular view of community.

In one meeting, Henry stated, "You do not have to scratch me very deep to see how important a loving community is to me." His statement was sincere and heartfelt, *and* he often finds himself incapable of understanding anyone who does not love the town as much as he. Yet Henry is the first to gossip about anyone or anything that is new or different in the town, calling into question whatever does not fit his version of community.

On the one hand, Henry is sincerely committed to community. On the other hand, he is careful about anyone who comes into "his" community. To agree with Henry is to find a friend, but to differ is to discover a silent adversary skilled at working interpersonal linkages to keep new people and new ideas controlled or banned. The interesting result of this seemingly dual set of actions goes unnoticed by Henry. It is highly likely that Henry does not understand his exclusive orientation. He is the first to welcome someone into the community, and the first to make sure that the new person knows his or her place. Only those on the outside of his community can understand the boundaries of exclusion that make Henry's view of community possible.

Ironically, Henry seldom tires of discussing community or gossiping about those who are different. Recently, he asked in all sincerity, "Why are so many new people leaving within a five- year time period? They do not seem to stay long." As one of my friends stated when I shared this example, "I would like Henry better if he talked more honestly about how community both includes and excludes. His view of community does both." The marks of both inclusion and exclusion define community—with only the first half of the equation understood by Henry.

Additionally, living in a contemporary Western culture that encourages us to take care of "number one" invites coopting of the notion of community by those who wish to further their own interests. As another colleague suggested, "Beware of organizations that are too friendly without knowing you. They are probably more interested in your numerical contribution than what you as a unique person might bring to the group."

"What a Wonderful Life" for Some

Some people feel little sense of home or rootedness in a given organization or group of people. As stated in my essay, "Existential Homelessness: A Contemporary Case for Dialogue," this feeling of community emptiness is not new. However, such a feeling now afflicts the white middle class, making the topic more salient for middle-class readers and authors (Arnett 1994:229–46). Being on the outside of someone else's idealistic project is the reality of outcast people in many different times and places (Tanno 1994).

Those on the inside of a community are often people of influence and power; they are the elite, governing what is appropriate and what violates the standards of their community. For some who assume this privileged position, the term community is a shield of protection for their elite standards and viewpoints. Community, of course, is genuinely desired by elites; they speak in terms of "my" and "our," limiting access to those on the outside. The elites have the "material, institutional, and ideological resources" (Parenti 1978:221) that keep "us" in power and give "us" a cohesive sense of community.

Those on the outside of such resources are unable to be participating members. Henry unknowingly excludes, but some elites knowingly attempt to keep "others" from securing power that might disrupt their way of life and their privileged position in the community hierarchy. A thorough examination of the way in which elites, supported by resources of wealth/education/status and most often the nobility of birth and behavioral style, attempt to maintain power by downplaying the notion of achievement is outlined by Ober in *Mass and Elite in Democratic Athens* (1989). Elites are more inclined to discuss *ethos* than actual achievement. The development of an aristocratic air that propels success through personality and behavior is less likely to be learned by the masses in short duration than are skills needed for genuine achievement.

Perhaps minority and oppressed people who achieve in athletic competition do so, at least to a degree, because the achievement cannot be refuted. If one runs faster, makes more baskets, or scores more runs, one becomes a valued member of the community. There is no way that the nobility of birth right and behavioral style can help, unless money is tied to the cost of participation, as is often the case in golf and tennis. We need to be careful about a romantic view of community that seeks to downplay achievement. Otherwise we open the door to aristocratic domination of the group, based on blood line and behavioral style.

Culture of Narcissism

The irony of exclusion, knowing and unknowing, in the midst of calls for community and intentional protection of one's elite position should not be a surprise in a narcissistic culture. Christopher Lasch's notion of *The Culture of Narcissism* (1979) reminds us that some of us live in such a way that "my" own interests should dominate, regardless of the needs of the community.

Lasch is detailing a culture in the Western world propelled on a dominant level by white men, of the middle and upper-middle classes socially and economically. There is considerable debate about how gender differences offer contrary insights into terms like "caring" and "narcissism." Noddings (1984) outlines a world view guided, not by narcissism, but by service and care. The hope is that multiple voices each admitting and claiming their own ground that nourishes a given perspective can together give us insight into notions like community. Lasch's view of narcissism is not just as self-love, but as a survival response to the lack of a unifying message that pulls people together according to community standards of a given narrative that includes others and ourselves. However, after admitting the limits of narcissism, caring is needed as an alternative foundation for self and other.

If we can agree that it is at least somewhat unusual to find many people willing to give up actualization of their needs in order to assist others, it should not be a surprise that a "culture of narcissism" is at odds with a sense of community that seeks to keep the "common good" at the center of discourse (see, for example, Aristotle, *Nicomachean Ethics,* and Bellah et al., *The Good Society* [1991]). As those who are part of a dominant culture take care of themselves in a narcissistic era, a communal sense of direction is neglected or subordinated.

Constituting a community that is based on everyone's personal aspirations is like linking a group of characters in a novel together without a plot. Christopher Lasch, in *The Minimal Self* (1984), outlines what it means to live without a story or narrative. In such a case, a person is left to depend on his or her own resources as a minimal self, unable to live from a sense of meaning larger than individual feelings. Lasch suggests that the "minimal self" survives by becoming so detached from others that only his or her own experience can offer guidance: "Selective apathy, emotional disengagement from others, renunciation of the past and the future, a determination to live one day at a time—these techniques of emotional self-management, necessarily carried to extremes under extreme conditions, in more moderate form . . . [have shaped the lives of ordinary people]" (57–58).

Lasch's "minimal self" is a person without a common or communal story to offer guidelines for living, giving birth to a narcissistic culture in which we take care of ourselves, lacking confidence in any narrative or story that might encourage a different way of living with others. Of course, all of this behavior and the motivation for it, having become part of our cultural norms, goes unnoticed by the majority of us in the dominant culture. We know nothing else. In short, our narcissistic view of community that calls for no pain and the protection of "me" and "my" resources has been normalized.

This "minimal self" view of community wants no bad news, as related to oneself and the demands of community. The "minimal self" wants to ignore the ontological reality of community, simultaneously an act of inclusion and exclusion in which only some will feel welcome. To attempt to make community happen for all is to court failure. *Paths in Utopia,* romantic views of community that meet the needs of *all* people, are only present in fiction (Buber 1958). Community is better comprehended as a double-bladed knife, cutting simultaneously in the directions of inclusion and exclusion.

Limits of Individualized Community

A romanticized view of community (individualized to the taste of those in power) is not working, according to writers such as Bellah and Lasch. An individualized view of community becomes a lighted path leading back to ourselves, not others, while fooling us into thinking that we have taken a "golden" journey afar to a higher quality lifestyle, which is actually more akin to "fool's gold."

Bellah et al. write in *The Good Society:*

> We described a language of individualistic achievement and self-fulfillment that often seems to make it difficult for people to sustain their commitments to others, either in intimate relationships or in the public sphere. We held up older traditions, biblical and civic republican, that had a better grasp on the truth that the individual is realized only in and through community; but we showed

that contemporary Americans have difficulty understanding those traditions today or seeing how they apply to their lives. We called for a deeper understanding of the moral ecology that sustains the lives of all of us. (5)

Bellah et al. and numerous other authors have informed earlier work on human dialogue, which differentiated the work of Buber and Carl Rogers—calling Buber's work a phenomenological dialogue and Rogers's view of dialogue, psychologized (Arnett 1981). Perhaps another way to distinguish between the different views of dialogue held by the two men is to look pragmatically at their starting points. Buber begins with the backdrop of a narrative context of a people while Rogers begins with the moment of discourse in a therapeutic exchange. In short, Rogers begins with the conversation, and Buber permits the conversation to link itself with an ongoing narrative of a people.

It is this narrative context that Bellah has recently discovered. He is suggesting that selves in conversation with one another are not enough to sustain a "good life." The good life calls one to find happiness in action for the common good, as outlined in Aristotle's *Nicomachean Ethics* and resurrected in contemporary form by Bellah. We can have no notion of the "common good" without some narrative that guides our actions and evaluations.

It is this focus on the lost notion of the "common good" shaped by the narrative life of a people that is at the heart of *The Good Society* (1991). Bellah et al. use Erik Erikson's term, "generativity," to express concern that one generation needs to live out the narrative in action for the next generation, reminding us that a narrative or common good understanding of community is not bound to an individual or even a current generation (273). Bellah et al. state that "a new moral paradigm—a paradigm of cultivation—replaces the old, outworn Lockean individualistic one" (279).

We need a narrative backdrop that permits us to link our lives to others and to ideas other than those that simply support a "minimal self." In summary, I can offer the following tentative observations, which are more or less applicable, depending on one's socioeconomic and power role in a narcissistic culture. First, community is desired and wanted. Second, community is often expected to entail few individual sacrifices from the dominant members of a narcissistic culture. And third, we are beginning to sense that a narrative view of communicative interaction may offer more hope for realistic community than an individualistic framework grounded in the individual psyche.

Community Revisited

The above critique of a romantic view of community strikes at the heart of a wishful view of community. In essence, it is as much a reminder that if we are to take such warnings seriously accommodations need to be made if the term "community" is to be relevant in an age of diversity. Any use of the term needs to embrace both sides of community: "welcome" and "no trespassing!"

Revisitation of the term community reminds one of an earlier work connecting communication and community, *The Human Dialogue,* by Matson and Montagu (1967).

Matson and Montagu suggested that we live in

> the dawning awareness of an age of alienation and anxiety—an awareness cutting across the planes of social science and social action—that the end of human communication is not to *command* but to *commune;* and that knowledge of the highest order (whether of the world, of oneself, or of the other) is to be sought and found not through detachment but through connection, not by objectivity but by intersubjectivity, not in a state of estranged aloofness but in something resembling an act of love.
>
> The theory of communication upon which these thinkers proceed, then, is also a theory of knowledge. It has to do with the manner in which we gain understanding of the world—in particular, the world of other selves. But it has equally to do with the manner in which we gain *self*-understanding; and it may be that this is the crucial point of the theory. It is the insight suggested by Dilthey when he spoke of "the rediscovery of the I in the Thou." (6–7)

In the nearly three decades since Matson and Montagu wrote these words, much has transpired in society. The optimism read into their call to community is now tempered by the influx of change that did not always seem invited, wanted, or constructive. Life's events must be met on their own terms, not just according to our best wishes.

We have witnessed the resignation of a president, the conclusion of a bitter war that divided the nation, growing awareness of problems for the environment and the economy, and, in general, the loss of national innocence. Our lives, on a personal note, have changed as well: perhaps through the influence of marriage and/or separation, graduate education, children, teaching on multiple campuses, surviving multiple faculty and administrative battles on campuses, and for some, witnessing the deaths of too many people we held dear. Like all who endure, life takes a different shape as social and personal changes necessitate adjustment, modification, and sometimes transformation.

At a recent gathering of alumni, a colleague recounted personal and social changes that have altered our lives since undergraduate school education. In the course of conversation, my colleague, who had studied *The Human Dialogue* with Paul Keller (a long time faculty member at Manchester College in Indiana and co-author with Charles T. Brown on *Monologue to Dialogue* [1973]), began to discuss the idealism and hope reflected by Matson and Montagu. He then pondered whether or not their optimism is still warranted.

The next statement was jarring, as my colleague questioned the work of dialogue—placing it in the camp of a "hopeless humanism." In a spirit of caution, I responded: "Perhaps we can believe in such communicative ideals. However, no longer is it possible to believe the invitation to community is as easy or even as personally fulfilling as we had once hoped." Our task, perhaps more than succeeding in the establishment of some ideal communication community, requires us to continue nourishing the fragile bounds of community between persons, both those who feel connected and those outside the inner workings of a group of people.

Such a perspective renovates the notion of community. There is no "heaven on earth" or interpersonal nirvana that eliminates problems and pain caused by human evil and loneliness; oppression is part of human life. Views of community without pain exist only in the minds of those pursuing a world that resembles their own limited understanding of how life should be.

Realizing that life needs to be met on ground that is sometimes unexpected and unknown is a propositional given as we accept the challenge of a realistic sense of community in the midst of diversity of persons. Inviting community that respects the complexity of diverse ethnic, religious, and cultural perspectives is a demanding task, one that at times seems impossible. This view of community does not enhance Henry's unreflective ideal of community; his view misses the complex demands of diversity.

Addressing the complexity of building community in a way that honors diversity requires a threefold commitment that brings together seeming opposites. First, we need to invite enough conceptual uniqueness that a sense of community is possible. A community needs to be centered around an action or idea that pulls people together, reminding them of the importance of their collective existence and searching for ways in which their individual abilities can be realized. Unlike the example of Henry, community needs more than geographical proximity and blind agreement. Community needs a conceptual uniqueness that brings people together; otherwise, without some collective focus the group is unlikely to survive the inevitable interpersonal struggles that accompany the life of a people.

Second, we need to keep a community open to others, offering genuine opportunities for inclusion and influence. The model of such a community is uniqueness of collective identity combined with opportunities for new members to offer insight and contribution that, in turn, continue to shape the collective agenda.

Third, and perhaps the most disconcerting commitment to community, is an honesty that admits that a community cannot include everything; it is defined as much by exclusion as by inclusion. We need an understanding of *communication ethics that embraces life as it is lived and simultaneously keeps alive the hope of a more ideal mode of interaction.* This revisited view of community attempts to be open to diversity, while simultaneously promoting collective uniqueness and difference, and attempts to be honest about public boundaries of a community that eventuate in exclusion.

The words of Maurice Friedman, a contemporary interpreter of Buber's work, outline a view of community that points to this oxymoronic view of community with the notion of "community of otherness":

> the notion of the "community of otherness," . . . can be briefly summarized as follows: Whenever one is concerned about the principles that ground a group or organization or the persons within that group, in addition to oneself, the beginning of a "community of otherness" surfaces. The "community of otherness" permits a struggle over ideas and principles, while confirming one's adversary. In short, the "community of otherness" holds in creative tension the importance of self, other and principles that ground a community, while encouraging confirmation of persons, even when their ideas clash with those of the majority. (quoted in Arnett 1986:7–8)

Friedman (1983) differentiates between a "community of otherness" and a "community of affinity" where one works only with the like-minded and those similar in professional and socioeconomic orientation. As one concurs with the general direction of Friedman's view of community, there remains an implementation question: How to take into account the demanding nature of this dual view of community in an age of diversity?

This implementation issue is more problematic than coming to some theoretical realization of the limits of a romantic view of community.

Articulating the limits of a romantic view of community is easier than outlining how to implement this realistic view while affirming diversity. The *praxis* of the twenty-first century will be our testing ground.

Answering the question of implementation revolves around three basic issues on which community depends: (1) understanding the confused state of public and private discourse, (2) recognizing the practical importance of narrative, and (3) understanding the need for "humble narratives," as opposed to blind adherence to a given static story that has become a dead tradition. Certainly these three issues are not an exhaustive list of implementation requirements for community. But these three elements may assist as we wed communal uniqueness with openness to diversity.

Public and Private

As we embrace diversity, community must turn to a public gathering, in which Bellah et al.'s (1985) call for "habits of the heart" is clearly announced. A privatized view of community simply cannot function *as the community becomes larger and more diverse.* Diversity and difference are seldom keys to private community; most of us are drawn to those similar to ourselves. As stated earlier, Friedman called this a "community of affinity."

Unfortunately, we live in a time when public and private discourse are confused. Bensman and Lilienfeld, in *Between Public and Private: Lost Boundaries of the Self* (1979), suggest that the confusion of what is public and private is not new, but has intensified. To verify such confusion, all one needs to do is tune in a daytime talk show and listen to the language and topics discussed. Without bringing to bear any discussion of right or wrong, it is clear that what was designated as private conversation only a short number of years ago is offered for public consumption. The blurring of what is and is not appropriate in a public setting is embedded in everyday life.

Blurring of private and public discourse encourages bringing private positions into the public arena unknowingly. At first blush such action may seem harmless or liberating. But danger to community is invited when a narrow set of acceptable options from private life precludes us from looking for more inclusive options in the public sphere. Narcissism is based on continual movement of private self-absorbed positions into the public domain—again, unknowingly. Rhetorical civility, on the other hand, requires an understanding of a public view of life composed of a much larger sense of diversity than one's private position might represent (Barrett 1991).

Many of us still live in the shadow of a negative reaction to the importance of the public role enunciated in the 1960s:

> The controversy has been intense. In the 1960s, for instance, it was said that public institutions and public definitions of the self were so alien and repressive, and that the boundaries of the private—i.e., what one could express to others—were so rigid that a whole new set of social relationships were necessary. The demands by public institutions (government, business, churches, universities) were out of phase with the needs of the private self, so much so that an entirely new set of institutions was necessary: communes, perhaps, or some other anarchical expression of social relations. (Bensman and Lilienfeld 1979:viii)

Bensman and Lilienfeld are correct in suggesting that some of us find ourselves in a 1960s-style reaction to overuse, and at times, misuse of public roles. It is out of this reaction that the field of Interpersonal Communication might even have found a foothold in the discipline of Speech Communication. A humanistic view of interpersonal communication moved us from ideas to feelings, from a public focus to a private orientation. Words from an early text on interpersonal communication, *Monologue to Dialogue: An Exploration of Interpersonal Communication,* by Brown and Keller (1973), reveal this movement toward privatized feelings:

> Let us stop here a moment and examine what we are doing as we build this case for communication on the foundation of the feelings of human relationships. Historically, because our view of man has come from Athens, we have conceived of human life as split into two worlds—the rational and the irrational, the cognitive and the affective, the logical and the emotional. . . . With due respect for Aristotle, the main voice of the past to which we are responding, the fact remains that this tendency to categorize . . . does not explain . . . all. . . . We opt for the view that we have a feeling-thinking system founded on our sensory world. As Descartes, taking the Greek view, arrived at the conclusion "I think, therefore I am," we would say, "I feel, therefore I am." (7)

This emphasis on the feeling level of communication was a reaction to role rigidity on the public level of discourse. What many of us, however, did not foresee was the pragmatic result of moving toward a feeling/privatized view of interpersonal communication. It is important to hear another's feelings, but a position based upon private feelings may not gather a hearing in a public arena where conflicting private feelings are felt from the different parties. Public discourse needs to look for ideas, examples, and evidence that can be examined by both parties, regardless of their private positions (Bernstein 1983). With much scholarly material pointing to the limitations of the Enlightenment, Richard Bernstein's argument is even more powerful. He simply reminds us that there is a place for public verification of evidence in the public sphere; the confusion of private and public discourse puts at risk this positive contribution of the Enlightenment to public dialogue. Privatized/emotive discourse leads us to an interpersonal "dark age" where power and similarity guide the notion of community, not public discourse.

Teachers and writers on interpersonal communication are correct in suggesting the importance of private feelings. The quality of life rests as much, if not more, with our affective interaction as with our ability to enter public dialogue with verifiable information. But when multiple private positions are at odds and each is taken unknowingly into the public arena, the contribution of the Enlightenment, bringing into the open ideas that can be publicly verified and examined ceases, is ignored and left unused. We put at risk the best of the Enlightenment contribution to open and free discourse when the public domain is entered with private narrowness. Instead of the private "truth" of the Church (the point of rebellion during the Enlightenment), we move to the opposite extreme (the privatized "truth" of personal feelings) with the same net effect. As we invite individual feelings to guide interaction, we simply move from the Church as autocrat to the individual as autocrat, with positions decided in private, not in the public domain.

Community with an interest in diversity requires a commitment to public discourse. If we are to outline what some of us can and cannot tolerate, many of us generally have a more gracious spirit at a public level than in our own private lives. The limits for what we call community need to be more expansive as we permit diversity to guide us. For instance, one can have a community of Methodists, or a community of Catholics. On the other hand, one may want to have a community centered around the moral core of Judaism and Christianity, as Maguire (1993) has done. One may be more interested in community being centered around "a religious issue," a willingness to be in conversation about religious issues with many traditions, Judeo-Christian and beyond. In each case, the community addresses a larger public, and in each case it must expand the conceptual center that brings the group together.

Narrative

The implications of narrative need to be understood as a foundation for public community that cannot be discovered with a privatized language that is egocentric and carries only one's own position into a larger public domain (Wood 1992:228–29). Walter Fisher's (1984) work points in the direction of public narratives that guide and bring people together. A community needs a "common center" from which to thrive. A narrative, a story of a people or an organization, can provide a common center that can pull people of difference together (Arnett 1992:20–21). The work of Stanley Hauerwas also suggests the importance of community being nourished by a narrative or story. In summarizing his reading of *Watership Down,* Hauerwas suggests, "Without trying to claim a strong continuity between rabbits and us, I think . . . that we, no less than rabbits, depend on narratives to guide us" (1981:34). Our lives together are shaped by trusting in the truth of good stories.

In short, the richness of our public life in an age of diversity may depend on the quality of our narrative life. It is this insight that guides Bellah et al. in *The Good Society.* They discuss rhetoric as the key to rediscovering the notion of the "good society," a narrative in the midst of a complex world. Rhetoric becomes the vehicle for making good arguments and holding organizations together by ideas.

The work on community and narrative has generated some concern from those not wanting a return to exclusive systems. There is legitimate fear that a narrative will become too powerful and oppressive and limit the freedom of opposing views. Such a warning needs to be heeded if we are to avoid the nourishing of small or large "Third Reich" narratives that seek to destroy "the other." From a dialectical perspective we need to limit the errors of a rigid narrative and the roots of self-centered decision-making in which there is no greater criteria than "me."

Perhaps we need to find ways that bring narratives into the public domain while acknowledging that there are good and bad narratives. Some narratives need to guide the public, and other narratives need to be challenged in the public arena with rhetoric. Perhaps the metaphor of *"humble narratives"* points to this vision. Not a narrative for all time or the "best," but a view of life in the public arena that guides and invites challenge. In the reading of this chapter in its early stages, a friend suggested detailing more clearly what constitutes a "humble narrative."

Perhaps another decade of living and writing is needed to be more explicit. At this time, the notion of "humble narrative" is more a research agenda than a definitive posture. Suffice it to say at this time, the metaphor of "humble narrative" is an oxymoron calling us to recognize the need for communal stories to guide our lives as we simultaneously walk in wariness of the blinders inherent in the perspective of a "true believer" (Hoffer 1951). In this vein, a willingness to openly discuss the notion of limits and differences of a narrative is vital as we move from a metaphor of *Bridges, Not Walls* (Stewart 1986) to a respect of diversity and difference, with the phrase, "Walls with Bridges."

As we approach the twenty-first century, a refashioned view of community might begin by suggesting an ethical communication base point: *acknowledging the oxymoronic demands of realistic community, calling for a public view of community more open to diversity, permitting "good" narratives to bind people in community more than interpersonal attraction, and finally, reminding us to be cautious—narratives that guide community are historically grounded, limited, and at times, wrong.* We might not have a warm fuzzy feeling when such a sense of community is discussed, but perhaps it will offer a framework through which diverse people can survive and prosper together in the twenty-first century. Communication ethics in an age of diversity points to a set of humble narratives that bring us together in public fashion, with the ever present knowledge of our own limits and caution toward any narrative that is taken as the ground for community.

References Cited

Aristotle. 1985. *Nicomachean Ethics.* Trans. Terence Irwin. Indianapolis: Hackett Publishers.

Arnett, R. C. 1981. "Toward a Phenomenological Dialogue." *Western Journal of Speech* 45:201–12.

———. 1986. *Communication and Community: Implications of Martin Buber's Dialogue.* Carbondale: Southern Illinois University Press.

———. 1992. *Dialogic Education: Conversation about Ideas and between Persons.* Carbondale: Southern Illinois University Press.

———. 1994. "Existential Homelessness: A Contemporary Case for Dialogue." In *The Reach of Dialogue: Confirmation, Voice, and Community.* Ed. Rob Anderson, Kenneth N. Cissna, and Ronald C. Arnett. Pp. 229–45. Cresskill, N.J.: Hampton Press.

Barrett, H. 1991. *Rhetoric and Civility: Human Development, Narcissism, and the Good Audience.* Albany: State University of New York Press.

Bellah, R. N., R. Madsen, W. M. Sullivan, A. Swidler, and S. M. Tipton. 1985. *Habits of the Heart: Individualism and Commitment in American Life.* Berkeley: University of California Press.

———. 1991. *The Good Society.* New York: Alfred A. Knopf.

Bensman, J., and R. Lilienfeld. 1979. *Between Public and Private: Lost Boundaries of the Self.* New York: Free Press.

Bernstein, R. J. 1983. *Beyond Objectivism and Relativism: Science, Hermeneutics, and Praxis.* Philadelphia: University of Pennsylvania Press.

Bonhoeffer, D. 1960. *The Communion of Saints: A Dogmatic Inquiry into the Sociology of the Church.* New York: Harper and Row.

———. 1975. *The Cost of Discipleship.* New York: Macmillan.

Brown, C. T., and P. W. Keller. 1973. *Monologue to Dialogue: An Exploration of Interpersonal Communication.* Englewood Cliffs, N.J.: Prentice-Hall.

Buber, M. 1958. *Paths in Utopia.* Boston: Beacon Press.

———. 1966. *The Way of Response.* New York: Schocken Books.

———. 1973. *Meetings.* Ed. Maurice Friedman. LaSalle, Ill.: Open Court.

Fisher, W. R. 1984. "Narrative as a Human Communication Paradigm: The Case of Public Moral Argument." *Communication Monographs* 51:1–22.

Friedman, M. 1983. *The Confirmation of Otherness in Family, Community, and Society.* New York: Pilgrim Press.

Hauerwas, S. 1981. *A Community of Character: Toward a Constructive Christian Social Ethic.* Notre Dame: University of Notre Dame Press.

Hoffer, E. 1951. *The True Believer.* New York: New American Library.

Lasch, C. 1979. *The Culture of Narcissism: American Life in an Age of Diminishing Expectations.* New York: W. W. Norton.

———. 1984. *The Minimal Self: Psychic Survival in Troubled Times.* New York: W. W. Norton.

———. 1991. *The True and Only Heaven: Progress and Its Critics.* New York: W. W. Norton.

Maguire, D. C. 1993. *The Moral Core of Judaism and Christianity: Reclaiming the Revolution.* Minneapolis: Fortress Press.

Matson, F. W., and A. Montagu. 1967. "Introduction: The Unfinished Revolution." In *The Human Dialogue: Perspectives on Communication.* Ed. F. W. Matson and A. Montagu. Pp. 6–7. New York: Free Press.

Mendes-Flohr, P. R., ed. 1983. *A Land of Two Peoples: Martin Buber on Jews and Arabs.* New York: Oxford University Press.

Noddings, Nel. 1984. *Caring: A Feminine Approach to Ethics and Moral Education.* Berkeley: University of California Press.

Ober, J. 1989. *Mass and Elite in Democratic Athens: Rhetoric, Ideology, and the Power of the People.* Princeton: Princeton University Press.

Parenti, M. 1978. *Power and the Powerless.* New York: St. Martin's Press.

Peck, M. S. 1987. *The Different Drum: Community Making and Peace.* New York: Simon and Schuster.

Sartre, J. P. 1973. *Being and Nothingness.* New York: Washington Square Press.

Stewart, J. 1986. *Bridges, Not Walls: A Book about Interpersonal Communication.* 4th ed. New York: Random House.

Tanno, D. 1994. "The Meaning of Morality: Views from Above and Below." Paper presented at the Communication Ethics Conference, Gull Lake, Mich.

Tinder, G. 1980. *Community: Reflections on a Tragic Ideal.* Baton Rouge: Louisiana State University Press.

Wiebe, R. H. 1978. *Peace Shall Destroy Many.* Toronto: McClelland and Stewart.

Wood, J. T. 1992. *Spinning the Symbolic Web: Human Communication and Symbolic Interaction.* Norwood, N.J.: Ablex.

3 Embracing Diversity in the Classroom

Josina M. Makau

In a recent editorial on the topic, columnist Joan Beck (1994) refers to diversity as both a "boon" and "bane." According to Beck, "America's current preoccupation" with diversity is "distorting our national life"; it is a dangerous trend that will "increase the fragmentation of our nation and handicap those outside of the mainstream." At the same time, Beck acknowledges that "ethnic and racial minorities contribute incalculable wealth to our social fabric and economic life." She recognizes further that "trying to homogenize us all into some sort of fast-food, cola-drinking, American pop culture would be a monumental mistake."

Beck's ambivalent view of diversity, like that of so many others in the American mainstream, reflects a fear that acknowledgment of diversity threatens to divide our nation's people. Focusing on ethnic, gender, racial, religious, class, and sexual orientation distinctions threatens to encourage separateness, thereby undermining the important task of pulling together toward common goals. This concern is coupled with the recognition that, to many people, diversity means "difference." Those outside our group are often perceived as "others," dangerous to the group's integrity and well-being. In its most destructive form, such a view can lead to forms of tribalism. The world today offers strong support for this concern, as we bear witness daily to horrors associated with xenophobia and tribal conflicts.

I will argue in this essay for a different view of diversity, one that celebrates this element of our nation's life. In the classroom, boardroom, legislative chamber, and living room, diversity enriches significantly the potential for defining and fulfilling our common goals. Realizing this potential requires, however, recognition that the problems commonly attributed to diversity are actually problems of communicative ethics. As Rakow (1994) notes, "it is communication that does or does not hold us together in our relationships and in our communities" (3). How, what, when, where, and why we communicate within and across our ethnic, racial, gender, religious, and class boundaries significantly affects the quality of our lives together. Our willingness and capacity to communicate openly and respectfully across differences affords the possibility of realizing diversity's potential.

In this chapter I will argue that engendering the will and capacity for ethical dialogic interaction requires responsible and responsive pedagogy. Such education is designed to prepare students for ethical participation in communication processes linking people in meaningful and just relationships of community (Rakow 1994). Responsible and responsive pedagogy inspires as it embodies a communicative ethic, developing the will and ability to participate in a process of inclusive, reciprocal, open, equitable, respectful, dynamic, empathic, caring dialogic interaction.[1] Diversity, I will argue, creates both a compelling need for and the possibility of such pedagogy.

I begin my exploration of this topic with a discussion of the concept of diversity. Drawing upon the work of Menand (1993), Mohanty (1991), Wood (1993), Spellman (1988), and Collins (1990), I note that the concept of diversity is not without problems. How we understand the concept carries implications for how we regard its value and consequences. This discussion is followed by an exploration of how diversity both creates and helps fulfill the need for communicative ethics. The final section of the chapter suggests strategies designed to fulfill goals of responsible and responsive pedagogy.

Constructing Diversity

Beck (1994) notes that the 1990 census divides "Americans into 197 groups according to foreign ancestry." Some predict that "by the middle of the next century, whites will be a minority. There will be no ethnic or racial majority group." As noted above, these changing demographics inspire both enthusiasm and worry. Few, however, question the empirical claim that our nation is becoming increasingly diverse ethnically and racially. One who does is Menand in the March 1993 issue of *Harper's*. According to Menand, the idea that the United States is becoming increasingly diverse is a myth. He contends that the nation remains roughly stable in its racial and religious proportions (about 80 percent "white," predominantly Christian), but that there has been real economic change. According to Menand, "this financial difference fragments a society like the United States, with its worship of the privileges of private ownership, far more effectively than any cultural difference" (28). Menand counsels us to avoid explaining "this economic ghettoizing in the language of diversity" (28).

Boorstin (1994) offers further insight into the nation's diversity. He points to the fact that the nation's founding fathers and mothers emigrated from a number of different nations. He notes, for example, that "the United States was the first great modern nation without its own language. Our country has been uniquely created by people willing and able to borrow a language" (5).

Further complicating our consideration of diversity is a growing literature challenging popular academic accounts of this concept. Diversity today is thought of primarily in terms of classifications such as class, ethnicity, race, gender, age, religion, and affectional orientation. These classifications offer potentially useful shorthands for groupings that provide "the genesis of patterned differences" (Wood 1993:5). As Wood notes, "location within social groups profoundly influences personal identity, what and how we know, values we embrace, and codes of conduct and communication we consider appropriate in sundry situations" (6). Cortese's (1990) work on ethnic ethics further supports consideration of people's group locations. He especially encourages the study of ethnic groups, noting that morality "presumes the existence of patterns and rules that transcend the individual. It is only through social relationships that comprehension of, respect for, and adherence to such rules occur" (2). According to Cortese, "the key to morality is in social relations, not abstract rational principles" (2).

Yet, while social location is useful, indeed critical, to an understanding of diversity, the process of identifying referent groups is not without risk. Menand's caution against using diversity language to mask or otherwise obscure problems of economic ghettoization is but one example. Spellman's (1988) critique of monolithic conceptions of women illuminates related risks. Her work challenges theorists to avoid separating race, class, ethnicity, and gender. According to Spellman, "gender exists and must be seen in the context of others factors of identity" (102). She notes, for example, that some white middle-class feminists have tended to generalize from their experiences to all women. This research leads them to mistakenly assume, among other things, that women of color share their experiences, agendas, values, and priorities. According to Spellman, feminists are no less subject to biases than others. "A description of the common world we share 'as women' may be simply a description of my world with you now as an honorary member" (142).

Mohanty's (1991) insightful critique of some western feminist scholarship supports Spellman's observations. According to Mohanty, broad categorizations can lead to a form of academic colonialism. To illustrate, Mohanty discusses the implications of assuming a conception of "women as an already constituted, coherent group with identical interests and desires, regardless of class, ethnic or racial location, or contradictions" (55). According to Mohanty, such conceptions imply "a notion of gender or sexual difference or even patriarchy which can be applied universally and cross-culturally" (55). She argues instead for a highly context-specific conception of identity, one that takes seriously the richness of diversity reflected across and within cultures. She notes, for example, that "male violence must be theorized and interpreted *within* specific societies, in order both to understand it better and to effectively organize to change it." According to Mohanty, "Sisterhood cannot be assumed on the basis of gender; it must be forged in concrete historical and political practice and analysis" (58).

To further illustrate her point, Mohanty critiques specific efforts to study colonial discourses. Responding to Cowie's (1978) work on women in Arab and Muslim societies, for example, Mohanty writes that there "is no discussion of the specific *practices* within the family which constitute women as mothers, wives, sisters, etc. Arabs and Muslims, it appears, don't change at all" (61). Of Daly's *Gyn/Ecology* (1978), Mohanty writes, it "obliterates the differences, complexities, and heterogeneities of the lives of, for example, women of different classes, religions and nations in Africa" (76n.7). According to Mohanty, "what matters is the complex, historical range of power differences, commonalities and resistances that exist among women in Africa which construct African women as 'subjects' of their own politics" (ibid.).

Wood's (1993) compelling critique of "unambiguous and invariant" images of women (2) further challenges scholars to avoid essentializing groups. She cautions against viewing women as a group (4–5), noting that such efforts obscure diversity among women and reinforce "views that have profoundly oppressed women historically" (5). Similarly, Collins (1990) notes that "African-American women as a group experience a world different from that of those who are not Black and female" (24). She cautions against internalizing "controlling images" resulting from essentialist views of gender. Wood (1993) concurs. She urges scholars and educators to "emphasize the enormous diversity among women and to explode long-standing and long-confining monolithic models of women" (7).

Yet, sensitivity to intra-group variability and particularities is not without its own risks. Some, for example, express this sensitivity by using multiple referents. While this strategy does indeed help enrich the notion of diversity, such comprehensive definitions can, as Wood (1993) notes, lead to absurdity. She writes:

> Taking myself as an example, if I fail to designate *all* aspects of my identity, then I am culpable for incompletely describing myself. On the other hand, if I do specify all constituents of my identify, there is no end. I might describe myself as Caucasian, Buddhist, heterosexual, married, child free, educated, orphaned, sister, wife, teacher, aunt, scholar, middle-class, southern, 20th century American woman, vegetarian, amateur investor, feminist, and on and on. It is not pragmatically feasible to enumerate all dimensions of any person, yet we lack criteria to distinguish which dimensions are "important enough" to need naming, much less to decide what comprises "important" or who should decide. (370)

Further complicating our understanding of the nature of human difference is consideration of philosophic diversity. Within each social location is the possibility for a wide range of alternative points of view. Even within a small group of white middle-class educated heterosexual young able-bodied Protestant men there is potential for a wide range of opinion. John Stuart Mill's classic treatise, *On Liberty* (1956[1859]), emphasizes the dangers of a tyrannical party line, whether the tyranny involves repressing creativity, inhibiting exploration of alternative views, or denying access to potential enlightenment through alternative visions. This insight of classical liberalism received renewed support in the September–October 1993 issue of *Ms.* in which the editors note that "feminists *don't* all think alike" (cover). The magazine's featured discussion between four feminist leaders reflects, among other things, differences of opinion on the nature and scope of feminist research and activism; media consumption, use, and criticism; and strategies for achievement of common goals.

In sum, the concept of diversity encompasses a broad range of possible meanings, generating complex problems. As Wood argues in her chapter in this volume, these problems result in a tension between those who would emphasize difference and those who would stress commonality, those embracing individuality and those pursuing a more communal orientation. With Wood, I encourage the preservation of these tensions and, especially, the dialogic communication they make possible. Rather than support a uni-dimensional notion of diversity, I propose that we acknowledge and valorize the inherent complexity of the term. In doing so, we heighten our dialogic possibilities.

In particular, I propose in this essay a conception of diversity encompassing the concerns raised above. Sensitive to the importance of resisting economic ghettoization, I call for a celebration of both the individual and the community, of group location and each person's authentic self. In my view, every individual brings to communication interactions a unique combination of genetic material, experiences, and a highly individual range of emotion and intellectual skills. At the same time, everyone brings to exchanges understandings informed by communal histories and stories, narratives shared with others within one's subcultures. Fulfilling the potential afforded by this view of diversity is dependent, however, upon people's ability and desire to engage in ethical dialogic interaction across differences. Burbules and Rice (1991) note accordingly that "pursuing dialogue across differences is essential to important aims of personal development and moral conduct. We ought to help foster the disposition to work toward understanding across differences, and the communicative virtues and skills that make this possible" (413). The following discussion explores critical links between diversity and communicative ethics.

Diversity and Communicative Ethics

Wood's (1993) consideration of standpoint theory provides a useful starting point for discussion of diversity and communicative ethics. This perspective rejects the poststructuralist tendency to undermine subjects' interpretive capacities, in favor of a view that "individuals interpret their own experiences and imbue them with meaning" (13). Standpoint theory invites us to consider how various standpoints "arise out of conditions surrounding them and how these are construed within subjective consciousness" (14). This perspective seeks to discover how subjects understand and represent their lives, focusing on individuals' "capacities to symbolize and give meaning to their experiences and identities" (14).

This perspective helps avoid a number of problems associated with diversity. Menand (1993) notes, for example, that "the more the marginal, the exotic, and the new become central to the culture, the more everything begins to send the same messages" (29). One risk is that celebrating diversity could mainstream it and thereby destroy its power as a voice of difference and resistance. In contrast, standpoint theory invites us to listen respectfully, openly, and critically to individual narratives, giving voice to a broad spectrum of experiences, values, interests, and beliefs. Such interaction helps prevent Tocqueville's vision of "a country in which people, permitted to say whatever they like, all somehow end up saying the same thing" (Menand 1993:29).

While standpoint theory helps mitigate this and related problems, its focus on social location and difference also poses risks. Preoccupation with social location has the potential to encourage boundaries between people based on class, racial, gender, ethnic, religious, or other arbitrary criteria used to define who and what we are. The politics of identity, while rich with potential, threaten to encourage preoccupation with difference at the expense of recognition of cross-cultural communal goals. As noted earlier, identity politics can encourage tribalism and conflict.

Living together peacefully and productively in an age of diversity requires a communicative ethics, a model of communication that links people in meaningful and just relationships of community. Rakow (1994) suggests inclusiveness, participation, and reciprocity as three elements for a "communicative ethic that could help guide our relations—between individuals, between cultures, between organizations, between countries" (18). Benhabib (1990, 1992) adds a fourth component, the capacity for reversing perspectives. According to Benhabib, the development of the "capacity for reversing perspectives and the development of the capacity to assume the moral point of view are intimately linked" (1990:359).

Benhabib's perspective rests on a revisioning of the "moral point of view." She challenges the traditional Kantian vision of the generalized other and calls instead for a local, concrete, particularized view. According to Benhabib, moral decision-making requires a process of understanding "concrete others'" perspectives. Rather than thinking of an abstract, universalized "other" in our decision-making, Benhabib urges us to consider "real," local, particularized concrete others whose lives are affected by the outcome of our actions and beliefs. Rather than seek detachment from "others," we should pursue moral decision-making "rooted in receptivity, relatedness, and responsiveness" (Noddings 1984:2). As Wood (1994) writes, "to be partial is to focus quite directly on the concrete perspectives, needs, concerns, and the like of particular others" (42). Such a stance "informs efforts to recognize and meet the unique needs and desires of particular persons, rather than to act on abstract and general ideas about what people need" (43).

Cooper (1994) and Johannesen (1990) provide a pedagogic framework for developing such a communicative ethic. Echoing work in human potential literature, they call for the development of response-ability. To be response-able implies "reaching out to another, of recognizing difference yet reaching out in love nonetheless" (Cooper 1994:3). A person who is response-able "exercises the ability to respond (is responsive) to the needs and communication of others in sensitive, thoughtful, fitting ways" (Johannesen 1990:9). As Johannesen notes in his essay in this volume, the "exercise of thoughtful and caring judgment" is "an essential element of responsible communication" for both senders and receivers. Response-ability—the capacity and desire to listen, to reach out to others, to "hear each other into speech," to engage in discursive practices that form bonds of identification in communication—creates the possibility of celebrating diversity without suffering its risks.

While response-ability helps diverse groups and individuals live peacefully and productively together, the link between diversity, pedagogy, and communicative ethics does not end there. In the discussion to follow, I argue that ethical decision-making in the postmodern world *requires* diversity. Like peaceful coexistence, decision-making in practical contemporary contexts depends upon response-ability.

Response-ability, Diversity, and Ethical Decision-Making

Standpoint epistemology opens links between communicative ethics and sound practical reasoning. If assumptions, values, and beliefs are affected significantly by social location and personal experiences, each individual's world view is necessarily constrained. We can know only what our limited experiences, cultural inheritance, and education teach us. Such inevitable constraint is problematic in any decision-making context but can be particularly debilitating in the complex postmodern world. Consider, for example, the issues confronting contemporary medical practitioners and their clients. Technological advancements create a multiplicity of difficult ethical problems for caring physicians. Should the physician harvest the anencephalic baby's organs so that another baby might live? Should she give an infant heart and liver transplants even if the prognosis is poor? Should she kill one Siamese twin to provide her sister a 10 percent chance of living another six months? These questions— derived from actual cases—represent a tiny fraction of the ethical dilemmas that surface in medical practice today.

Standpoint epistemology suggests that each decision maker's approach to these complex issues is influenced significantly by his or her social location. Individual decisions are therefore likely to be subject to prejudices, particularized interests, and limited epistemic frames. Traditionally, philosophers proposed application of abstract, context-invariant universal principles to prevent the type of individualistic, prejudicial decisions social locations could otherwise generate.

The vast majority of contemporary bioethicists have come to recognize, however, the untenability and potential harms of adhering to this perspective. In their collected volume, *A Matter of Principles?* (DuBose et al. 1994), scholars from medicine, philosophy, law, and theology unite to denounce abstract universalist approaches to bioethical problems. Despite many differences of opinion on specific issues, these scholars share the increasingly accepted view that resolving bioethical issues requires practical reasoning skills.[2] Because such decisions are local, temporal, and highly particularized, it is neither possible nor desirable to identify and apply universal principles. Recognition of the resulting "ambiguity and lack of certainty" is "what makes ethical reflection both possible and important" (Churchill 1994:329–30).

This view of bioethics reinforces the importance of recognizing diversity in decision-making. Combined with constraints of social location, limited epistemic frames and ambiguity impose almost impossible burdens on individual or monolithic groups of decision makers. Only through dynamic dialogic interaction with concrete others whose beliefs, values, and interests differ from our own can we hope to reason competently and morally.

Elliot (1992) identifies additional reasons why bioethical decisions require diversity. He notes that it is "extraordinarily difficult, if not impossible, to capture the countless subtleties that go into perceptions and judgments of each person involved" in a difficult medical case (28). Only "novelists and poets," he writes, have the talent to both perceive and record the prayers, guilt, pride, remorse, and other conflicting emotions experienced by each person. The process of providing a case narrative is particularly difficult. According to Elliot, "one of the most interesting and disturbing discoveries to be made in a medical ethics case conference is how one's moral intuitions change as each player in the drama says his piece, as another perspective is added to one's own" (28). Because one's "conceptual framework structures one's perception of the case" (29), dialogic interaction inviting others to consider alternative narratives is critical to bioethical decision-making.

In sum, given the complexity of issues, the constraints of epistemic frames, the inherent ambiguities associated with bioethical cases, the paucity of context-invariant principles, and the need for diverse narrative accounts, bioethical decision-making requires multiple perspectives that provide the tools needed to expose and challenge underlying assumptions, to provide alternative narrative accounts, and hence to provide the narrative richness needed to make reasoned ethical decisions. In medical practice, as in most postmodern practical decision-making settings, diversity enhances competent moral decision-making.[3]

Even more fundamentally, diversity offers the potential to create conditions necessary for ethical decision-making. Benhabib (1990) writes persuasively, for example, that "moral blindness implies not necessarily an evil or unprincipled person, but one who cannot see the moral texture of the situation confronting him or her" (357). Seeing this moral texture requires dialogic interaction with others whose perspectives differ substantively from our own. Assuming the moral point of view and developing the capacity to see the moral texture of situations requires the capacity to listen, to understand others' points of view, to represent to ourselves the world and the other as seen by the concrete other (359). According to Benhabib, "judgment requires for its successful exercise the ability to take the standpoint of the other" (1992:137).

Mill (1956[1859]) speaks to this point. Personal and group enlightenment, according to Mill, requires that we hear alternative perspectives "from persons who actually believe them, who defend them in earnest and do their very utmost for them." This allows us to know the perspectives "in their most plausible and persuasive form" (45). According to Mill, without throwing ourselves "into the mental position of those who think differently from" us and considering "what such persons may have to say," we do not "in any proper sense of the word, know the doctrine" which we ourselves "profess" (45). Access to people whose social locations differ substantially from our own provides the best and most reliable means for such enlightenment. We have good reason, therefore, to celebrate diversity and its expression in the classroom.

According to Benhabib (1992), "the cultivation of one's moral imagination flourishes" in a "culture in which the self-centered perspective of the individual is constantly challenged by the multiplicity and diversity of perspectives that constitute public life" (141). The very essence of critical "judgment involves the capacity to represent to oneself the multiplicity of viewpoints, the variety of perspectives, the layers of meaning which constitute a situation. This representational capacity is crucial for the kind of sensitivity to particulars which most agree is central for good and perspicacious judgment" (53–54). Wood (1993) notes further that "diversity can be an agent, not an enemy, of change in its power to stimulate new ideas, which are suppressed in monolithic thinking" (371). As she observes, to exclude any voices from our dialogues "is to impoverish ourselves and our understandings of communication" (373).

Pedagogic Strategies

What remains is consideration of pedagogic strategies designed to facilitate development of the will and capacity to engage in ethical dialogic interaction across differences. Wood and Lenze (1991) speak of the important role pedagogical processes play in creating constructive learning environments. They identify "instructors' language, classroom style, and ways of responding to students" as elements of the process "which convey a great deal about what instructors value and endorse in their classrooms and, more generally, in human interaction" (17). They note that in most traditional classrooms "individual achievement is valued more highly than collaborative efforts, talking is encouraged more than listening, presenting new ideas is emphasized whereas responding to and synthesizing classmates' ideas is not, competition is stressed more than co-operation, and advancing firm conclusions is more highly regarded than holding tentative ones" (17).

Such instructional practices are likely to discourage the development of response-ability. If ethical communication is "a mode of being, something which is created rather than possessed" (Cooper 1994:3), a competitive, individualistic classroom environment is likely to inhibit the development of the will and capacity to engage in ethical communication. To be responsible is "to be *response-able,* able to respond" (Cooper 1994:2). Response-ability allows us to "hear each other into speech," thereby helping constitute "ourselves and others as ethical agents" (4). Individualistic, competitive instruction undermines the heart of response-ability.[4]

Three related elements are required to develop response-ability: creating conditions conducive to reaching out in respect to one another, developing a willingness to listen, and developing the will and capacity to develop a sensitivity to the perspective of others (Cooper 1994:3).

Creating conditions conducive to reaching out with openness and respect is critical to responsible and responsive pedagogy. Reciprocity, inclusiveness, and participation depend upon a sense of immanent value and safety (Foss and Griffin 1995). Creating a safe space for dialogue requires, among other things, generating a sense of mutual respect and equality. As hooks (1989) notes, "we must acknowledge that our role as teacher is a position of power over others" (52). Although such acknowledgment is important, however, it need not and indeed should not entail acceptance of personal inequality. A safe classroom is a place where everyone experiences "equality in terms of personal value, where students and the professor have equal respect for each other as persons and where this respect affects all aspects of the interaction and learning in the class" (Foss 1991:2). Circular seating arrangements, noncompetitive assignments and grading, the use of respectful, inclusive, and sensitive examples, reciprocal interaction in which students sense their contributions are genuinely valued, and other strategies facilitating connected knowing (Belenky et al. 1986) all contribute to the creation of such a safe, constructive learning environment.

Creating a constructive learning environment in an age of diversity also requires sensitivity to different and sometimes competing experiences of "safety." Ng (1994) argues, for example, that "to speak of safety and comfort is to speak from a position of privilege, relative though it may be" (45). She argues that any form of "anti-oppression work is not easy, comfortable, or safe. It is protracted, difficult, uncomfortable, painful, and risky" (45). Our task, according to Ng, is to "speak up against normalized courses of action which serve to maintain existing inequality." She speaks in particular of the "need to consciously open up spaces for previously silenced or marginalized voices to be heard. We need to create spaces for students to interrogate existing paradigms and explore alternate ones, and to support them in other endeavors" (44). According to Ng, "universities should expose students to a range of perspectives and experiences, not simply confirm or reinforce the students' limited views of the world" (44). Deep critical reflection of the sort prescribed by Ng has the potential to challenge students at such a fundamental level that some may feel "unsafe."

The notion of safety is challenged further by Srivastava (1994). In her critique of anti-racist workshops, she speaks to the "pain of exposing personal experiences of racism to a mixed group, the crushing invalidation by white students and teachers who may have been the source of these experiences, the feeling of invasion and vulnerability in having their experiences probed by the facilitator, and then displayed 'for all to see'" (107). According to Srivastava, people of color "should be able to share our experiences in situations under our own control, or when we have chosen to—and when it is in our interest" (107).

In sum, the construction of power in the classroom is critical to responsible pedagogy. It is a highly complex process requiring understanding of and sensitivity to historical patterns of inequality and domination. Engendering and developing response-ability requires, above all, a relational view of power "characterized by mutuality rather than sovereignty" (Christians et al. 1993:106). Assignments designed to help students pursue and value "cooperation with peers" rather than "hegemony over subject" (107) facilitate realization of this view of power in the classroom. In such an environment, students are more likely to develop the capacity and will to understand, to have both "knowledge of the perspectives of others" and "knowledge of the interests underlying those perspectives" (Rucinski 1991:188). In Buber's words, dialogue involves "real outgoing to the other, reaching to the other, and companying with the other" (1965:21).

Development of the ability and will to listen and to develop sensitivity to others' perspectives is facilitated by creating an environment in which "individuals are allowed to tell of their experiences without listeners interrupting, comforting, or inserting anything of their own" (Foss and Griffin 1995:11). Perhaps most important, however, is the need to recognize that "dialogue implies talk between two subjects, not the speech of subject and object. It is a humanizing speech, one that challenges and resists domination" (hooks 1989:131).

Houston's (1994) study of conversations between African- American and white women reveals important challenges to this process. She notes that "expectations for talk are culturally learned" (135). Dialogues between people from different cultures is difficult in part because participants bring different "expectations for how to express specific attitudes and emotions" (135). These differences often result in misunderstandings and potentially harmful conflicts. Houston admonishes teachers and scholars to recognize the important impact cultural, sexual, and generational differences have on social experiences and interpretations of shared experiences (137). Creating a constructive learning environment requires understanding of and sensitivity to these differences. Freire (1994) suggests that "multiculturality as a phenomenon involving the coexistence of different cultures in one and the same space is not something natural and spontaneous." According to Freire, "it calls for a new ethics, founded on respect for differences" (157).

Realizing Diversity's Potential in the Communication Classroom

The discussions above reveal the centrality of communication to responsible and responsive pedagogy. Consideration of how communication classrooms can realize diversity's potential therefore seems particularly useful.

Shepherd's (1992) critique of dominant approaches to communication research and pedagogy suggests that realizing diversity's potential in the classroom requires a transformation of vision. He notes that the traditional view of communication as influence relies on the "subjugation of an alternative" view that "defines communication in terms of relations, concern, care, and responsibility, rather than influence" (206). Traditional conceptions of communication as influence view communication as functioning primarily to maintain dominance and subordination. Shephard proposes an alternative view of communication as power that functions to "illuminate interdependence and foster concern for others" (207).

Traditional argumentation courses provide useful exemplars of these differing perspectives. Until recently, many argumentation instructors embraced an adversarial view of argument. Courses were designed to develop advocacy skills within a competitive framework. Muir's (1993) defense of contemporary debate, for example, maintains the efficacy and value of this perspective. Such classes encourage what Buber (1965, 1970) describes as the world of I-It relations. Others in the class are seen as opposing objects. Students are encouraged to "win" debates, to pursue individualized, separated, detached goals. Success in this environment is achieved by gaining control over others, rather than risking with others.[5] In contrast, the I-Thou or dialogic relationship is characterized by communion, directness, open-heartedness, mutuality, and nonmanipulative intent.

A cooperative approach to argumentation instruction encourages students to embrace this view of ethical dialogic interaction. Argumentation in this class is defined as a process of reasoned interaction designed to improve the quality of participants' decision-making (Makau 1990, 1992, 1995). Students are encouraged to work collaboratively, inviting each other to dialogue. They share information with each other and are graded on the basis of their contributions to decision-making. Students are discouraged from viewing debate as a "game" of reason (Belenky et al. 1986). In the alternative class, there are no winners or losers; students are encouraged to see debate and argumentation as opportunities to learn and grow, rather than as occasions to advance their individual perspectives. Students are discouraged from pursuing conversion of others; they are rewarded for their willingness and ability to invite others to dialogue. In this class, there is no competition for scarce resources; participants benefit from collaborative efforts. Further, in this revisioned course, participants' experiences and emotions join with "expert" testimony as valuable grounds for decision-making. All sources of information—from narrative accounts to statistical tables—are interpreted, analyzed, and used for the betterment of the group's decision-making. In the revisioned argumentation course, dialogue is viewed as possible throughout humanity. "There are no gifted and ungifted here, only those who give themselves and those who withhold themselves" (Buber 1965:35). Students in this class are taught to appreciate "enlarged thought," to "make present to oneself what the perspectives of others involved are or could be" (Benhabib 1992:137). Class participants are encouraged to see others who disagree most fundamentally with them and whose life experiences differ most substantively from their own as among the most potentially insightful teachers. In sum, students in the alternative argumentation class are encouraged to view each other as valuable resources; every facet of the course is designed to help students pursue reasoned decisions together.[6]

Sonja Foss (1992) and Sonja Foss and Karen Foss (1994) provide an overview of how the public speaking course can be revisioned to incorporate this transformed vision of communication. Among the speaking goals included in the revisioned course are: to articulate a perspective, to assert individuality, to maintain community, to discover knowledge or belief, or to resist. Organizational patterns include the metaphor, narrative, complementary opposites, web, circle, and Rogerian.[7]

Karen Foss's (1992) overview of a revisioned American Public Address Course offers additional suggestions for transforming communication pedagogy. Foss's course "includes a variety of formal and informal texts by a diverse group of individuals and concentrates on the understanding and analysis of texts rather than on historical events associated with famous speeches" (67). Foss notes, "attention to diversity in genres, texts, and rhetors will demonstrate to students the richness and variety of symbol use in our time" (67).

Conclusion

Freire (1994) writes that educators have the ethical duty to express "respect for differences in ideas and positions" (79). Fulfilling this duty requires pursuit of ethical communication practices and processes. Responsive and responsible pedagogy inspires the will and capacity to engage in ethical dialogic interaction across differences.

Many who write about diversity in the classroom emphasize the need for and importance of tolerance. The educational journal *Teaching Tolerance,* for example, is devoted fully to this endeavor. While tolerance can serve important social functions, stressing the need for tolerance can jeopardize the perspective proposed in this essay. People tolerant of one another may fail to appreciate the riches diversity offers them.

In this essay I have attempted to illustrate the importance of replacing tolerance with celebration. Diversity is not simply an obstacle to overcome. Competent moral decision-making in the postmodern world is dependent upon the narrative richness, exposure of underlying assumptions and values, and critical understanding made possible only when decision makers have access to and have the vision, talent, and insight to hear a wide diversity of voices. Similarly, personal growth and development depend upon the will and ability to interact dialogically across differences. Perhaps most significantly, discovery and realization of common goals and purposes are possible only through such interaction.

Problems commonly associated with diversity actually find their roots in incompetent and unethical communication processes. Living peacefully together in an age of diversity requires responsive and responsible pedagogy designed to develop response-ability, the capacity and will to interact with others openly, receptively, and respectfully.

In sum, to achieve its goals in this age of diversity, postmodern pedagogy requires a shift in attitude. Rather than strive for tolerance, educators will serve themselves and their communities best by helping students develop response-ability. This goal "is best realized through a dialogic or discursive ethic" (Benhabib 1992:137) in which educators and students sincerely embrace diversity in the classroom.

Notes

1. These elements bear a striking resemblance to Martin Buber's elements of dialogue. For an overview of Buber's concept, see Johannesen 1990:62–64.

2. Toulmin was among the first and most influential contributors to the development of this awareness. See, for example, his 1988 essays on cosmic

prudence and practical philosophy and his work with Jonsen on the nature of *phronesis* (1989).

3. It is important to note that dialogic interaction is a necessary, but not a sufficient, condition for competent moral reasoning and decision-making. Good decision-making requires, among other things, all the elements of *phronesis*. While dialogic interaction provides some of these elements, *phronesis* includes more than is offered by such interaction. The point here is that without access to diverse experiences and perspectives, decision makers are ill-equipped to make competent judgments. Thus, although not sufficient, dialogic interaction across differences is *necessary* for competent decision-making. Until recently, few philosophers acknowledged this necessity. For discussions of other elements of *phronesis,* see Jonsen and Toulmin (1988).

4. Treichler and Kramarae (1983) argue that competitive, individualistic classroom environments fail to "foster the patterns of interaction many women have grown up with, are accustomed to, and are good at" (126). They contend, however, that "female and male interaction *patterns* can exist in classrooms side-by-side, as important resources for both females and males" (126). They recommend "a sensitivity to structure and more flexibility and diversity in the forms of interaction teachers use, value, and foster" (128).

5. For insightful explorations of differences between an ethic of control and an ethic of risk, see Jonas (1984) and Welch (1990).

6. Herrick (1992) argues that his view of rhetoric "as persuasive and adversarial by its nature" (143) is compatible with this view of cooperative argument. In my view, these perspectives are incompatible. For elaboration, see Makau 1993, Gearhart 1979, and Foss and Griffin 1995.

7. Foss and Foss's textbook (1994) provides a resource for the revisioned public speaking course.

References Cited

Beck, J. 1994. "Diversity Can Be Both Boon, Bane." *Columbus Dispatch,* June 28, p. 7-A.

Belenky, M. F., B. M. Clinchy, N. R. Goldberger, and J. M. Tarule. 1986. *Women's Ways of Knowing.* New York: Basic Books.

Benhabib, S. 1990. "Afterword: Communicative Ethics and Contemporary Controversies in Practical Philosophy." In *The Communicative Ethics Controversy.* Ed. S. Benhabib and F. Dallmayr. Pp. 330–70. Cambridge: MIT Press.

———. 1992. *Situating the Self.* New York: Routledge.

Boorstin, D. J. 1994. "Why an Eminent Historian Unequivocally States: 'I Am Optimistic.'" *Parade,* July 10, p. 4.

Buber, M. 1965. *Between Man and Man.* Trans. R. G. Smith. New York: Collier.

————. 1970. *I and Thou.* Trans. W. Kaufmann. New York: Charles Scribner's Sons.

Burbules, N., and S. Rice. 1991. "Dialogues across Differences: Continuing the Conversation." *Harvard Educational Review* 61:393–416.

Christians, C. G., J. P. Ferre, and M. P. Fackler. 1993. *Good News: Social Ethics and the Press.* New York: Oxford University Press.

Churchill, L. R. 1994. "Rejecting Principlism, Affirming Principles: A Philosopher Reflects on the Ferment in U.S. Bioethics." In *A Matter of Principles?: Ferment in U.S. Bioethics.* Ed. E. R. DuBose, R. P. Hamel, and L. J. O'Connell. Pp. 321–31. Valley Forge, Pa.: Trinity Press International.

Collins, P. H. 1990. *Black Feminist Thought: Knowledge, Consciousness, and the Politics of Empowerment.* New York: Routledge.

Cooper, M. 1994. "Postmodernism, Feminism, and the Ethical Subject." Paper presented at the Communication Ethics Conference, Gull Lake, Mich.

Cortese, A. 1990. *Ethnic Ethics.* Albany: State University of New York Press.

Cowie, E. 1978. "Women as Sign." *m/f* 1:49–63.

Daly, M. 1978. *Gyn/ecology: The Metaethics of Radical Feminism.* Boston: Beacon Press.

DuBose, E. R., R. P. Hamel, and L. J. O'Connell, eds. 1994. *A Matter of Principles?: Ferment in U.S. Bioethics.* Valley Forge, Pa.: Trinity Press International.

Elliot, C. 1992. "Where Ethics Comes from and What to Do about It." *Hastings Center Report* 22 (July–August):28–35.

Foss, K. 1992. "Revisioning the American Public Address Course." *Women's Studies in Communication* 15:66–78.

Foss, S. K. 1991. "What Is Feminist Pedagogy?" Paper presented at the annual meeting of the Organization for Research in Gender and Communication, San Antonio, Tex.

————. 1992. "Revisioning the Public-Speaking Course." *Women's Studies in Communication* 15:53–65.

Foss, S. K., and K. A. Foss. 1994. *Inviting Transformation: Presentational Speaking for a Changing World.* Prospect Heights, Ill.: Waveland.

Foss, S. K., and C. Griffin. 1995. "Beyond Persuasion: A Proposal for a Feminist Rhetoric." *Communication Monographs* 62:2–18.

Freire, P. 1994. *Pedagogy of Hope.* New York: Continuum.

Gearhart, S. 1979. "The Womanization of Rhetoric." *Women's Studies International Quarterly* 2:195–201.

Herrick, J. A. 1992. "Rhetoric, Ethics, and Virtue." *Communication Studies* 43:133–49.

hooks, bell. 1989. *Talking Back: Thinking Feminist, Thinking Black.* Boston: South End Press.

Houston, M. 1994. "When Black Women Talk with White Women: Why Dialogues Are Difficult." In *Our Voices: Essays in Culture, Ethnicity, and Communication.* Ed. A. Gonzalez, M. Houston, and V. Chen. Pp. 133–40. Los Angeles: Roxbury.

Johannesen, Richard L. 1990. *Ethics in Human Communication.* 3d ed. Prospect Heights, Ill.: Waveland.

Jonas, H. 1984. *The Imperative of Responsibility.* Chicago: University of Chicago Press.

Jonsen, A., and S. Toulmin. 1988. *The Abuse of Casuistry.* Berkeley: University of California Press.

Makau, J. M. 1990. *Reasoning and Communication.* Belmont, Calif.: Wadsworth Publishing.

———. 1993. "Revisioning the Argumentation Course." *Women's Studies in Communication* 15:79–91.

Menand, L. 1993. "The Myth of American Diversity." *Harper's Magazine,* March, pp. 26–28.

Mill, J. S. 1956 [1859]. *On Liberty.* Indianapolis: Bobbs-Merrill.

Mohanty, C. T. 1991. "Under Western Eyes: Feminist Scholarship and Colonial Discourses." In *Third-World Women and the Politics of Feminism.* Ed. C. T. Mohanty, A. Russ, and L. Torres. Pp. 51–80. Bloomington: Indiana University Press.

Muir, S. A. 1993. "The Ethics of Contemporary Debate." *Philosophy and Rhetoric* 26:277–96.

Ng, R. 1994. "Sexism and Racism in the University: Analyzing a Personal Experience." *Canadian Women's Studies* 14:41–46.

Noddings, N. 1984. *Caring: A Feminine Approach to Ethics and Moral Education.* Berkeley: University of California Press.

Rakow, L. 1994. "The Future of the Field: Finding Our Mission." Paper presented as part of Communication Day activities, Ohio State University, Columbus.

Rucinski, D. 1991. "The Centrality of Reciprocity to Communication and Democracy." *Critical Studies in Mass Communication* 8(2):184–95.

Shepherd, G. J. 1992. "Communication as Influence: Definitional Exclusion." *Communication Studies* 43:203–19.

Spellman, E. V. 1988. *Inessential Woman: Problems of Exclusion in Feminist Thought.* Boston: Beacon Press.

Srivastava, S. 1994. "Voyeurism and Vulnerability: Critiquing the Power Relations of Anti-racist Workshops." *Canadian Women's Studies* 14:105–9.

Toulmin, S. 1988a. "The Case for Cosmic Prudence." *Tennessee Law Review* 56:29–41.

———. 1988b. "The Recovery of Practical Philosophy." *American Scholar* (Summer):337–52.

Treichler, P., and C. Kramarae. 1983. "Women's Talk in the Ivory Tower." *Communication Quarterly* 31:18–22.

Welch, S. 1990. *A Feminist Ethic of Risk.* Minneapolis: Fortress Press.

Wood, J. T. 1993. "Gender and Moral Voice: From Woman's Nature to Standpoint Epistemology." *Women's Studies in Communication* 15:1–24.

———. 1994. *Who Cares?: Women, Care, and Culture.* Carbondale: Southern Illinois University Press.

Wood, J. T., and L. F. Lenze. 1991. "Strategies to Enhance Gender Sensitivity in Communication Education." *Communication Education* 40:16–22.

PART 2

Culture, Diversity, and Ethics

Introduction

The chapters in part 2 reflect many of the tensions inherent in any consideration of diversity and communication ethics. Dolores V. Tanno's essay, "Ethical Implications of the Ethnic 'Text' in Multicultural Communication Studies," reminds us that people "outside" the status quo or group norm have a different perspective. For instance, as some white middle-class people in mainstream America bemoan a loss of direction and a lack of confidence in the future, we realize such a view is not new, just recent to those in the dominant culture. Research of the lives of human beings requires the capacity and will to listen with sensitivity and respect to multiple voices.

Barbara Paige Pointer and Gale Auletta Young's essay, "Derailing the Equity Process: Language as a Mechanism of Sabotage," for example, asks the provocative question of how the deeply conservative conception of political correctness took hold of the American psyche. Their exploration of relationships between ethnicity and ethics challenges universalist views, noting that such perspectives historically serve inevitably to marginalize various groups. Because theory is inherently ideological, deeply internalized biases and prejudices influence public perceptions of moves to challenge oppressive ideological frames. The authors call for an honest and open speech environment in which communicators develop critical abilities for inquiry about feelings as well as ideas. They call, in essence, for a communicative ethic in which participants speak honestly and with compassion for their own and others' feelings.

Lea P. Stewart makes similar observations in her essay, "Facilitating Connections: Issues of Gender, Culture, and Diversity." After noting the considerable role culture plays in shaping gender, Stewart calls for reclaiming notions of voice for all interactants, regardless of their gender. Stewart's starting point leads to advice different, however, from Paige Pointer and Young's. She calls for us to transcend specific culture. Fostering dialogue, embracing multiple discourses, empowerment, inclusion, and critical reflection form the essence of her guidelines for ethical communication between masculine and feminine cultures.

James W. Chesebro's "Ethical Communication and Sexual Orientation" also emphasizes the role of culture in defining self. His focus, sexual orientation, provides a particularly salient exemplar for illustrating this key point. In his search for a communication ethic for same-sex relationships, Chesebro emphasizes equality, respect of and for differences, elimination of domination, and developing a framework of creative social change.

In short, all the authors in this section contend that society has the potential to play a key role in fostering as well as inhibiting communicative ethics. They all note the importance of creating conditions that foster such interaction. They disagree, however, on the degree to which scholars, teachers, and practitioners should pursue universalist versus more particularized ethical standards. As these essays reveal, this issue remains among the more complex and difficult questions facing those who wish to foster constructive human interaction in an age of diversity.

4   Ethical Implications of the Ethnic "Text" in Multicultural Communication Studies

Dolores V. Tanno

Understanding the role of communication in multicultural communities continues to gain importance in our discipline. Our increased awareness of a diverse society has helped make the context of "culture" seem less strange alongside other communication contexts such as the interpersonal, organizational, political, and so on.

Within a multicultural context, communication acts are enriched as they are informed by a variety of value systems, philosophies, traditions, and histories. A multicultural discursive community results from an interplay between a specific culture's values and philosophies and those of the society at large as they play out in language. In some cultural communities, bilinguality adds a third dimension to this interplay. These dimensions manifest themselves in "thick" communication (Geertz 1973), suggesting not layers of communication but rather an intertwining, so that it becomes difficult to know where one dimension ends and another begins. Any knowledge about multicultural communication, therefore, must account for the often indistinguishable interdependence among these dimensions of communication.

Both the complexity and the relative newness of the multicultural communication context in our discipline calls for what Bazerman (1992) has described as the "reflexive rhetorical turn" that focuses attention on language and its impact. The "reflexive rhetorical turn" in this chapter focuses on the multicultural communication research process, paying particular attention to the language of multicultural research, its relationship to knowledge gained through comparison rather than dialogue, some ethical imperatives arising therefrom, and what these may imply for researchers. The ethnic "text" is the pivotal point around which this examination takes place.

Introduction

An explanation about my use of the terms "multicultural," "ethics," and ethnic "text" is appropriate at this point. I use the term "multicultural" to describe all the contexts (variously known as intercultural, cross-cultural, intracultural, international, etc.) within which communication between, among, and within cultural communities takes place. At the same time that the term "multicultural" captures the diversity of cultural communities and contexts, it is also a reminder of the multitude of cultural voices waiting to be engaged in empowering dialogue.

The issue of empowerment is embodied in the term "ethics" as one ties it conceptually to choice. Choice is one part of the essence of ethical communication, the other part being responsibility for the impact of our communication. In 1968, Winterowd captured this dual essence of ethical communication when he defined language as "perhaps the only human and humane act" by which "we can literally talk ourselves to death" (14).

When using the term "text" in relation to the word "ethnic" I follow Bazerman's lead in "The Interpretation of Disciplinary Writing" (1992). Arguing that his study of social scientific texts "reverses" traditional hermeneutic assumptions, Bazerman writes: "When looking at a text in isolation, I look at how the text reaches out beyond the page, what connections it makes with the reader, the ambient natural world, the ambient social world. I look at how a text defines or reorders relationships and defines activities" (35). This "rhetorical self-consciousness" (37) begins with a keen awareness of language use and its relationship to knowledge. Within critical and social scientific multicultural studies, our language choices for definitions, identifying labels, interpretations, and conclusions have the potential to leap "beyond the page" and impact groups of people in ways we never intended nor imagined. Furthermore, the language of our studies composes the knowledge base of multicultural understanding. I will argue that the term "ethnic" becomes an exemplar of a specific "text" in multicultural studies that extends into society, creating a particular and not always accurate perception about members of cultural groups.

Currently, much of our understanding of multicultural communication is based on the pursuit of *comparative* knowledge. We gather information and evaluate it by comparing it to often unconsciously assumed a priori norms or by comparing it to consciously developed frames of reference. One result of this is an attribution of relative worth of one norm over another. Discussing genres of discourse, Hariman (1986) argued that "the act of comparing discourses implies both manifest definitions of substance and latent attributions of status for each genre" (38).

In and of itself, comparison is not an unproductive approach for pursuing knowledge and understanding. In the context of multicultural communication research, however, the act of comparing communication practices between and among cultures has the potential for the same consequences of the attribution of greater or lesser status that Hariman speaks about. As an example of how this might happen, I offer a brief glimpse of the passage through time of the word "ethnic."

The Ethnic "Text," Then and Now

In 1975, Glazer and Moynihan provided a short history of the word "ethnicity," indicating that, in its sense of describing the "character or quality of an ethnic group," it was first used in 1953 by David Riesman in his essay "Some Observations on Intellectual Freedom" (1). In 1986, Werner Sollors provided a more comprehensive examination of the use of "ethnicity," tracing it back again to Riesman, but reporting that the "apparently first occurrences" of this term were found in W. Lloyd Warner's study of a Massachusetts city (1945:23). In fact, the root word "ethnic" can be traced back to Greek times. It derived from *ethnikos,* the Greek word for nation, and the Ecclesiastical Late Greek word for heathen or pagan; thus, to be ethnic was to be a member of a heathen nation. This meaning survived relatively intact through the eighteenth century.

Ethnic as Heathen or Pagan

Examples of "ethnic" as it relates to paganism are found in social, philosophical, and historical treatises as well as in poetry. In 1588, in *An Admonition to the Nobility,* William Allen warned: "This I faie, yf he obeie not, or heare not the churche, let him be taken for an ethnike" (xxxvii). In *Leviathan,* published in 1651, Hobbes addresses the apostles' efforts to warn converts about "their then Ethnique Princes" (338). In his *A Complete History of Algiers*, Morgan (1731) describes those he perceives as barbarous as "the blindest and most wretched of all *heathens, Ethnikes, Pagans,* and *Idolaters*" (77). The English traveler Thomas Coryate (1611) carries through on this theme of barbarity; observing visitors to St. Mark's square in Venice, he notes: "here you may both see all manner of fashions of attire, and hear all the languages of christendom, besides those that are spoken by the barbaripus [*sic*] Ethnicikes" (177). Writing about John Sterling, Thomas Carlyle (1851) describes Sterling's break with the church "as good as altogether Ethnic, Greekish" (51).

In its sense of heathen or pagan, "ethnic" is also found in poetry. Longfellow's "Drinking Song" reflects this meaning: "These are ancient ethnic revels / of a faith long since forsaken / Now the Satyrs, changed to devils / Frighten mortals wine-o'ertaken."

Ethnic as Empirically Inferior

During the Age of Enlightenment, the meaning of the word "ethnic" changed. This period marked the shift from pietism to scientism and from faith to fact, so it is not surprising that ethnicity was no longer defined on the basis of religious difference. Instead, ethnicity was defined on the basis of observable and verifiable physical features. One who documents this state of affairs with great insight and completeness is Charles Rosenberg (1976) in *No Other Gods: On Science and American Social Thought*. Rosenberg addresses how the scientific community resorted to "facts" to prove the inferiority of women and to argue for the value of eugenics by comparing and "grading" racial traits. As an example, Rosenberg reports that Charles Davenport, the father of eugenics, argued that skin color was directly correlated to superiority—the lighter the color, the more superior the individual.

In *The Inequality of Human Races* (1915), Arthur de Gobineau defined as superior those races more prone toward civilization and defined the civilized as those "compelled, either by war or peaceful measures, to draw their neighbors within their sphere of influence" (28). Gobineau "scientifically" rank-ordered the superior, civilized races according to skin color, with the "ethnics," or dark-skinned, relegated to the most inferior positions.

In 1914, Edward Alsworth Ross (*The Old World in the New: The Significance of Past and Present Immigration to the American People*) referred to African, Chinese, Japanese, Greeks, and others as the "lesser ethnics" (168), and went on to state: "to the practiced eye, the physiognomy of certain groups unmistakably proclaims inferiority of type" (286), particularly the "hirsute, low-browed, big-faced persons of obviously low mentality" (285). In 1939, C. S. Coon attempted to understand differences in height, shape of face, size of head, and nose structure, but appeared to reserve the term "ethnic" to describe only the Jewish population.

In and of itself, the focus on differences in observable and empirically verifiable physical features might be granted some respectability. But it was the value judgments placed on those differences that effectively set the standard for the pursuit of scientifically based comparative knowledge. The aforementioned Edward Alsworth Ross concluded that differences in facial features were correlated with "ethical endowments": "That the Mediterranean peoples are morally below the races of northern Europe is as certain as any social fact. . . . The Northerners seem to surpass the southern Europeans in innate ethical endowments" (239). The relating of ethnicity and morality was still occurring in the 1950s and 1960s when Lawrence Kohlberg discussed the relationship between complex societies and high moral reasoning. As Anthony Cortese (1990) argues in his book *Ethnic Ethics,* Kohlberg's moral development theory is based on the placement of societies "on a continuum from simple to complex," but then is extended to relate complexity to moral superiority and simplicity to moral retardation (147). As Cortese describes it, Kohlberg's measurement of the relative simplicity or complexity of societies occurs through the comparative process whereby he examines the relative sophistication of social and political infrastructures. But like Edward Alsworth Ross before him, Kohlberg proceeded to place a value judgment on the relative worth of "simple" societies by designating them as morally inferior.

Ethnic/White Ethnic as Foreign or Exotic

In the early-to-mid twentieth century, the influx of immigrants to the United States gave a new meaning to the word "ethnic." Captured in this word were the styles, rituals, traditions, and value systems of the Irish, Italians, Dutch, Jews, Poles, Russians, and others. Indeed, during this period, the word "ethnic" and the phrase "white ethnic" were used interchangeably, indicating how differences in rituals, traditions, and language identified the outsider. Julian Huxley and A. C. Haddon (1935), although addressing the issue of ethnicity in Europe rather than in America, nevertheless offer one of the most enlightening treatises on the issue of ethnicity. Huxley and Haddon use the term ethnic "to signify the complexity of such factors as language, ritual, and tradition as defining factors of a group" (30), and argue for the relative importance of *socialization* processes over *biological* factors.

As a result of a study conducted between 1930 and 1935, Warner and Srole examined the adjustment to the United States of "the ethnic groups [of] the Irish, French, Canadians, Jews, Italians, Armenians, Greeks, Poles, and Russians" (1) and described these groups as "foreign" in the sense of strange or unfamiliar rather than in the sense of coming from another land (283). S. M. Miller (1964) addressed the political and economic issues of "the white ethnics—first the Irish, later the Jews, and still more recently the Italians" (297). In a 1979 *Journal of Communication* article, Jeffries and Hur define "white ethnic groups" as, among others, Irish, Italians, Poles, Slavs, and in a departure from the norm, the Puerto Rican/Chicano (116).

Using "ethnic" and "white ethnic" interchangeably suggests that differences in cultural behaviors and language, rather than a skin color, served to identify groups of people. The stigma of inferiority prevailed, however. In the *Times Literary Supplement* of November 17, 1961, a book review critique describes "the former 'ethnics,' a polite term for Jews, Italians, and other lesser breeds just inside the law" ("Eggheads," 823).

Ethnic as "People of Color"

As our cultural consciousness has matured, we have attempted to find other words or phrases that we think move us away from implications of value. "People of color" is such a phrase. Today, "ethnic" largely means to be a person of color. Ethnicity as a function of language, rituals, and so on, has not been dismissed; but increasingly it appears it is *only* the languages, rituals, and traditions of people of color that undergo intellectual scrutiny. Although African Americans, Latino/as, Asian Americans, and Native Americans have always constituted a part of the American population, they were rarely mentioned in connection with American ethnicity studies done before the 1950s and 1960s. This changed with the Civil Rights Movement, the Chicano Movement, and the American Indian Movement. Protesting their invisibility, members of these cultural groups worked to be seen and heard by proclaiming their respective black, brown, and red power movements. The strategy of choosing a color as an identifying label cannot have been accidental, and it served to set the stage for the eventual change of meaning for the word "ethnic." In the introduction to *Interethnic Communication: Current Research,* Kim (1986) provides a definition of ethnicity as the combination of the "objective . . . symbolic markers [such] as race, religion, language, national origin" and the "'subjective' identification of individuals with an ethnic group" (10). The compelling aspect of this definition is that it does not limit ethnicity as a descriptor only of people of color; it encompasses all ethnic groups, including "white" ethnics. It is revealing, however, that the greater number of articles comprising this anthology focus exclusively on people of color—Eskimos, Hispanics, and blacks—so although Kim's definition is encompassing, studies continue to define ethnics as "people of color." Within that same volume, ethnicity is sometimes defined even more narrowly: "ethnicity (black versus white)" (205), or ethnicity as "the social demands of being, for instance, a black, or a Mexican-American" (102).

There are two themes running through these various definitions of "ethnic." The first theme is marginalization; like the groups of people it defines, "ethnic" has historically been used as an exclusionary rather than a merely descriptive label. Our pursuit of knowledge about ethnics began when individuals or communities were identified as being outside the defined standards of religious practices, physical appearances, traditions, or skin colors. Thus the label "ethnic" encapsulated assumptions, conscious or otherwise, about cultural others. The studies described above serve as representative cases illustrating how language choices reinforced marginalization through the use of "scientific" studies. The relationship between language and knowledge points to the second theme cutting across the various definitions of "ethnic," one that is essentially the foundation for marginalization, that is, comparison followed by value judgment. Clearly, marginalization happens whenever one group is compared to another and found "deficient" in some way or another. As stated earlier, comparison is not a bad approach to the pursuit of knowledge, especially when what is being compared is devoid of cognition or emotion. Furthermore, were the process to stop at comparison, we could have understanding—and perhaps appreciation—of difference.

Limits of Comparative Knowledge

But the comparison technique is fundamentally grounded in what Woelfel and Napoli (1984) have described as a "standard reference frame" (118). When applied to sentient beings, unexamined standards of reference have the potential for great harm because a set of values is embedded in any definition of the "standard." As examples, we have only to recall the standards revealed in the different meanings of "ethnic" that led to value judgments about the *worth* of the differences observed. Thus religious difference could be projected to mean "irreligious" or "unenlightened," shapes of noses could mean "moral bankruptcy," varying rituals could mean "alien," and skin color could relegate groups of people to "subcultures." In 1965, Edwin Black wrote: "the aims of a man [woman] will display their symptoms in what he[she] says and how he [she] says it" (17). This is as true of the individual who engages in public discourse about political and socioeconomic issues as it is of researchers who engage in the discourse of cultural discovery and understanding. Words—labels—convey volumes about assumptions and perceptions, as do conclusions of studies that generalize to an entire community on the basis of a single identifying label, in this case the label "ethnic." The language of multicultural ethnic studies creates a "text" that often serves as the only knowledge connection among researchers and between researchers and the cultural communities they attempt to study and define.

A recent debate illustrates how "texts" are often created. Published in volumes 14, 17, and 18 of the *International Journal of Intercultural Relations* (Hecht et al. 1990, 1993; Mirandé and Tanno 1993a, 1993b; Delgado 1994), the debate centers around issues of researcher perspectives, contextual validation, and ethnic labeling in the study of multicultural communication in the Latino community. Researcher perspective addresses the value of etic or emic approaches to the study of cultural communities. The argument for contextual validation through dialogue is grounded in the idea that a richer and deeper understanding of multicultural communication would occur if we allowed "members of the culture an opportunity to literally 'talk back' to the researcher" (Mirandé and Tanno 1993a: 154). But it is the issue of labeling that lies at the heart of both researcher perspective and contextual validation. By inventing the multiple labels by which they wish to be identified, members of cultural groups are communicating a very important fact about their heterogeneity. When researchers choose to use data only from participants who use a particular label (e.g., Mexican American), reject data from those who self-identify differently (e.g., Chicana, Latino, Mexican, etc.), and then generalize to an entire cultural community, they are communicating homogeneity. This inaccurate perception of cultural homogeneity finds its way into print and becomes the knowledge base or "text" of the Latino community that is read by other researchers. This "text" of cultural homogeneity may also become the frame of reference for subsequent studies.

If frames of reference are to be used, they should be constructed from within the culture being studied, with the help of members of that particular cultural community. Geertz's (1973) suggestion that the study of cultures should be to seek meaning rather than laws provides a powerful rationale for the co-construction of frames of reference that will eventually lead to co-constructed texts. Fisher's (1987) concept of narrative as the process by which we give meaning and order to our lives offers a strategy for gaining insight into different cultural "texts" or stories created by the cultural members themselves. Understanding the different meanings of communication in multicultural contexts is bound to be enriched when the values and assumptions underlying selected frames of reference are commensurate with the values and assumptions of the particular culture being studied.

An ethnic "text" based on lack of rhetorical sensitivity about labels and frames of reference serves to marginalize groups, even if such is not the conscious intent of researchers. As Starosta (1984) argued, it matters little "that one attempts to 'empathize' with native conditions; one maintains the change emphasis of the rhetorician. And identificationist-extractionist distinctions dissolve into matters of strategy, not substance. Both aim to create that 'frame of reference' within which things or new ideas can take root" (234).

Foucault's (1972) argument that inequality is the product of a standard discourse of a culture and Starosta's comment about the researcher as change agent ring true in the context of multicultural communication studies. Tafoya (1984) reinforces the idea of discourse as a force of marginalization and inequality when she argues that, "One of the paradoxes found in some cross-cultural texts and studies is that their authors, while claiming to adhere to process notions defining a culture as something that is constantly evolving or changing, somehow feel confident that they can label or identify particular or specific characteristics or behaviors of members of the culture(s) reviewed. It is distressing to see so few qualifiers when so much is dynamic and diffuse" (48). Foucault's insights speak to the power of discourse generally and Tafoya's insight speaks to the particular power of multicultural research studies and conclusions. These insights also illuminate what has been, until recently, the monologic characteristic of the ethnic "text" in multicultural studies, a characteristic rooted in what Robert Bellah (1975) has described as the American "rational, technical, utilitarian, ideology" that has given us much information, but little wisdom (xiv).

Research-as-Dialogue

Bellah (1975) also has argued that "the first step toward . . . wisdom is humility" (xv). In a research context, wisdom may come when researchers are able to participate in authentic dialogue with members of cultural communities and thus co-create a richer "text." Walter Fisher (1992) has argued that "genuine communication cannot be the usual forms of monologic discourse . . . whether in debate [or] in conversations" (201), or, it could be argued, in multicultural research studies.

This idea of dialogue as a means of gaining knowledge (and wisdom) is not peculiar to multicultural communication studies. It is, for example, at the core of current debates in higher education and visual communication.

With regard to higher education, dialogue has been addressed by several individuals (for example, Boyer 1990; Christensen et al. 1991; Arnett 1992). Arnett (1992) provides the grounding for dialogue: a willingness to be open, a commitment to affirmation, and a desire to ask value questions about the application of knowledge (10). While Arnett focuses on dialogue between teacher and student, his observation about "viewing dialogue as reaching out to the other in an authentic fashion, [and being] willing to try to meet and follow the unpredictable consequences of the exchange" applies equally to the interaction between researcher and participant (11).

In the context of visual communication, Ruby (1991) argues: "While most documentaries are Vertovian, that is, the filmmakers/'authors' present us with their vision, some documentarians have aspired to replicate the subject's view of the world. . . . The documentary is assumed to give a 'voice to the voiceless,' that is, portray the political, social and economic realities of oppressed minorities and others *previously* denied access to the means of producing their own image. From this perspective, the documentary is not only an art form, it is a social service and a political act" (51). The documentary is thus created through dialogue that gives force also to the image of the "documented" where before it gave force only to the image of the documentarian. In addition, integrating the possibility of social service and political empowerment serves to give equal force to the discourse of the participant in higher education, in visual communication, and in multicultural research. But research-as-dialogue demands that some ethical imperatives be in place.

Ethical Imperatives for Multicultural Studies

In *A Short History of Ethics* (1966), Alasdair MacIntyre helps us understand how ethical analysis can "insulate itself from correction": "In ethics it can happen in the following way. A certain unsystematically selected class of moral concepts and judgments is made the subject of attention. From the study of these it is concluded that specifically moral discourse possesses certain characteristics. When counter-examples are adduced to show that this is not always so, these counterexamples are dismissed as irrelevant, because [they are] not examples of moral discourse; and they are shown to be nonmoral by exhibiting their lack of the necessary characteristics" (4).

In similar fashion, we can "insulate" ourselves against the process of re-examining how we go about gaining understanding about multicultural communication. We do this by accepting, without constant reassessment, certain methodological characteristics and certain language choices. If we are truly to gain rich understanding of the communication patterns of different cultural groups, it seems to me that the overarching ethical imperatives are first, a keen awareness about and concern for the language we use in our studies and critical analyses, and second, an emphasis on dialogue in the research process.

Geertz (1973) described the study of culture as "not an experimental science in search of law but an interpretive one in search of meaning" (5). Rhetorical sensitivity and dialogue will allow the creation of shared meanings, the co-writing of a cultural "text." As researcher/critics we must be concerned about the language we use insofar as it affects how we describe, prescribe, or otherwise rhetorically characterize cultural groups. We can address this concern about language in three ways.

First, *whatever labels we anticipate applying to groups of others, we must first apply to ourselves.* What does the label mean when I apply it to myself? How would I feel if it were frequently used to describe me? As an example, let me use the label which gave rise to this essay. In spite of the current practice of defining it narrowly as "people of color," ethnic in its broadest meaning refers to groups with a common cultural heritage. If we accept that, all of us can be so labeled, and yet many of us would not think to use that word as a self-descriptor. Why? In the process of pursuing answers, we may unearth those assumptions behind the label with which we are most comfortable or uncomfortable and in that way come closer to understanding the moral consequences of applying that—or any similar—label to others exclusive of oneself. Krippendorf (1989) referred to this process as the "self-referential imperative," which admonishes us to "include yourself as a constituent of your own constructions" (83).

Second, *the language of our studies should reflect the relationship between diversity and universality.* While the form of communication may differ from culture to culture, it may be that the purpose behind the communication may be universal. As Lu and Frank (1993) argue: "A multicultural perspective of rhetoric should assume cultural diversity and universality. . . . we should seek out and learn from the differences in cultural expressions. . . . However, this diversity may be connected by a culturally invariant recognition of the role played by speech in human affairs" (461). All cultures have been influenced by philosophic ideas, by events that tear people apart, and by traditions and rituals that keep them together. These influences manifest themselves in a diversity of *patterns* of language. But as Lu and Frank rightly point out, language itself is a universal endeavor, and the surest way of not losing sight of this important insight is by assiduously avoiding making value judgments about the various patterns of discourse.

Third, *the language of our studies should promote the relationship between social enhancement and research.* In general, the use of language entails moral responsibility. But in multicultural studies specifically, moral responsibility requires that we incorporate into the study and analysis process the answer to several questions: Does this knowledge enhance the lives of the cultural groups we are studying? How does the language of our studies serve to empower them? Does our language minimize isolation or marginalization? Does it promote acceptance? For example, in assessing how ancient Eastern and Western religions provide us with a rich source of guidelines for communication ethics, Jensen (1992) concludes that ancient religions "go beyond the three fundamental purposes of rhetoric . . . —to inform, to persuade, and to please—and add a fourth, to edify" (65). Does the language of the conclusions of our various studies uplift members of cultural groups morally, spiritually, and politically? Arguably, this question suggests the possibility that while knowledge in and of itself is a necessary motive, it may no longer be a sufficient motive for conducting multicultural communication research.

One of the means by which we, as researchers/critics, can enhance our sensitivity about language choice is by emphasizing dialogue as part of the research process. Elsewhere in this chapter I have addressed the relationship between language and knowledge and between dialogue and wisdom. *The relationship between language and wisdom may be enhanced by seeking knowledge through genuine dialogue with the participants of multicultural studies.* In his book *Dialogic Education,* Arnett writes: "Dialogic education asks the question, what will be the impact on others when information is implemented?" (9). This question applies equally well to multicultural studies, and we cannot hope to gain answers to it until and unless we incorporate dialogue into the research process.

General Implications for Multicultural Researchers/Critics

The major implication of research-as-dialogue is essentially one of re-visioning our role in the research process. In the pursuit of multicultural understanding, we need to see ourselves more as participants in the co-construction of meaning and less as autonomous experts seeking generalizable laws to explain what are, in essence, groups with great internal diversity. We need also to see ourselves as potential persuaders and possible change agents, since our studies do "define" cultural groups and in that sense impact general as well as particular perceptions of them.

The re-visioning process requires commitment and time, and if we are successful, it means that the research process itself will become more time consuming. The results of the process, however, cannot but yield a truer, richer body of knowledge.

Summary

Tracing the label "ethnic" as it has been used over time, addressing the limits of comparative knowledge as it affects perceptions of marginalization, and arguing for dialogue as a necessary part of the research process constitute an attempt at "rhetorical self-consciousness" (Bazerman 1992) that culminated in what I consider to be the ethical imperatives of multicultural communication research and the implications for researchers/critics. This self-consciousness represents a beginning, and it is communicated in the hope that it will engender a dialogue about research-as-dialogue and its impact on the language and process of inquiry.

Considering that multicultural communication studies have the potential to create ethnic texts with a potential for negatively impacting cultural groups, the ethical imperatives of research in this context are ones that we should take to mind and to heart.

References Cited

Allen, W. 1971 [1588]. *An Admonition to the Nobility.* Yorkshire, England: Scolar Press.

Arnett, R. 1992. *Dialogic Education: Conversation about Ideas and between Persons.* Carbondale: Southern Illinois University Press.

Bazerman, C. 1992. "The Interpretation of Disciplinary Writing." In *Writing the Social Text: Poetics in Social Science Discourse.* Ed. R. H. Brown. Pp. 31–38. New York: Aldine De Gruyter.

Bellah, R. 1975. *The Broken Covenant: American Civil Religion in Time of Trial.* New York: Seabury Press.

Black, E. 1965. *Rhetorical Criticism: A Study in Method.* Madison: University of Wisconsin Press.

Boyer, E. 1990. *Scholarship Reconsidered: Priorities of the Professorate.* Princeton, N.J.: Carnegie Foundation for the Advancement of Teaching.

Carlyle, T. 1903 [1851]. *The Life of John Sterling.* New York: Scribner's.

Christensen, C. R., D. Garvin, and A. Sweet, eds. 1991. *Education for Judgment: The Artistry of Discussion Leadership.* Boston: Harvard Business School Press.

Coon, C. S. 1939. *The Races of Europe.* Westport, Conn.: Greenwood Press.

Cortese, A. 1990. *Ethnic Ethics: The Reconstruction of Moral Theory.* Albany: State University of New York Press.

Coryate, T. 1611. *Coryats Crudites.* London.

Delgado, F. 1994. "The Complexity of Mexican American Identity: A Reply to Hecht, Sedano, and Ribeau and Mirande and Tanno." *International Journal of Intercultural Relations* 18:77–84.

"Eggheads and Floating Voters." 1961. *Times Literary Supplement,* November 17, p. 823.

Fisher, W. 1987. *Human Communication as Narration: Toward a Philosophy of Reason, Value, and Action.* Columbia: University of South Carolina Press.

———. 1992. "Narration, Reason, and Community." In *Writing the Social Text.* Ed. R. H. Brown. Pp. 199–217. New York: Aldine de Gruyter.

Foucault, M. 1972. *The Archaeology of Knowledge and the Discourse on Language.* Trans. A. M. Sheridan Smith. New York: Pantheon Books.

Geertz, C. 1973. *The Interpretation of Cultures.* New York: Basic Books.

Glazer, N., and D. P. Moynihan, eds. 1975. *Ethnicity: Theory and Experience.* Cambridge: Harvard University Press.

de Gobineau, A. 1915. *The Inequality of Human Races.* Trans. Adrian Collins. New York: Putnam and Sons.

Hariman, R. 1986. "Status, Marginality, and Rhetorical Theory." *Quarterly Journal of Speech* 72:38–54.

Hecht, M., S. Ribeau, and M. Sedano. 1990. "A Mexican American Perspective on Interethnic Communication." *International Journal of Intercultural Relations* 14:31–55.

Hecht, M., M. Sedano, and S. Ribeau. 1993. "Understanding Culture, Communication, and Research: Application to Chicanos and Mexican Americans." *International Journal of Intercultural Relations* 17:157–65.

Hobbes, T. 1946[?] [1651]. *Leviathan; or, The Matter, Forme and Power of a Commonwealth Ecclesiastical and Civil.* Oxford: Basil Blackwell.

Huxley, J. S., and A. C. Haddon. 1935. *We Europeans: A Survey of "Racial" Problems.* London: Jonathan Cape.

Jeffries, L. W., and K. K. Hur. 1979. "White Ethnics and Their Media Images." *Journal of Communication* 29:116–22.

Jensen, J. V. 1992. "Ancient Eastern and Western Religions as Guides for Contemporary Communication Ethics." In *Proceedings of the Second National Communication Ethics Conference.* Ed. J. A. Jaksa. Pp. 58–67. Kellogg Biological Station Education Center, Gull Lake, Hickory Corners, Mich.

Kim, Y. Y. 1986. "Introduction: A Communication Approach to Interethnic Relations." In *Interethnic Communication: Current Research.* Ed. Y. Y. Kim. Pp. 9–18. Newbury Park, Calif.: Sage.

Krippendorf, K. 1989. "On the Ethics of Constructing Communication." In *Rethinking Communication.* Vol. 1: *Paradigm Issues.* Ed. B. Dervin, L. Grossberg, B. O'Keefe, and E. Wartella. Pp. 66–96. Newbury Park, Calif.: Sage.

Longfellow, H. W. 1893. *The Complete Poetical Works of Henry Wadsworth Longfellow.* Boston: Houghton, Mifflin.

Lu, X., and D. A. Frank. 1993. "On the Study of Ancient Chinese Rhetoric/Bain." *Western Journal of Communication* 57:445–63.

MacIntyre, A. 1966. *A Short History of Ethics.* New York: Macmillan.

Miller, S. M. 1964. "Poverty, Race, and Politics." In *The New Sociology: Essays in Social Science and Social Theory.* Ed. I. L. Horowitz. Pp. 290–312. New York: Oxford University Press.

Mirandé, A., and D. Tanno. 1993a. "Labels, Researcher Perspective, and Contextual Validation: A Commentary." *International Journal of Intercultural Relations* 17:149–55.

———. 1993b. "Understanding Interethnic Communication and Research: 'A Rose by Any Other Name Would Smell as Sweet.'" *International Journal of Intercultural Relations* 17:381–88.

Morgan, J. 1970 [1731]. *A Complete History of Algiers.* New York: Negro Universities Press.

Riesman, D. 1953–54. "Some Observations on Intellectual Freedom." *American Scholar* 23:9–25.

Ross, E. A. 1914. *The Old World in the New: The Significance of Past and Present Immigration to the American People.* New York: Century Co.

Rosenberg, C. 1976. *No Other Gods: On Science and American Social Thought.* Baltimore: Johns Hopkins University Press.

Ruby, J. 1991. "Speaking for, Speaking about, Speaking with or Speaking Alongside." *Visual Anthropology Review* 7:50–67.

Sollars, W. 1986. *Beyond Ethnicity: Consent and Descent in American Culture.* New York: Oxford University Press.

Starosta, W. J. 1984. "On Intercultural Rhetoric." In *Methods for Intercultural Communication Research.* Ed. W. B. Gudykunst and Y. Y. Kim. Pp. 229–38. Beverly Hills: Sage.

Tafoya, D. W. 1984. "Research and Cultural Phenomena." In *Methods for Intercultural Communication Research.* Ed. W. B. Gudykunst and Y. Y. Kim. Pp. 47–65. Beverly Hills: Sage.

Warner, W. L., and L. Srole. 1945. *The Social Systems of American Ethnic Groups.* Vol. 3 of Yankee City series. New Haven: Yale University Press.

Winterowd, W. R. 1968. *Rhetoric: A Synthesis.* New York: Holt, Rinehart and Winston.

Woelfel, J., and N. R. Napoli. 1984. "Measuring Human Emotion: Proposed Standards." In *Methods for Intercultural Communication Research.* Ed. W. B. Gudykunst and Y. Y. Kim. Pp. 117–27. Beverly Hills: Sage.

5 Derailing the Equity Process: Language as a Mechanism of Sabotage

Barbara Paige Pointer and Gale Auletta Young

Either we learn a new language of empathy and compassion, or the fire this time will consume us all. — Cornel West (1993)

Through the subtle and sometimes not so subtle use of language as a form of distortion, conservative educators and journalists largely defined the parameters within which the debate over questions of diversity and equity took place in American institutions of higher learning in the 1970s and 1980s. In fact, much of the momentum that advocates of educational equity and diversity gained in the 1960s was lost as the debate shifted, and free speech rather than equity began to dominate the politics of education landscape. What was the ideological source of this shift? How was the intellectual elite (i.e., middle- and upper-middle-class white males) so easily convinced that two academically marginal groups, white women and racial minorities, suddenly had the ability to shape and control educational policy? Perhaps more to the point, how was the general public convinced that their ability to speak openly and freely was at risk? How did individuals, who were often at polarized ends of the American political continuum, reach a general consensus that the people who were leading the movement for greater equality of opportunity were a threat to principles of academic freedom and pursuit of excellence in American higher education? How, in short, did the diversity and equity thrust (i.e., the push for basic fairness and human decency) come to be labeled "politically correct," and in the process devalued and, in some cases, even vilified? In our attempt to address these questions, we will examine the structure and function of racially coded speech, and the extent to which it has historically impeded the development of *genuine* communication. We will focus, in particular, on the role that the absence of a language of socio-ethics (i.e, an emphasis on greater accountability in speech) has played in our inability, as a nation, to either more effectively negotiate our differences, or commit ourselves to the removal of structural barriers to equality of access and retention in higher education.

Political Correctness: Language as Symbolic Aggression

Duplicitous speech has been used universally to disguise the roots of important social problems. We believe that racially coded speech has functioned as a particularly effective form of linguistic distortion in the United States because this nation has yet to come to terms with the obvious disparity between its constitutional commitment to principles of liberty, equality, and justice, and the existence of social practices that sanction racial and gender exclusion. While this inconsistency has become less pronounced over time, the mechanism for resolving the cognitive dissonance that is a by-product of it has remained remarkably stable. Through the duplicitous use of language, racist and conservative whites have waged a sustained attempt to define and control the parameters within which discussions of ethnicity and equity take place in the United States. By creating and manipulating racial and cultural stereotypes, they have consistently cast themselves in the role of victims and their victims in the role of oppressors. Ronald Takaki (1979) refers to this rhetorical strategy of shifting blame as the "metaphysics of civilization," and he traces this sociolinguistic trend to the immediate post-American revolutionary period. It was only after the barrier to westward expansion was removed, and people of European descent were forced to confront their inability to control their territorially aggressive impulses, Takaki emphasizes, that the psychological need emerged for "more complex disguises"; mechanisms through which, he points out, whites attempted to reconcile their "unleashed greed" and their need to continue to view themselves as basically "virtuous and decent" people. Inversion, he concludes, a clever form of linguistic displacement, became one of the primary mechanisms through which white Americans denied any moral responsibility for killing the native population or removing them from their land, as well as the rhetorical strategy for enslaving Africans and justifying white privilege (80–144).

Takaki's discussion of inversion, especially as a form of group psychological warfare, provides some important insights into the role of print media in sustaining systems of oppression. He points out, for example, that it was through the manipulation and control of the socio-structural contexts within which the debate over "Indian removal" took place, that whites shifted blame from themselves to their victims. By defining civilization in basically material terms (e.g., technology and progress), white Americans were able to shift the debate from the ethics of either forcibly removing the native population from their land, or creating a caste system of involuntary servitude (e.g., racial slavery) and move it to a more abstract plane. The framework for the debate became civilization versus heathenism, and within this context, Takaki emphasizes, a context in which morality took on absolute overtones, "Indian" became a synonym for "immoral," as did "African." The concept of heathenism, in short, dehumanized the indigenous and transported African populations. Once the emphasis was transferred to the assumed spiritual poverty of these two groups, role switching was a fait accompli.

"Political correctness" is thus a label that represents simply the most recent, and perhaps most clever attempt at linguistic displacement. It is an approach that, like its historical predecessors, relies on the reluctance of most Americans to acknowledge the deep institutional roots of either racism or sexism. Collective denial is deeply rooted in the American past, and it is a psychological construct, particularly when it is placed within the context of an analysis of the socio-structural dynamics of power, that enables us to better understand the often subtle ways in which oppressive structures are maintained. We believe, for example, that white America's long-term ability to so effectively walk a moral tightrope has been a function primarily of its ability, given its position of political dominance, to censor the historical past. Racial minority groups, given their more marginal position of power, have often been so effectively objectified, silenced, or both, that when they managed to find their collective voice, and demand that their humanity be acknowledged, many white Americans, as Ralph Ellison (1964) so eloquently points out, have been genuinely baffled. Minority voices have so infrequently found a public forum for their views because of the almost total control of the political and economic system in the United States by white males. As that base eroded, as more women and racial minorities entered the American mainstream, a process that accelerated in the change-oriented decade of the 1960s, it became increasingly more difficult to censor dissident voices.

As a form of linguistic displacement, PC is both simple-minded and brilliant. In its failure to articulate honestly its opposition to affirmative action and other diversity pursuits, the PC movement has generated a level of discourse that, even at its best, can only be described as mundane and sophomoric. On the other hand, in their ability to avoid a debate that they cannot win, either intellectually or morally, Americans who have effectively used PC to manipulate public perceptions and shape public attitudes demonstrated tremendous political savvy. What they accomplished, in effect, was the appropriation of the "moral" tone of racial minority movements of the 1960s. In the liberal environment of the 1970s, a context in which, as Omi and Winant (1994) perceptively observe, attempts to justify racial exclusion with crude "biologic" arguments predictably failed, opponents of affirmative action made an astute adjustment: they adopted a strategy of "rearticulation." They took the language of affirmative action (e.g., discrimination) and inverted it (e.g., reverse discrimination) in ways that suggested that it was they and not oppressed groups (i.e., women and racial minorities) who were victimized. This manipulation of "code words" (e.g., reverse discrimination, political correctness) enabled them, Omi and Winant conclude, to articulate a commitment to principles of democracy and egalitarianism (to maintain the tone of morality), but reject the primary mechanism through which institutional social change could take place (e.g., group action).[1] It was thus in their ability to create an intellectual climate in which diversity and equity became synonymous with political correctness, and political correctness became a synonym for censorship, that groups who were threatened by minority gains (a coalition of conservatives, of which the "new right" was at the center), largely derailed the affirmative action movement.

The incident that perhaps most perceptively underscores the extent of this derailment was the weak-kneed Democratic response to George Bush's threat to veto the Civil Rights Act of 1990–91. This act "was an attempt to expand employment discrimination protection for minorities and women, as well as to overturn a series of 1989 Supreme Court decisions limiting the scope of employment discrimination law" (Forman 1991:746). The principal strategy of the opposition (i.e., the Bush Administration) was to employ the mechanism of language as distortion; they characterized the act as an attempt to reintroduce quotas, an argument that had tremendous popular appeal in the weak economic climate of the early 1990s (even though this was clearly a mis-statement of the facts).[2] Instead of taking the high moral ground (e.g., calling the Republicans liars) and confronting the risk of being labeled "politically correct," Democrats dissociated themselves from the use of any language that might even vaguely suggest that the proposed Civil Rights Act was an affirmative action bill. John Jacob, for example, the president of the National Urban League, lambasted critics of the act for even suggesting that it was an affirmative action bill (Forman 1991:746).[3]

How do we explain the readiness with which Democrats conceded so much ideological ground? It was perhaps rooted, in part, in the tendency of Democrats, conservative and liberal, to too easily capitulate. As an imperfect solution to a complex problem, affirmative action legislation was after all, from its inauspicious beginnings, highly vulnerable to criticism. It therefore needed committed rather than "lukewarm" advocates, and its supporters, all too often, unfortunately, fell into the latter category. We believe, however, that James Forman Jr. (1991) provides the most compelling explanation for the Democratic retreat: in their preoccupation with sustaining their public image as "libertarians" (i.e., protectors of democratic freedoms, including freedom of expression), Democrats failed to advance the ideological argument that was the basis for the proposed legislation— the ongoing need for affirmative action (746, 748). As Forman emphasizes, "nowhere to be found, either in the numerous press statements or in months of testimony before House and Senate committees, was there a principled defense of affirmative action, of hiring with an eye to race" (746). In the absence of such a defense, the Democrats did not simply lose a single battle, he concludes, they undermined the ethical foundation that was the basis for civil rights legislation.

Role of the Professorate

In an article that, given its visionary thrust, is still timely, Robert Blauner (1972) provides some additional insight into the Democratic or liberal retreat from principle. His conclusions, in fact, given his focus on the academy, are particularly important. In an attempt to understand the retreat of a group (University of California, Berkeley, liberal professors), who were initially predisposed to support efforts to actively recruit women and racial minorities (both faculty and students), Blauner explores several explanatory factors; they range from university professors' relative isolation within their own departments and corresponding loyalty primarily to their fields, to their tendency to view prejudice rather than racism as the primary source of institutional exclusion. Blauner concludes that what is most significant about this retreat is that it took place only at the point that "preferential programs" and/or "diversity course" requirements were introduced. He thus explains this reversal of commitment in terms of a crisis of conscience. At the core of the American liberal's perceived absence of "backbone," whether the context is political or educational, he suggests, is a fundamentally flawed idealism: the belief that society should judge a person "in terms of his individual uniqueness and his universal humanity, not in terms of 'accidental' features like skin color." It's a belief, Blauner emphasizes, that fails to take into account that even after the more obvious material barriers to racial mobility are removed (e.g., separate public facilities, etc.), the system is structured in ways that "manage and preserve, in many ways, a reality of particularism and of ascription, elaborately disguised by a mythology of universalism and achievement orientation" (256–94). Thus, in the absence of group "restitutive" action, those individuals who are members of groups that have institutionalized power maintain their privileged positions. Ironically, therefore, even though conservatives and liberals disagree on most important social issues, in their philosophical commitment to democratic idealism they share a common and binding thread that explains the growing decline in support, among white Americans, for affirmation action programs.

It is thus only within the context of the United States' long-term failure to fully acknowledge or address a historical pattern of institutionalized racial and gender bias that the relative success of the anti-affirmative action forces in the 1970s and 1980s can be understood. In a nation that was willing to place as much emphasis on responsible speech as it did free speech, censorship could not have displaced equity and diversity as a pivotal social issue. Similarly, conservative educators and journalists would not have been as able to persuade either the lay or academic public that racial minorities and women, groups with little power to alter or change American institutional structures, had, in fact, acquired the ability to limit their freedom of expression. While this distortion of reality had its roots in a general erosion of public support for diversity and equity issues, it was also largely a function of the failure of American educators to link affirmative action and intellectual diversity. In their tendency to view affirmative action either as a threat to *academic excellence* or as an intellectual placebo (a response to campus climate problems) they have failed to examine the potential of diversity programs to transform the curriculum in complex and challenging ways.

In their tendency to be fairly critical of affirmative action legislation, university professors, given their intellectual status, have provided anti-affirmative action forces with greater credibility than conservative journalists, despite the wider readership of the latter group. It is not a coincidence, for example, that so much of the anti-affirmative action literature is anecdotal,[4] or that the university campus has been the primary context in which the political correctness versus freedom of speech debate has played itself out. "Anti-intellectual components of American culture and historic forays against leftists in U.S. higher education in the 1950s," Patrick Drinan (1991) points out, "should have supplied key warnings." The political right, he continues, simply "turned on the left in one of its [more visible] bastions of strength—higher education" (7).[5] This should not have surprised either leftist of liberal educators; the battle for and against affirmative action legislation and policies has been (and continues to be) waged largely on an ideological plane.

Despite the inane content of much of the anti-affirmative action literature and, more importantly, its inability to address relevant educational policy issues, it has nonetheless managed to reach, in the past two decades, a much wider readership than carefully researched and interpretive works on equity and diversity.[6] An excellent case in point is Dinesh D'Souza's *Illiberal Education* (1991). D'Souza's central premise is that "preferential" minority programs are undermining the "liberal" structure of the American academy. He therefore concludes that what he labels "the 'victim's revolution' is beginning its siege of the final bastion of 'pure scholarship'" (19). While D'Souza's position is only tenable if we ignore, as he does, the continuing legacy of institutionalized racial bias, and the contextual (i.e., Eurocentric) roots of American humanistic and social science scholarship, his book has been favorably reviewed by several highly respected scholars.

The greater interest in the chaff rather than the wheat has been a function, in part, of a declining economy. Yet, it is a mistake, as Omi and Winant conclude, to view the broad-based appeal of "rightist" ideology as simply a response to changing market trends; it is instead, they conclude, a response to a complex category of fears, many of which are racial and xenophobic in content (114–15). We agree. In an environment in which race as a social category has acquired greater acceptance, and "biologistic" arguments no longer work, opponents of affirmative action have retreated behind a strategy of distortion and deception. This retrogressive social trend, and its appeal within the academy, we believe, has its roots in the academy's universalist and Eurocentric structure, and the corresponding reluctance of many educators to acknowledge that American higher education is neither apolitical nor (solely) rational.

Ethics, Affirmative Action, and Social Change

Ethical questions have always been at the center of the human quest for knowledge. Whether these questions were philosophical and addressed concerns about the intrinsic value of knowledge, or behavioral and rooted in discussions of appropriate guidelines for regulating conduct within the academy, they played a pivotal role in shaping the nature of academic discourse. The contention that the academy is apolitical and that affirmative action policies threaten the intrinsically objective structure of the educational process is thus theoretically flawed. The current debate on multicultural education and the corresponding controversy over the academic parameters within which that discussion should take place is part of a traditional and evolving educational process.

Several factors obscure the political structure of educational institutions, particularly public education. The most obvious political structures, of course, come disguised under the rubric of institutionalization. Once new ideas or concepts become part of an existing structure, they no longer seem controversial or threatening, and thereafter take on the status of "apolitical." It is thus within the parameter of newness or untested that ideas are more likely to take on political overtones. A less obvious element of obfuscation is the culturally monolithic structure of Western philosophical discourse. Western social scientific structures, including ethical paradigms, have their roots in Western environmental contexts. So these structures are not necessarily universal, and are thus limited as paradigms for mediating racial and cultural difference.

An excellent case in point is the existing literature on ethics. This body of research is deeply rooted in a European philosophical tradition that marginalizes the role of culture in shaping structures of morality. Yet, since there is little cross-cultural research on ethics, the existence of a universal system of morality remains, according to Anthony Cortese, open to question. In an excellent critical overview of the theoretical research on morality, Cortese (1990) concludes that "moral development is culturally and socially determined," and that "moral judgment reflects the structure of social relations, and not the structure of human cognition" (4). The basic limitation of the extant research on moral theory, he continues, is that "it appears to view Anglo-American culture as universal in defining moral development," and yet is "unable to recognize virtually all-white research samples as a methodological problem" (1).

This myopic vision is at the core of the often polarized structure of the debate on multicultural education. American educators are, for the most part, unwilling to acknowledge that the theoretical models that give order and consistency to their research interests and pursuits are not necessarily universal. And yet these models are clearly not multicultural in origin. We believe that much of the resistance to multicultural education stems from the reluctance of many American educators to consider the possibility that their academic training, and thus their teaching and research, are incomplete. And then there is the question of intellectual parity. To acknowledge that the works of some past, as well as contemporary, authors of color deserve a place, alongside the "classical greats" is, in effect, to acknowledge that the domain of the classic is not exclusively European. For a society that is still committed, on many levels, to sustaining racist structures, this is not an easy acknowledgment.

The problem is thus cyclical. The continuing importance of race, and the corresponding inability of many white Americans to confront their racial bias, has created an environment in which deception is not uncommon. This deception is reinforced by American educational institutions that, given their reluctance to become more inclusive, perpetuate a system of academic genocide. There is, in short, a very close relationship between the tacit assumption that universal systems of morality exist and the continuing resistance to positive and aggressive actions that address historical patterns of racial and gender exclusion.

Implicit within the structure of traditional philosophical theories of morality, for example, is the assumption that a close connection exists between intellectual and moral development. The thread that runs throughout the intellectual musings of Kant, Rawls, Piaget, and Kohlberg, all of whom conclude that morality is cognitively based, is that "higher stages" (i.e., universalist structures) of morality are transcendental, that they exist independently of specific sociocultural contexts, and are achieved through rational rather than social consciousness.

It is not a coincidence, for example, that Kohlberg's six-stage model of moral reasoning bears a remarkable resemblance to Piaget's stage-based model of cognitive development. The underlying premise of each model is that "individuals move from a stage of heteronomy to one of autonomy," and that the process by which this transition takes place involves "an irreversible sequence [or stages] of qualitative transformations" (Cortese 1990:16–20). Both models thus border on a biological evolution-ism that has dangerous social implications; it is Kohlberg's paradigm, however, given his focus on adults rather than children, that most closely links lower intelligence and the absence of higher ethics.[7] What he terms "postconventional" morality is only reached, he concludes, by a minority of adults. In his failure to identify the criteria by which "this chosen few" are elevated to a level of higher moral consciousness, and his equating of the morality at stages one and two with childish reasoning (i.e., age nine and younger), he clearly suggests that intelligence is the primary index of moral development.

Given the primarily Eurocentric and male context in which ethical literature has been produced, the belief that Eurocentric ethics equals universal has become a self-fulfilling fallacy, and a perpetual noose around European Americans and people of color alike. It has stifled our collective intellectual and creative potential. Standpoint theory (Wood 1992), for example, which is currently being explored by feminist scholars, challenges us to divorce ourselves from both biological and universal arguments, and to focus instead on trying "to understand the distinctive features of women's experiences as they take place in a gender-stratified culture and as they are interpreted by women" (Wood 1992:12–13). Such a perspective, as Julia Wood notes, invites "scholars to inquire into conditions that cultivate distinct understandings of morality" (16).

Cultivating an Authentic Socio-ethics

As educators, we cannot begin to develop a language of socio-ethics; that is, a coding system that will enable us to more effectively mediate our racial, class, and gender differences, until we come to terms with the culture-bound content of the academy's existing knowledge base. The fly, in a word, is in the milk. Philosophy and Communication: the very disciplines with the greatest potential for providing the paradigms for such mediation are perhaps most deeply mired in the fallacy of universalism. As an academic endeavor that preoccupies itself with ideas (mind), apart from their practical application, philosophy (the disciplinary context in which most discussions of ethics take place) is perhaps the most abstract of either the humanities or social sciences. The very nature of Eurocentric philosophical discourse, ironically, precludes a preoccupation with socio-cultural context. Tinder (1980), for example, in a sometimes intriguing philosophical discussion of communication as a mechanism for achieving "genuine" community, concludes that community, as a socio-cultural construct, does not exist (19). Such a position, of course, flies in the face of traditional anthropological theory. To the extent that beliefs are encoded within traditional cultural forms, those beliefs provide a unifying or communal ethos. Therefore, in conceptualizing community as temporal, and as only taking place during moments of honest verbal exchange, Tinder simultaneously underscores the intrinsic value of communication and marginalizes the systemic relationship between speech and action. Philosophy is thus a victim of the very academic trend that it should be leading the way in reversing; the equating of Eurocentric with universal.

Theory, in short, does not emerge in an ideological vacuum. As Cortese (1990) has perceptively observed, "ethics is a product of human interaction; knowledge is socially constructed" (61). A genuine multicultural approach to research, teaching, learning, and communicating thus means rethinking traditional paradigms of analysis. Unfortunately, the fairly widespread assumption that restructuring the curriculum means giving equal time to each racial and/or cultural group, and the scissor and paste approach implicit in this assumption, mirrors the greater resistance to rethinking theory and method, as opposed to content.

Communication, the discipline that studies linguistically constructed social realities, and that has twenty-five years of research into intercultural relations, is just as mired in a universalist approach as philosophy. Communication scholars have, for example, identified "specific competencies"; that is, effective and appropriate attitudes and skills for successfully negotiating interethnic relations. These competencies consist of empathy and tolerance (for ambiguity, uncertainty, and anxiety), the ability to create new categories, and working cooperatively with others across race and culture lines (Forman 1991; Gudykunst 1993; Martin 1993; Koester and Olebe 1988; Devine 1991). These attributes would seem to reduce the language of aggression and sabotage and encourage instead openness, and honest and culturally sensitive interaction and discourse. However, while researchers in intercultural communication have identified and validated these attributes, they have not developed an effective means for cultivating or teaching them. The underlying and untested assumption is that enough of the right kind of knowledge will trigger these competencies. Even more disappointing has been the almost exclusive comparative focus on international relations, involving (European) "Americans" and a "foreigner."

While accurate and adequate knowledge about other cultural paradigms is obviously essential before informed and ethical policies and practices can be established, this information alone is insufficient. Elshtain (1988) found, for example, that information about "other" people from within national borders can actually increase hostility. Perhaps even more disturbing are Jackman and Crane's (1986) findings that intercultural competencies do not necessarily reduce racist or culturally based prejudices (482). In other words, the very social and political context that philosophy and communication has ignored is the very terrain that we need to more fully understand. Absence of more comparative research on American ethnic minority groups has retarded our ability to develop the relevant paradigms, the necessary compassion, and a genuine critical spirit, an essential component of which is a greater openness to racial, gender, and cultural difference.

Race relations in the United States is both an intensely intellectual and an extremely emotional issue. Honestly grappling with the socio-cultural issues and the different perspectives of groups within our national borders is inconsistent with our Eurocentric reliance on rational understanding. Emotions are immediate, volatile, spontaneous, and complex. They are thus not easily contained within the narrow confines of rational discourse. Our reluctance to step outside of confining structures—to acknowledge the critical role that emotion plays in sustaining inequalities based on race, gender, and other differences—limits our ability to explore the nature of our resistance to change. In an excellent critique of "new right" orthodoxy, Reed and Bond (1991) point out that the "movement beyond race strategy is doomed. . . . Our only hope lies not in rejecting but in resuscitating the project of confronting racism in the white electorate for what it is and struggling with whites to overcome their commitment to racial privilege. No more euphemisms, no elaborate circumlocutions." They continue: "Those who want to dispense with egalitarian agendas should declare themselves forthrightly and stand on their convictions. That way we can all know who stands for what, and act accordingly" (737).

Easier said than done. One of the essential roles of the ego is to protect us from painful realities. It could be that race relations brings us up against those moments that John Welwood (1983) terms "world collapse," those moments when our ego structures and categories begin to crumble and we are faced with the raw and vivid realization of our racially constructed world. These masks and facades of our distorted reasoning thus hide our fear of honestly pulling away the curtain and exposing the wizard, the naked truth of white privilege. White privilege is so potent because it is, as Peggy McIntosh (1988) argues, largely invisible; it thus allows European Americans in good conscience to believe in the fallacy of equal opportunity. The fairly fashionable conclusion that much of the Democratic party's loss of power in the 1970s and 1980s was rooted in its unexamined support of racial minorities and women, and its desertion of the so-called beleaguered middle-class, has as its source, Reed and Bond (1991) conclude, the assumption that the "put-upon Joe Six-Pack and the 'average family' . . . were victims rather than beneficiaries of a 'racially stratified system' " (735).[8] White privilege is thus not easily acknowledged, for it involves both a potential loss of power and a responsibility for initiating change.

Broken Cycles: The Process of Rebuilding

The distortions inherent in coded phrases like "political correctness" and "reverse discrimination" reveal the weakness of our racial defenses; these words also paradoxically offer an opportunity to face our more basic human vulnerability and genuine power to confront our biases. John Welwood (1983), in his groundbreaking work on East/West approaches to the healing relationship, makes an important distinction between what he "call[s] basic human vulnerability from another kind of vulnerability—the fragility of the ego, the shell that we construct around our soft receptive center where we take the world into us" (156). Ironically, the very fragility and brittleness that weakens us, in terms of our racial defenses, point the way toward genuine openness and tenderness. Genuine growth can therefore only take place when the cycle is broken.[9]

The current brittleness of race relations offers us the rare opportunity to put down our language of aggression and reaction and allow the denial of white privilege and its facade of universal righteousness and its oppositional mentality to crumble. The resulting void, the raw, naked void of not knowing what to be to one another, what to think, do, or say in race relations, will hopefully be replaced with the ability to speak honestly and with compassion for our own and each other's feelings. If we can acknowledge that our emotions matter, we can then begin to develop critical abilities for inquiring into our feelings. We encourage our students to think and write critically. Why can't we also provide them with analytical paradigms that train them to value their feelings? As Daniel Goleman (1995) reminds us: "In the dance of feeling and thought the emotional faculty guides our moment-to-moment decisions, working hand-in-hand with the rational mind, enabling—or disabling—thought itself. Likewise, the thinking brain plays an executive role in our emotions—except in those moments when emotions surge out of control and the emotional brain runs rampant."

In a February 1994 televised interview with Oprah Winfrey, Maya Angelou made the following observation: "Someday we'll acquire the ability to measure the intensity of words and their ability to harm or hurt." What an intriguing concept—the notion that people should be held accountable for their potentially harmful verbalizations as well as their potentially harmful behavior! Such a position is, of course, at variance with most of the philosophical literature on ethics and communication. Tinder (1980), for example, develops such an abstract theoretical structure in his discussion of communication and community that he avoids the question of speech accountability altogether. For Tinder, it is the speech act, apart from its behavioral implications that is significant; it is the basis of communal connections.

In a nation that is ostensibly committed to freedom of expression,[10] the concept of verbal accountability is obviously somewhat threatening. And yet, when it is couched in the philosophical terms in which Maya Angelou discusses it, the concept is clearly consistent with our constitutional commitment to freedom of speech. Our constitutional right to freedom of speech is protected within the structure of an amendment that has as its focus the relatively powerless individual or relatively powerless groups: "*CONGRESS* shall make no law respecting an establishment of religion, or prohibiting the free exercise thereof, or abridging the freedom of speech, or of the press, or the right of the people peaceably to assemble, and to petition the Government for a redress of grievances" (First Amendment to the Constitution of the United States, ratified December 15, 1791).

Every inclusive constitutional privilege contains within its structure the potential for abuse and/or misrepresentation. Hate groups (e.g., the Ku Klux Klan) or simply groups that want to impose their version of morality on the country as a whole (e.g., anti-abortion forces) have either used or abused the constitutional right to freedom of speech. Ironically, it is easy to misrepresent the intent of the First Amendment because of the sometimes thin line between censorship and verbal insensitivity. Despite the potential of certain interest groups to abuse the privileges that come with First Amendment rights, we believe strongly in the greater creative latitude that these privileges provide. In fact, we agree with Laurence Stains's (1993) contention that "in the end, speech codes didn't protect minorities as much as they protected administrators" (49). With speech codes on the books and the "public fanfare" that usually followed their institutionalization, administrators could more easily avoid the more thorny issue of accelerating the diversification of curriculum, faculty, and student body.

We are not suggesting, of course, that hate speech should go uncensured. We are simply exploring the possibility, as Stains does, that "counterspeech and education" represent an alternative and perhaps a more appropriate response (49). Some of the more abusive forms of vile speech, for example, "obscenity, libel, threats of violence, incitements to lawlessness and so-called 'fighting words'" already fall outside the purview of First Amendment rights. Additional structural constraints on speech, especially at the campus level, have not been effective. They have, in fact, most often backfired, making, as Stains points out, "First Amendment martyrs of fraternity boors" (49) and providing an otherwise "morally bankrupted movement" (i.e., anti-affirmative action forces) with a target issue.

No single affirmative action strategy, in fact, has been more effectively misrepresented than restrictive speech codes; they have been manipulated by "rightist" and neoconservative forces to "change the focus of the issue from civil rights to civil liberties" (Stains 1993:49). Such a rhetorical switch allowed those who bought it to decapitate the ethical head of the "rights" issue, and to dissociate themselves from any moral responsibility for affirmative action and/or multicultural education. The switch also became a mechanism for avoiding power questions. Equity and diversity issues are, at the core, about power and privilege. Who has the right to scarce educational resources? Likewise, who has the power to determine whose experiences constitute knowledge? Franklin Haiman (1993), in his finely crafted argument for separating speech from action, makes the following concession: "institutional restrictions on such speech by employees who wield power over others is thus a justified, and even necessary kind of social control over potential abuses of authority" (30–33).

Maya Angelou believes that it is counterproductive to censor harmful words, for censorship precludes the establishment of either an honest exchange or a meaningful assessment of opposing positions. She preoccupies herself instead with the importance of personal accountability in speech, and the potential that such accountability has for the creation of a more ethical society. American educators should take note. In championing the right to freedom of speech, even hate speech, without a corresponding emphasis on individual accountability in speech, the far right, new right, and neo-conservative forces have helped to create and sustain an environment in which Americans have lost faith in moral victories. Reed and Bond (1991) point out, for example, that in their "misrepresentation of the goals of the 1960s," opponents of equity and diversity have attempted to justify "a view that commitment to principle has little, if any, place in politics" (737).

The implications of a flight from principle are obvious. For it is principle that represents the strongest argument against any form of injustice. In addressing the problem of hate speech, more of an emphasis on "counterargument and education" and less of a focus on punishment will rob opponents of affirmative action of their most effective target issue; it will also place supporters of equity and diversity in a position to begin to initiate a public discourse that will more closely examine the relationship between individual freedom and personal accountability. Such a discourse is critical if American educators are going to preoccupy themselves with defining the parameters of a language of socio-ethics.

A special relationship has always existed, as George Orwell (1968) pointed out, between "politics and the debasement of language." "Political language," he argued, "is designed to make lies sound truthful and murder respectable, and to give an appearance of solidity to pure wind" (139). We should not lose sight of the fact, however, that language (political or otherwise) does not emerge in a sanitized context. To the extent that "the [multicultural] debate," as Henry Louis Gates Jr. (1991) eloquently points out, was miscast from the beginning, it was a function of the erosion in the 1970s and 1980s (a radical departure from the often idealized politics of the 1960s) of a commitment to a politics of principle.

The United States' inability to sustain a collective commitment to a politics of principle has been due primarily to the absence of a national consciousness that was willing to either acknowledge the multicultural structure of our society, or the potential implicit within that structure for developing a language of socio-ethics. "Those who fear 'Balkanization' and social fragmentation," Gates points out, "have got it exactly backwards. Ours is a world that already is fissured by nationality, ethnicity, race, and gender. And the only way to transcend those divisions—to forge, for once, a civic culture that respects both differences and commonalities—is through education that seeks to comprehend the diversity of human culture" (555). That education, we believe, must incorporate a commitment to accountability in speech. As Orwell concluded, "One cannot change this all in a moment, but one can at least change one's habits, and from time to time, one can, if one jeers loudly enough, send some worn-out and useless phrase(s) . . . into the dustbin where [they] belong" (1945:135).

Jeering alone, unfortunately, will not refocus the affirmative action debate. In their retreat from principle, liberal politicians and educators created a moral vacuum. It was this vacuum, rather than a creative oppositional strategy, that enabled neoconservative forces to miscast the affirmative action debate. As an imperfect solution to a complex problem, affirmative action was an easy target for Americans who were unwilling to view it as a mechanism for bridging the gap between European-American males and American racial and gender minority groups, and chose to view it instead as an unethical (e.g., the allegation of "preferential treatment") and unacceptable solution to the problem of racial and gender bias. Supporters of affirmative action can therefore only regain control of the debate if they are willing to recast it in moral terms, to reclaim the moral authority that was the initial basis for affirmative action legislation. To assert strongly, as Cornel West (1993) puts it, that race (and gender) matter.

Overall, the so-called free speech movement has had a debilitating impact on American public and social policy. Rather than engaging advocates of greater inclusion in the kind of open and honest dialogue that could have resolved some of the contradictions that invariably exist in any reformist (i.e., affirmative action) approach to social change, anti-affirmative action forces retreated behind the door of collective denial. The concept of free speech is a double-edged sword. It has the ability to clarify as well as distort. Clarity, however, takes courage. Supporters of multicultural policies and programs need to begin to take the offensive, to become stronger advocates for freedom of speech than their critics, and to emphasize that a focus on freedom of speech without a corresponding emphasis on social responsibility is, in effect, a departure from a free speech environment. Tinder (1980) makes an important observation. Meaningful verbal exchange can only take place, he contends, in an honest and open speech environment; in a context in which hidden agendas either do not exist or are, at least, put on the table. An ethical stance is thus an essential prelude to meaningful verbal exchange as well as social action. If American educators can acknowledge that we are emotional as well as rational animals, and that it is ultimately the nature of our emotional response that will determine whether we destroy each other or, hopefully, learn to coexist, then perhaps we can provide the leadership that will begin the process of healing.

Notes

1. Since structural inequalities based on race and gender cannot be effectively addressed through individual action, in rejecting group action as a

strategic approach to social change, opponents of affirmative action programs were, in effect, rejecting social change.

2. No single factor more effectively underscored the fact that the act was not a quota bill than the willingness on the part of the American business community, prior to President Bush's negative intervention, to negotiate with supporters of the bill over their concerns (e.g., establishing reasonable limits on affirmative action suits). The appeal of the "quota" argument was, in part, a response to a weak economic climate. It was also, however, as Reed and Bond emphasize, a function of America's reluctance "to admit the endemic and pervasive character of explicitly racial stratification in American society . . . [or] . . . to accept the equally explicit struggle for racial justice as a necessarily integral component of . . . political life" (736).

3. It was this inaction that led James Forman Jr. (1991) to conclude that "the greatest threat to affirmative action stems not from attacks by the right but from its abandonment by the left." He continues: "It is becoming increasingly apparent that the conservative attack on affirmative action has been accompanied and nurtured by the collapse of affirmative action supporters, who have shown an unfortunate willingness to abandon it and the vision of civil rights and government/corporate responsibility that sustains it" (746). Cornel West (1993) explains this abandonment as a symptom of a failure of leadership; the absence, he maintains, of leaders who have neither the courage or conviction of the leadership of the 1960s.

4. One of our personal favorites is a story that was told by Lynne Chaney, the former chairperson of the national Endowment for the Humanities, during a *McNeil and Lehrer News Hour* interview in 1991. She relates a story about a young man who, in the process of trying to fulfill a diversity requirement found himself in the classroom with a "politically correct" (i.e., close-minded) professor. The distressed student purportedly escaped with an "A" grade by manipulating the instructor into believing that she (and the class) had transformed him from "a male chauvinist pig" into a sensitive human being. Whether this incident happened or not is less important than its sheer irrelevance, given the absence of a basis for assessing its representativeness.

5. Equally as pertinent, Drinan (1991) points out, was the fact that "state and local governments pursued a variety of adaptive strategies which could not become an easy target for the political right, particularly since the legitimacy and vitality of local government had been a part of the right political philosophy for some time. . . . The visibility and stature of higher education," on the other hand, "made it a [more] likely target" (7).

6. See, for example: Lani Guinier, *The Tyranny of the Majority* (1994), Omi and Winant, *Racial Formations in the United States* (1994), and Cornel West, *Race Matters* (1993). Guinier's objective and balanced approach to civil rights is particularly noteworthy, for her political career was derailed by the ability of the new right to label her a "quota queen."

7. The long-term value of Piaget's research is that even though cross-cultural research has thrown into question the universality of some of his conclusions (e.g., his contention that certain conceptual tasks cannot be mastered before a certain age), he clearly establishes the relationship between maturational and intellectual development. While it has been demonstrated that children in some cultures master conceptual tasks like depth perception at an earlier age, Piaget's contention that conceptual development takes place in a series of invariant stages has not been challenged. In documenting the developmental structure of intelligence, Piaget thus demonstrates that the child is not simply a small adult, an observation that has withstood the test of time and has important social policy implications. Also, in stressing the invariant nature of conceptual development in humans, he clearly underscores the hereditary origins of much of human behavior. Kohlberg, on the other hand, does not simply marginalize the role of culture, he attempts to negate it. For implicit within his stage theory of moral development is the assumption that some adults fail to complete *all* of Piaget's stages of development, and he links this failure with undeveloped moral consciousness. Unfortunately, even Piaget falls victim to this evolutionist thinking; it seems to come with the "stage theory" territory. For example, he associates "the language of children prior to age eight with 'savages and imbeciles'" (Cortese 1990:40). What is unfortunate about the evolutionist cast of Kohlberg's theory of moral development is that he identifies some of the processes by which people possibly resolve moral conflict or dissonance (e.g., the concept of "moral musical chairs"). Placed within a sociocultural rather than an evolutionary framework, these concepts can enhance our understanding of the development of ethical consciousness.

8. "This sentiment," Reed and Bond (1991) contend, "rests in the reluctance to admit the endemic and pervasive character of explicitly racial stratification" (736). They emphasize that neither working-class antagonism toward blacks nor the privilege it attempts to protect are new (734).

9. Welwood goes on to explain that it is the process of having to maintain and patch ourselves up that creates a certain brittleness and that this is the vulnerability we usually think of in our culture as something weak. In an attempt to ward off feelings of weakness, we compensate by becoming preoccupied with controlling our world and preventing its collapse. This preoccupation only fuels the cycle; it keeps us from getting in touch with our more basic human tenderness and seeing vulnerability in race relations as a source of real power (156).

10. A nation ostensibly committed, in the sense that many Americans are not willing to acknowledge that people in positions of power not only have greater latitude to challenge infringements of their individual freedoms, they are also in a position to limit the individual freedoms of the less powerful.

References Cited

Blauner, R. 1972. *Racial Oppression in America.* New York: Harper and Row.

Cortese, A. 1990. *Ethnic Ethics: The Restructuring of Moral Theory.* Albany: State University of New York Press.

D'Souza, D. 1991. *Illiberal Education.* New York: Vintage Books.

Devine, P. P. 1991. "Political Correctness and Multicultural Education." Paper presented at California State University at Hayward's conference "The Inclusive University: Multicultural Perspectives in Higher Education," November 7–10.

Drinan, Patrick. 1991. "Political Correctness: A Critique." Paper presented at California State University at Hayward's conference "The Inclusive University: Multicultural Perspectives in Higher Education," November 7–10.

Ellison, R. 1964. *Shadow and Act.* New York: Random House.

Elshtain, J. B. 1988. "Lessons from Amherst: Dragnet or Agenda for Action?" *Commonwealth,* March 25, pp. 164–65.

Forman, A. K. 1991. "Managing Multiracial Institutions: Goals and Approaches for Race Relations Training." *Communication Education* 40:255–65.

Forman, J. Jr. 1991. "Saving Affirmative Action." *The Nation* 253 (20):746–48.

Gates, H. L., Jr. 1991. "The Debate Has Been Miscast from the Start." *Boston Globe Magazine* 13 (October):26, 36–38.

Goleman, Daniel.1995. *Emotional Intelligence: Why It Can Matter More Than I.Q.* New York: Bantam Books.

Gudykunst, W. B. 1993. "Towards a Theory of Effective Interpersonal and Intergroup Communication: An Anxiety/Uncertainty Management Perspective." In *Intercultural Communication Competence.* Ed. R. Wiseman and J. Koester. Pp. 33–71. Newbury Park, Calif.: Sage.

Guinier, L. 1994. *The Tyranny of the Majority: Fundamental Fairness in Representative Democracy.* New York: Free Press.

Haiman, F. S. 1993. *"Speech Acts" and the First Amendment.* Carbondale: Southern Illinois University Press.

Jackman, M. R., and M. Crane. 1986. "Some of My Best Friends Are Black . . . : Interracial Friendship and Whites' Racial Attitudes." *Public Opinion Quarterly* 50:459–86.

Koester, J., and M. Olebe. 1988. "The Behavioral Assessment Scale for Intercultural Communication Effectiveness." *International Journal of Intercultural Relations* 12:233–46.

McIntosh, P. 1988. "White Privilege and Male Privilege: A Personal Account of Coming to See Correspondence through Work in Women's Studies."

Working Paper no. 189. Mass.: Wellesley College Center for Research on Women.

Martin, J. 1993. "Intercultural Communication Competence: A Review." In *Intercultural Communication Competence.* Ed. R. Wiseman and J. Koester. Pp. 16–29. Newbury Park, Calif.: Sage.

Omi, M., and M. Winant. 1994. *Racial Formations in the United States: From the 1960s to the 1990s.* 2d ed. New York: Routledge.

Orwell, G. 1968. "Politics and the English Language." In *In Front of Your Nose, 1945–1950.* Ed. Sonia Orwell and Ian Angus. Pp. 127–40. New York: Harcourt, Brace, and World.

Reed, A. Jr., and J. Bond. 1991. "Equality: Why We Can't Wait." *The Nation* 253 (20):733–37.

Stains, L. 1993. "Speech Impediment." *Rolling Stone,* August, pp. 45–49, 79–80.

Takaki, R. 1979. *Iron Cages: Race and Culture in Nineteenth-Century America.* New York: Alfred A. Knopf.

Tinder, G. 1980. *Community: Reflections on a Tragic Ideal.* Baton Rouge: Louisiana State University Press.

Welwood, J. 1983. "Vulnerability and Power in the Therapeutic Process." In *Awakening the Heart: East/West Approaches to Psychotherapy and the Healing Relationship.* Ed. J. Welwood. Pp. 148–62. Boston: Shambhala Press.

West, C. 1993. *Race Matters.* Boston: Beacon Press.

Wood, J. T. 1992. "Gender and Moral Voice: Moving from Woman's Nature to Standpoint Epistemology." *Women's Studies in Communications* 3 (Spring):1–24.

6   Facilitating Connections: Issues of Gender, Culture, and Diversity

Lea P. Stewart

In an essay titled "Women's Culture and Communication," Fern Johnson (1989) supports the popular notion that women and men live in "two different worlds," that they inhabit the same literal space but diverge in dramatic ways. She cites evidence from a number of disciplines, including communication, "to support the existence of a women's culture separable from men's" (302). This analysis solves the common problem of subordinating gender to culture and the equally pervasive problem of assuming that women's communication behavior is different from, and by implication inferior to, men's. The question remains, however, if men and women truly inhabit separate cultures, how can they ethically coexist with one another? This essay attempts to answer this question by examining the cultural worlds of women and men and then suggesting ethical guidelines for communication between women's and men's cultural spheres.

Gender and culture are not totally separable, of course. Gender "is established by the existential experience of ethnicity, race, culture, social class, caste and consciousness" (Cortese 1990:101). Men and women are gendered within a cultural context, yet, as Johnson (1989) suggests, form their own cultural contexts. Culture shapes the rules and norms for communication behavior. As Johnson eloquently states, "there are patterns from the past that have been brought to the present; and in the present, new patterns and forms of symbolic meaning are being created that will enter the future as the past" (308).

The manifestation of culturally defined roles for females and males is referred to as gender. All cultures have a gender system that functions to construct what it means to be feminine or masculine (de Lauretis 1987). As Rakow (1986) contends: "Gender . . . is usefully conceptualized as a culturally constructed organization of biology and social life into particular ways of doing, thinking, and experiencing the world. . . . It is in communication that this gender system is accomplished. Gender has meaning, is organized and structured, and takes place as interaction and social practice, all of which are communication processes. That is, communication creates genders who create communication" (23).

In any gendered system, some communicative behaviors may be stereotypically associated with males and females, although such associations are not often accurate reflections of individual behavior. For example, in many societies women are viewed stereotypically as friendlier than men. Many men are more friendly than some women, but the stereotype still exists. Gender stereotypes exist when a large portion of a society agrees that certain traits or behaviors are commonly associated with a given group of people (Harriman 1985). Stereotypes may have some basis in reality and may help us to understand our social world in some ways, but they are not accurate descriptions of particular individuals. Nevertheless, gender stereotypes affect our perceptions and, consequently, our communication with others. For example, a male nurse may be communicated with differently because he is filling a role traditionally occupied by women. He is engaged in a nurturing, caretaking role that is seen in terms of traditional stereotypes as unusual for men.

There are cultural variations in social roles ascribed to men and women. The anthropologist Maria Lepowsky discovered a group of people on a South Pacific island with a gender-egalitarian society in which women and men live and work equally in almost all aspects of the society (Wilford 1994). In this setting, the cultures of men and women are quite similar. In most societies, however, women and men form somewhat more separate spheres. One way to recognize the existence of these spheres is through language usage. According to Weedon (1987), language is the place where actual and possible forms of social organization and their likely social and political consequences are defined and contested. Yet it

is also the place where our sense of ourselves, our subjectivity, is constructed. This framework illuminates the hidden meaning in everyday life and
allows us to examine the taken-for-granted assumptions in language that
direct our behavior. This method is particularly useful in analyzing
conflict between cultures and surfacing meanings that would otherwise
be hidden.

Of course, cultured behavior changes over time. The societal role of
middle-class women in the United States has changed tremendously over
the years. In the early 1800s, for example, it was thought inappropriate
for women in the United States to speak in front of public gatherings.
Until recently, women were expected to be the primary caretakers of
young children. Now more and more women are pursuing careers outside the home while co-parenting a family. Increasingly men, who were
once seen primarily as the major source of financial support for their
families, are taking a more active role in day-to-day parenting. These
changing social roles are accompanied by changes in communication
behavior. For example, it is no longer unusual to see women anchoring
network television newscasts or to hear men discussing the paternity leave
policies of the companies where they work.

Analyzing gendered communication from a cultural perspective does
not mean that all women or all men behave similarly or that there is no
similarity between women and men. We are all members of multiple
cultural groups that influence our behavior and others' behavior toward
us. Societal changes that have affected one group to which we belong may
not affect us because of our membership in some other group. For example, many of the recent social changes in U.S. society only apply to a
comparatively small portion of the population. While large numbers of
white, middle-class women and many Asian Indian women pursue job
opportunities outside the home, for example, other groups of women
continue to choose to define their primary responsibilities as centered in
their homes.

Nevertheless, in most societies, there are communication behaviors
that are culturally defined as more appropriate for one gender than for
the other. In many ways, we communicate in feminine or masculine ways.
In North American culture, women may find it acceptable and enjoy-
able to talk at great length about their relationships; men may begin their
conversation in a gathering of male strangers with talk about sports,
politics, or music. In other societies men may be encouraged to display
overt signs of emotion in public, and women may use a more deferen-
tial form of speech.

The Case for Separate Ethical Orientations

Different Voices

One way to respond to the idea of different cultures for men and women is to posit a separate ethic for each gender. In her landmark book, *In a Different Voice,* Carol Gilligan (1982) expands the understanding of human development by including the study of women that was lacking in previous theories, especially those proposed by Kohlberg (1981). As a psychologist, Gilligan argues that the early social environment is experienced differently by male and female children and, thus, leads to basic differences in personality development. She contends that "given that for both sexes the primary caretaker in the first three years of life is typically female, the interpersonal dynamics of gender identity formation are different for boys and girls" (7). She bases her argument on Chodorow's (1974) observation that for females identity formation takes place in the context of an ongoing relationship with their mothers while males must separate from their mothers in defining themselves as masculine. For Chodorow (1978), male development entails a "more emphatic individuation and a more defensive firming of experienced ego boundaries" (167). Females experience themselves more like their mothers and fuse the experience of attachment with the process of gender identity formation. A separate ethic for males and females arises from these early experiences.

As a result of this early experience, Gilligan (1982) concludes that male gender identity is threatened by intimacy (since it is defined through separation) while female gender identity is threatened by separation (since it is defined through attachment). As an example, Gilligan notes that little boys are much more likely to argue about the rules when playing games. Little girls will suspend the game if an argument about rules appears to threaten their relationship. To boys, arguing about rules is part of the game; to girls, the continuation of the game is subordinated to the continuation of the relationship (10).

Gilligan (1982) contends that "women not only define themselves in a context of human relationships but also judge themselves in terms of their ability to care" (17). Gilligan sees the ability of women to care for others as a great strength. She notes that: "Women's construction of the moral problem as a problem of care and responsibility in relationships rather than as one of rights and rules ties the development of their moral thinking to changes in their understanding of responsibility and relationships, just as the conception of morality as justice ties development to the logic of equality and reciprocity. Thus the logic underlying an ethic of care is a psychological logic of relationships, which contrasts with the formal logic of fairness that informs the justice approach" (73). In this view, women are more likely to see problems in terms of conflicting responsibilities and their effects on their relationships with others while men base their judgments on a hierarchical set of principles. These viewpoints result in the assumption of an ethic of care relied on more by women and an ethic of justice more often used by men.

Cortese (1990) defends Gilligan's work against critics who question the existence of gender differences in moral judgment. He argues that: "the point is that Gilligan has expanded the domain of moral judgment by showing that women define themselves through their relationships with others, focusing on care and intimacy rather than separation and achievement. If we define morality according to conceptions of justice and systems of rules that are more attainable by one segment of the population than others—whether that segment is based on gender, race, ethnicity, or social class—this notion of morality is probably biased" (99–100).

Positing separate ethics for males and females is troubling in some ways, however, since it seems to imply that the choice to value care or value justice may be inherent in one's gender ideology and is essentially "value free." Of course traditional discourse has always implicitly valued the ethic of justice by supporting the notion of hierarchical standards for human behavior. Gilligan's great contribution (built on by many others) is to expand our notion of hierarchical standards to include caring for others as justification for moral action. Nevertheless, the implication that either ethic is appropriate in any given circumstance is problematic.

Significance of Gilligan's Work for Communication

Gilligan's theory is important from a communication perspective, however, because she bases her ideas on the assumption "that the way people talk about their lives is significant, that the language they use and the connections they make reveal the world that they see and in which they act" (2). Gilligan has been criticized for moving from relatively limited and unrepresentative data to generalizations of women as caring and responsive (Wood 1992). But Cortese (1990) argues that her close textual analysis of language and logic results in identifying common themes that recur in women's conceptions of morality. Cortese contends that Gilligan's greatest contribution is the "recognition of an interactive level of morality, mediation between individuals and the social structure" (146). Thus, communication is necessary for care.

Although her theory has been interpreted quite narrowly at times, Gilligan has stated that the association between the ethic of care and women is not absolute. More recent theorists contend that both men and women can demonstrate an ethic of care in their everyday lives (Pritchard 1991). Although Wood (1992) argues that "the narrative weight of the book inarguably associates the voice of care with women" (3), according to Cortese (1990), "the responsibility and justice orientations to morality are thematic, not gender differences. A person of either gender could have either or both orientations. Both are important for moral reasoning" (77). Noddings (1990) contends that any given person is capable of being either the caring-one or the cared for. Little attention is paid to women's choice of an ethic of justice, however.

Although theorists argue that men can approach situations from the position of an ethic of care, numerous examples of males relying on a hierarchical model of self-definition can be enumerated. For example, young boys may emphasize their masculine dominance by using girls as a negative reference group. One researcher asked students, "Who would you least wish to be like?" All of the boys named girls (and only girls). The characteristic of girls most vehemently rejected by these boys was their apparent marginality in classroom encounters. The term "faceless" was used repeatedly by the male students interviewed (but by none of the female students) to describe their female classmates, and seemed to reflect their feeling that silence robs female students of any claim to individual identity and respect (Stanworth 1981).

As Smith (1985) notes, "there is considerable evidence that the norms of femininity and masculinity encourage women and men to construe communication situations and the goals of interaction somewhat differently" (135). The traditional concept of masculinity is highly correlated with the control dimension—the extent to which a person can exert active control over the process and outcomes of an interaction. The affiliative dimension—the tendency to elicit warmth and approach—is associated with the traditional norms of femininity. Thus, men may be more concerned with aspects of control while women are more concerned with the goal of affiliation. Smith (1985) contends, however, that "Men are not 'dominant' and women 'muted': rather, men who are encouraged to be masculine, are concerned to manage and monitor the control-related aspects of interaction; while women, encouraged to be feminine, will tend to manage and monitor interaction in the pursuit of affiliative goals" (136). This conclusion is empirically supported by Mulac et al. (1988), who found that men are more likely to use direct control tactics such as directives ("Why don't you write down our answers?") and to maintain their speaking turns by using fillers to begin sentences ("And another thing . . ."), while women are more likely to use indirect control strategies such as questions ("What next?") and to express interest in others through the use of personal pronouns such as "we."

In interaction with each other, women and men form a social sphere in which their separate cultures come in contact to form a more complete world. This interaction serves as a bridge among cultures. Through interaction, separation diminishes and connections form.

Moving Beyond Separation

To move beyond separation and toward an ethic of connectedness, it is important to understand the multiple cultural groups that influence individuals' lives.

Embracing Multiple Cultural Groups

Much of the work on moral theory has been based on a narrow sample of people. This literature primarily focuses on Anglo-American culture and is built on virtually all-white research samples (Cortese 1990). Gilligan's and Chodorow's works have been criticized for a heavy reliance on the analysis of white, middle-class respondents' behavior. As Collins (1990) notes, "while these two classics make key contributions to feminist theory, they simultaneously promote the notion of a generic woman who is white and middle class" (8). bell hooks (1990) reminds us that "feminist thinkers engaged in radically revisioning central tenets of feminist thought must continually emphasize the importance of sex, race, and class as factors which *together* determine the social construction of femaleness" (189).

Much of the scholarly work on gender and communication has been criticized for making the implicit assumption that all women experience the world in the same way. Communication research and theory rarely deal with issues of social class, for example. As Spellman (1988) notes, "Just because people don't think of themselves as having any class identity, it doesn't mean that they have none. Indeed, under certain circumstances, the very lack of awareness of elements of one's identity is a significant reflection of that identity" (96). Stanback (1985) argues that many language and gender scholars have ignored the social class and subcultural differences among female speakers because they believe sexism creates a common ground of communicative experiences for all women.

Those who study women's language must pay greater attention to the discourse of nonwhite women and to the interplay of race and gender in communication (Johnson 1988). Many communication scholars are responding to this challenge, however. Collins (1990) provides an excellent synthesis of the long tradition of black feminist scholarship that is too often ignored in studies of communication and gender. According to Collins (1990), "Black women intellectuals have laid a vital analytical foundation for a distinctive standpoint on self, community, and society and, in doing so, created a Black women's intellectual tradition" (5).

Essentialist Bias

As discussed earlier, Gilligan's theoretical perspective has been lauded for including the perspective of women in studies on moral judgment and criticized for its methodology and assumptive framework. Although recognizing some value in Gilligan's work, Wood (1992) notes that "the voice of care and the essentialist assumptions about women that undergird it also may be read as not only false in obscuring diversity among women, but regressive in reinforcing views that have profoundly oppressed women historically. . . . The view of women that Gilligan and those working from her ideas appear to hold resonates with entrenched conservative, patriarchal identities prescribed for women" (5). This criticism assumes that all women are expected to exhibit an ethic of care. Gilligan acknowledges that the focus on care in moral reasoning is not characteristic of all women (Cortese 1990). Of course, Gilligan may be read to be arguing that it should be characteristic of all women.

Nevertheless, the essentialist nature of Gilligan's argument diminishes if one separates ethical orientation in moral judgment from societal role. One can make moral judgments based on an ethic of care without being a caretaker or, even in may cases, without being stereotypically caring. Conceiving morality in terms of caring means that decisions are made within a context of responsibility and relationships. For example, a person might drive a drunken friend home because the thought of the friend being injured is unbearable. Making moral decisions based on an ethic of justice is concerned with a logic of reciprocity and fairness. You drive your friends home because you expect them to do the same thing for you. The power of this theoretical perspective comes from its ability to include relational thinking in moral judgments. These ideas need to be developed further and, as Wood (1992) notes, it is important "to develop a theory of care as an ethic per se" (17).

Feminist Standpoint Theory

An understanding of the separate cultural spheres of women and men based on moral theory leads to the search for a path to connect these spheres through ethical communication.

To begin to develop guidelines for ethical communication between masculine and feminine cultures, a theoretical perspective that helps us consider the viewpoints of individuals from many aspects is necessary. Feminist standpoint theory (grounded in the theories of John Stuart Mill) as elucidated by Sandra Harding (1986) helps to supply this perspective. Harding notes that emancipatory stories of discourse have produced less distorted accounts of history because the dominant group's understanding of themselves is only partial and, therefore, distorted. These studies have turned a critical eye on folk beliefs in various cultures and pointed out the limitations of these beliefs. For example, the history of science emphasizes the objective nature of science, but the conventional notion of objectivity is only weak objectivity, according to Harding. Emancipatory movements demand strong objectivity and require symmetrical causal accounts. Since the subjects of knowledge are locations in a social matrix, they can learn to take the viewpoint of the other. Thus the researcher is speaking *from* peoples' lives and not *for* them.

Harding contends that competing discourses are positive, since richness comes from contradictions and creates opportunities. In this way, contradiction is a positive resource. To approach cultural understanding between men and women, feminist standpoint theory encourages individuals to take the viewpoint of the other to truly understand any situation. In this way, people can begin to embrace diverse or competing discourses.

To avoid exclusion, it is important to consider multiple standpoints when developing ethical viewpoints, including a consideration of the perspective of women. The construction of an ethics that includes the standpoint of women can contribute significantly to both ethical thinking and general human welfare (Noddings 1990).

Hearing the Voices of Others

To begin to develop a sense of connectedness arising from separation, we need to look for ethical guidelines for our communication with others.

Developing Ethical Guidelines

From an ethical perspective, individuals need to resist the privileged discourse and communication norms that often privilege white male forms of discourse or definitions of cultural terms. To accomplish this resistance, Fine (1991) calls for the creation of a "harmonic discourse," creating a discourse in which all voices retain their individual integrity yet combine to form a whole discourse that is orderly and congruous. Fine maintains that since metaphors connect the known with the unknown, we should adjust our metaphors to describe this new communicative reality. Men and women have much to learn by analyzing the meaning of the metaphors they use from the perspective of others who may not share similar norms. For example, a woman attending a business meeting in which military metaphors predominate (for example, "let's win this war" or "let's run this up the flag pole and see who salutes") may feel excluded. In a similar fashion, an African American male who grew up in the inner city may use different metaphors to describe his world than a white male from suburbia.

In addition, any ethic of conciliation between cultures must reclaim the notion of voice for all interactants. Interestingly, one of the earlier conceptualizations of the concept of voice was introduced to the communication field by the work of Albert Hirschman (1970), an economist. Hirschman proposed that organizational management discovered its failings through two alternative routes: exit and voice. The exit option occurred when customers stopped buying a product; the voice option occurred when customers expressed their dissatisfaction directly to management or to some authority to which management was subordinate or through general protest addressed to anyone willing to listen. In this situation, voice is generally the preferred alternative because once customers have exited from a transaction, they have lost the power to use voice to bring about change. Significantly, according to Hirschman, voice is the preferable alternative when individuals feel that the complaints of others and their own faithfulness will be successful and the individual is loyal to the product or organization. In other words, using one's voice is based on faith in one's ability to bring about change and loyalty to a societal institution or individual.

Using this early conceptualization, it is clear how voices from women's culture can be unsilenced. Silence is broken when women believe that their voices can be joined with the voices of others and, therefore, be successful in affecting change. The contemporary women's movement provides numerous examples of this method of breaking silence and affecting social change. In addition, individuals are more likely to use voice when they are loyal to an institution or individual because they truly want to improve something that they are part of. If women feel disenfranchised from male culture, they have little motivation to voice their views. For example, a woman who feels excluded from a political process she perceives as consisting of argumentative debate, majority rule, or quid pro quo dealings may choose not to vote.

A preliminary conceptualization of ethical guidelines for cultural communication between genders based on the above discussion would include the following:

Fostering Dialogue   Johannesen (1990) contends that "the essential movement in dialogue, according to Buber, is turning toward, outgoing to, and reaching for the other. And a basic element in dialogue is 'seeing the other' or 'experiencing the other side'" (59). Dialogue is characterized by authenticity, inclusion, confirmation, presentness, spirit of mutual equality, and supportive climate. Men and women truly must engage in dialogue as a first step toward valuing each others' cultures.

Embracing Multiple Discourses   Conflict may arise because of the multiple discourses of diverse individuals. Viewing women and men as separate cultures may be described as a paradigm shift. Addressing this conflict ethically means recognizing its growth potential. It is imperative to recognize that individuals perceive conflict differently. Thus, ethically responding to conflict calls for a valuing of differences in approaches to conflict and other aspects of discourse. Table 6-1 illustrates a valuing-differences approach to encouraging dialogue based on an organizational model. This model can be applied to the sometimes conflicting cultures of men and women.

The United States is a multicultural society that does not always effectively deal with or value its diversity. This societal problem affects our scholarship. One solution for overcoming this difficulty in the scholarship on women and pluralism is to make culture the central concept for analysis. In this framework, culture consists of "the system of verbal, nonverbal, and discourse patterns that characterize the expressions of a group of people. The system of artifacts comprises artistic expressions of a group of people . . . including . . . music, poetry, arts, and crafts. And the system of abstractions includes values, moral principles, ethics, logic, religious and spiritual notions, and so forth" (Johnson 1988:39). Dealing with these aspects of culture should be a central focus of communication scholarship leading to an ethics of connectedness.

Table 6-1. Valuing Differences through Dialogue

Qualitative
Emphasis on the appreciation of differences and the creation of an environment in which everyone feels valued and accepted.

Ethically driven
Moral and ethical imperatives drive this culture change.

Idealistic
Everyone benefits. Everyone feels valued and accepted in an inclusive environment.

Diversity model
Assumes that groups will retain their own characteristics and shape the organization [or society] as well as be shaped by it, creating a common set of values.

Opens attitudes, minds, and the culture
Efforts affect attitudes of individuals.

Resistance
Resistance is due to a fear of change, discomfort with differences, and a desire to return to the "good old days."

Source: Adapted from Galagan (1993) and Gardenswartz and Rowe (1993).

Empowering All People   Individuals should be empowered to make decisions about what they are most familiar with and to provide meaningful input. Empowerment cannot occur without true listening and commitment to understanding different cultural perspectives. As Spellman (1988) notes, "if the meaning of what we apparently have in common (being women [or men]) depends in some ways on the meaning of what we don't have in common (for example, our different racial or class identities), then far from distracting us from issues of gender, attention to race and class in fact helps us to understand gender. In this sense it is only if we pay attention to how we differ that we come to an understanding of what we have in common" (113).

Abandoning the Notion of Women's Issues   Jaggar (1991) provides a comprehensive overview of feminist ethics in which she argues that attention to so-called women's issues may, in fact, disenfranchise women from other societal and public spheres. She emphasizes that using words such as "women's issues," no matter what the positive intention, tends to suggest that there is something natural or inevitable about women's concerns for these issues, and, conversely, that men do not have to be concerned about them. Work must be done to reconceptualize the public/private sphere dichotomy that often haunts discussions of women's role in society and, by extension, their ethical concerns.

Of course, the public/private dichotomy has always been problematic when discussing women's roles across cultural, racial, ethnic, and social class lines. Some groups (typically white, middle-class women) have gained access to the public sphere by relegating their domestic tasks to poorer women from other ethnic groups. Thus, the concept of women's issues varies dramatically among social class, racial, and ethnic groups. As Spellman (1988) reminds us, women can perpetuate racism, too.

Connections to Intercultural Theory

The previous guidelines have been based on a dialogic theory of communication. The following guidelines are developed from intercultural communication theory and are a necessary foundation for implementing any of the previous guidelines.

Encouraging Individuals to Understand Themselves

Gudykunst (1991) notes that we are members of many social groups, based on gender, race, ethnicity, sexual orientation, and so on. These group memberships influence our communication. Gudykunst argues that "our personal and social identities influence all of our communication behavior, even though one may predominate in a particular situation" (21). Because of this multiple group membership, we need to understand the groups to which we belong before we can communicate effectively with members of other groups. As Johnson (1988) notes, "Placing value on diversity and respecting the integrity of different cultures requires increasing knowledge about that diversity; and knowledge is always interpreted through a person's own cultural perspective" (40).

Replacing Hierarchical Thinking with Relational Thinking

Noddings (1990) argues that: "An ethics of caring is based on a relational ontology. It takes as a basic assumption that human beings are defined in relation. It is not just that 'I' as a preformed, persistent individual enter into relations; the 'I' of which we all speak so easily is itself a relational entity. I am defined by the set of relations into which my physical self has been thrown" (172–73). Relations are created through interactions among people. Relationships may be more crucial than conceptions of justice in some circumstances (Cortese 1990). Work needs to be done to explore the connections between subcultural moral systems and universal standards of ethics. The view that universal principles are the highest good must be challenged through communication.

Conclusion

This preliminary conceptualization is intended to be the beginning of a discussion of ethical ways in which men's and women's cultures may speak to one another to begin a dialogue that can lead to true acceptance of each culture. It is no longer acceptable to assume that all women should be rooted in the so-called private sphere of relationships and that all men must exclusively function in the public sphere of hierarchical decision-making. As Johnson (1988) reminds us, "feminist scholars of communication must hold especially high goals for the attainment of a theoretical perspective that fosters work on the diversity as well as the similarity among women" (41). Men's and women's special knowledge and abilities are needed in each context. True peace will never be achieved until these cultures can ethically speak to one another.

References Cited

Chodorow, N. 1974. "Family Structure and Feminine Personality." In *Women, Culture, and Society.* Ed. M. Z. Rosaldo and L. Lamphere. Pp. 43–66. Stanford: Stanford University Press.

———. 1978. *The Reproduction of Mothering.* Berkeley: University of California Press.

Collins, P. H. 1990. *Black Feminist Thought: Knowledge, Consciousness, and the Politics of Empowerment.* New York: Routledge.

Cortese, A. 1990. *Ethnic Ethics: The Restructuring of Moral Theory.* Albany: State University of New York Press.

de Lauretis, T. 1987. *Technologies of Gender: Essays on Theory, Film, and Fiction.* Bloomington: Indiana University Press.

Fine, M. G. 1991. "New Voices in the Workplace: Research Directions in Multicultural Communication." *Journal of Business Communication* 28:259–75.

Galagan, P. A. 1993. "Navigating the Differences." *Training and Development* 47 (April):29–33.

Gardenswartz, L., and A. Rowe. 1993. *Managing Diversity: A Complete Desk Reference and Planning Guide.* Homewood, Ill.: Business One Irwin.

Gilligan, C. 1982. *In a Different Voice: Psychological Theory and Women's Development.* Cambridge: Harvard University Press.

Gudykunst, W. B. 1991. *Bridging Differences: Effective Intergroup Commu-nication.* Newbury Park, Calif.: Sage.

Harding, S. 1986. *Whose Science? Whose Knowledge?* Ithaca: Cornell Univer-sity Press.

Harriman, A. 1985. *Women/Men Management.* New York: Praeger.

Hirschman, A. O. 1970. *Exit, Voice, and Loyalty.* Cambridge: Harvard Uni-versity Press.

hooks, b. 1990. "Feminism: A Transformational Politic." In *Theoretical Per-spectives on Sexual Difference.* Ed. D. L. Rhode. Pp. 185–93. New Ha-ven: Yale University Press.

Jaggar, A. M. 1991. "Feminist Ethics: Projects, Problems, and Prospects." In *Feminist Ethics.* Ed. C. Card. Pp. 78–104. Lawrence: University of Kansas Press.

Johannesen, R. L. 1990. *Ethics in Human Communication.* 3d ed. Prospect Heights, Ill.: Waveland.

Johnson, F. L. 1988. "Feminist Theory, Cultural Diversity, and Women's Communication." *Howard Journal of Communications* 1(2):33–41.

———. 1989. "Women's Culture and Communication: An Analytical Per-spective." In *Beyond Boundaries: Sex and Gender Diversity in Communi-cation.* Ed. C. M. Lont and S. A. Friedley. Pp. 301–16. Fairfax: George Mason University Press.

Kohlberg, L. 1981. *The Philosophy of Moral Development.* San Francisco: Harper and Row.

Mulac, A., J. M. Wiemann, S. J. Widenmann, and T. W. Gibson. 1988. "Male/Female Language Differences and Effects in Same-Sex and Mixed-Sex Dyads: The Gender-Linked Language Effect." *Communication Mono-graphs* 55:315–35.

Noddings, N. 1990. "Ethics from the Standpoint of Women." In *Theoreti-cal Perspectives on Sexual Difference.* Ed. D. L. Rhode. Pp. 160–73. New Haven: Yale University Press.

Pritchard, M. 1991. *On Becoming Responsible.* Lawrence: University of Kansas Press.

Rakow, L. F. 1986. "Rethinking Gender Research in Communication." *Jour-nal of Communication* 36(4):11–26.

Smith, P. M. 1985. *Language, the Sexes, and Society.* Oxford: Basil Blackwell.

Spellman, E. V. 1988. *Inessential Woman: Problems of Exclusion in Feminist Thought.* Boston: Beacon Press.

Stanback, M. H. 1985. "Language and Black Women's Place: Evidence from the Black Middle Class." In *For Alma Mater: Theory and Practice in Fem-inist Scholarship.* Ed. P. A. Treichler, C. Kramarae, and B. Stafford. Pp. 177–93. Urbana: University of Illinois Press.

Stanworth, M. 1981. *Gender and Schooling: A Study of Sexual Divisions in the Classroom.* London: Women's Research and Resources Centre.

Weedon, C. 1987. *Feminist Practice and Poststructuralist Theory.* Oxford: Basil Blackwell.

Wilford, J. N. 1994. "Sexes Equal on South Sea Island." *New York Times,* March 29, pp. C1, C11.

Wood, J. T. 1992. "Gender and Moral Voice: Moving from Woman's Nature to Standpoint Epistemology." *Women's Studies in Communication* 15:1–24.

7 Ethical Communication and Sexual Orientation

James W. Chesebro

When human beings communicate, they are motivated by several simultaneous objectives. Seeking to persuade others, for example, they may be goaded by pragmatic objectives and therefore attempt to regulate the symbols other people use to define themselves, others, and their environment. Regardless of the pragmatic end sought, when human beings communicate, they also implicitly presume that certain kinds of symbol-using are good or bad, right or wrong. When people employ a commonly shared set of values about how people should communicate, they fulfill one of the requirements for creating a system of human communication.

Yet, not all people share the same values. Multiple systems of human communication exist, in part, because different sets of values govern symbol-using (see, e.g., Chesebro 1973). But, far more important in this essay, the values regulating any particular human communication system are influenced by societal systems. Indeed, societal systems can foster or inhibit the development of any symbol system. Societal controls may take the form of formal legal sanctions or informal stereotypes. In all, societies influence and control the kinds of communication systems that can exist. Correspondingly, by regulating human symbol-using, the system of ethical standards that can emerge within a human communication system are also inhibited and restricted.

When societies control human communication systems—and therefore the related ethical standards governing these systems—the essence of the human being is directly challenged. Ethical systems determine what should and should not be said, and in so doing, at least three recognizable dimensions are affected (Chesebro 1969:195–96). First, "ethics introduces a *dimension of social identity,*" determining how a group will define and understand itself. But ethics also introduces "a second *dimension of cultural integrity,*" directly affecting the kind of community structure and processes affecting human interactions. Finally, "ethics also introduces a third *dimension of temporal motivation,*" forcing members of a group to "reconsider their commitment to an enlarged humanity," which is most clearly reflected in the history and future a group believes it has and can realize (105–6).

These preliminary observations provide the immediate context for how communication ethics in same-sex relationships[1] are approached in this essay.[2] The thesis developed in this essay is that same-sex relationships have traditionally been influenced, if not dramatically regulated and controlled, by societal forces largely beyond the control of the men and women involved in same-sex relationships. As Adam (1985:19) has reported, "cross-cultural evidence demonstrates that homosexuality is an inextricable component of the structural codes of the societies in which it appears." Specifically, in the United States, these societal forces have severely inhibited and restricted the development of the system of communication ethics that might govern same-sex relationships. Accordingly, this essay is developed in two major parts. In the first section, the societal forces are specified that inhibit the development of same-sex communication ethics. Recognizing that this system of communication ethics has not yet had an opportunity to develop, the second part of this essay posits the potential core of a same-sex communication ethics.

The Politics of Diversity and Ethical Communication Systems

Before he died of AIDS in 1984, Michel Foucault identified the explicit processes by which sexuality is defined and regulated in societal systems.[3] In *The History of Sexuality,* a three-volume collection published between 1978 and 1984, Foucault maintained that sexuality has been systematically and increasingly regulated and controlled by societal forces. In his historical reconstruction, Foucault reported that the "fundamental link between power, knowledge, and sexuality" began in "the classical age" (1978:5). In Foucault's view, "the demand for sexual freedom" and the "right to speak" about sexuality was achieved, at the societal level, by carefully regulating and sanctioning the kind of "discourse" that could be employed to describe sexuality (1978:6–8). Particularly, Foucault maintained that each successive set of discourses, from Victorian to Freudian conceptions, constitutes a socially imposed definition of what sexuality was and provided built-in prescriptions regarding how sexuality was to be expressed. Accordingly, by regulating how sex was discussed, the meaning of different kinds of sexual activity was also socially defined, characterized, understood, and controlled.

In the United States, same-sex relationships were not explicitly and formally recognized as an identifiable sociocultural system until the nineteenth century, when the term *homosexuality* was coined by Benkert in 1869 (Herdt and Boxer 1992:4). Certainly, same-sex sexual behaviors existed and specific acts were characterized prior to the nineteenth century. But it was not until the nineteenth century in the United States that same-sex relationships were recognized as a distinct or discrete human system, with its own values, a unique sociological structure, and distinct social processes. As Hayes (1981) has reported: "Although there is thorough documentation that homosexual *behavior* is both universal and timeless in some variety or other, evidence of a homosexual *identity* has been found only in recent and specific phenomena. Homosexuality exists everywhere, but only in certain cultures or under certain circumstances is it *structured* into a subculture or made an official institution of a closed community (e.g., the courts of some monarchs, nunneries, the Greek gymnasium). Elsewhere it seems to lack any structure whatsoever" (29).

Recognition as a sociocultural system occurred, however, with a high price tag for those in same-sex relationships. The definitions and characterizations of same-sex relationships were predominantly provided by those removed from and external to these relationships, such as social scientists (Chesebro 1980). For example, while he did recognize its sociocultural existence, Freud conceived and characterized homosexuality as a form of retarded social development, a form of sexual repression, and a pathological fixation (see, e.g., Freud, 1950[1913]:67, 217, 245, 261, 262–63, and 268).

Following the end of World War II, a new set of conceptions regarding homosexuality began to emerge. While apparently more "liberal" and "tolerant," even this new set of conceptions continued to inhibit the development of a system of communication ethics for those in same-sex relationships. These conceptions turn on how homosexuality was defined, the attitudes expressed toward homosexuals, and the devastating effect of AIDS.

Definition as a Strategy of Disorientation

With the advent of the Kinsey report on male sexual behavior in 1948 (Kinsey et al. 1948), defining homosexuality became the domain of the "experts," including psychologists, psychiatrists, and social scientists. And the definition of *homosexuality* contained within this volume initially promised tremendous clarity. Kinsey and his colleagues reported that "37 percent of the total male population has at least some overt homosexual experience to the point of orgasm between adolescence and old age" and that "an additional 13 percent of the males (approximately) react erotically to other males without having overt sexual contact after the onset of adolescence" (650). Subsequently, Warren B. Pomeroy (1969), one of Kinsey's coauthors of *Sexual Behavior in the Human Male,* reported that "about 37 percent of the males above the age of puberty have had at least one overt homosexual experience to the point of orgasm" and that "about 13 percent of the females above the age of puberty have had at least one overt homosexual experience to the point of orgasm" (8). Such conclusions would seem to offer a vividly clear definition of homosexuality as well as its scope.

However, the Kinsey report also introduced a research scheme that began to cloud the meaning of the term *homosexuality.* Indeed, for many, the shocking impact of the Kinsey report was quickly replaced by confusion. From 1948 through 1969, the Kinsey Institute (see, e.g., Pomeroy 1969:5–6) discussed *homosexuality* in terms of two continua. One continuum was behavioral, and it classified human sexual acts along a scale of seven categories from "exclusively homosexual" at one end to "exclusively heterosexual" at the other. The second continuum was psychological, and it classified sexual preferences or orientations along a scale of seven categories from "exclusively homosexual" at one end to "exclusively heterosexual" at the other. Pomeroy explained the continua in these terms: "Individuals can be classified on this scale according to their overt behavior, their psychic response, or both. Ordinarily, overt behavior is closely related to psychological reactions. When this is not true—as, for example, in the case of a married man whose overt behavior would be classed as 2 (more heterosexual than homosexual), although his psychic response might be 4 (predominantly homosexual)—one can average the individual's ratings or can classify him on two different scales" (ibid.).

Rather than clarifying homosexuality, these two scales launched a series of contradictory conceptions of *homosexuality.* For example, Humphrey (1970) reported that 25 percent of males who engage in sex with other males in quasi-public places espoused some of the most oppressive condemnations of homosexuals, while Masters and Johnson (1979) reported that "ambisexuals" or bisexuals were a clinical entity. Defined as "men and women" who "reported frequent sexual interaction with members of both sexes" and who "described the additional exceptional characteristic of an apparent complete neutrality in partner preference between the two genders" (145), ambisexuals or bisexuals were assigned to male and female as well as heterosexual and homosexual "sexual interactions in the laboratory" (152). Masters and Johnson concluded that "there was no loss of physiologic responsivity that could be statistically determined, and there certainly was no loss of subjective involvement that could be observed for the assigned partners of either preference" (160).

While undoubtedly designed to clarify, such discussions initiated a series of complex conceptions that ultimately created, not only confusion, but contradictory understandings of homosexuality, perhaps even fostering negative attitudes toward gay men and lesbians. Employing the definitions provided in these studies, homosexuality could be a mere psychological reaction. Or, homosexual behavior might be only a physical release without an accompanying and related emotional reaction. It was no longer even clear if homosexuals actually had orgasms with others of the same sex. Indeed, homosexuals might be deceiving themselves and others (e.g., the "repressed homosexual" and the "closet case"). When all was said and done, the homosexual had been objectified and dehumanized. At best, homosexuals could possess physical or psychological or physical and psychological attractions for others of the same sex. At worst, homosexuals were schizophrenic. Given the twenty-five years of "research" defining homosexuality after World War II through the early 1970s, the January 1975 decision of the American Psychological Association to remove homosexuality from its official list of mental disorders ultimately had no effect upon American public opinion about homosexuality (Morin 1977:629).

Unfortunately, these definitions may have confused homosexuals as much as they confused others. For example, when attempting to define homosexuality in his book *The Gay World* in 1968, Martin Hoffman reasoned:

> When I use the term "homosexual" to describe a man, by this I do not mean that he may not also be heterosexual, for I think there are a significant number of people . . . who are sexually attracted

to and seek out sexual partners of both sexes. These people we could very conveniently call bisexual, and I will do so, providing only that it is understood that the nature of the sexual attraction to men may not be the same as the sexual attraction to women. In other words, just because we say that a man is sexually attracted to both men and women does not imply that his feelings on seeing a man and his feelings on seeing a woman are the same. . . .

The fact is that there are almost as many different kinds of homosexual, bisexual, and heterosexual responses as there are individuals.

Hoffman's definition may aptly reflect the diversity of sexual variations possible within a human culture, but the definition does little to achieve his original objective of providing a definition (or delimiting and specification of the unique and essential class features) of *homosexuality*. To complicate an already complicated situation even more, Carrier (1992) has also reported that cross-cultural differences determine how homosexuality is defined. He has noted that "mainstream Anglo culture in the United States" makes a "harsh judgment" of "*all* males involved in homosexual behavior, no matter how infrequent" (207),[4] while "in Mexican society," "only the feminine male is labeled a 'homosexual,'" for "by societal standards, the masculine self-image of Mexican males is not threatened by their homosexual behavior as long as they play the anal insertive role and also have a reputation for having sexual relations with women" (206). In all, particularly before the Stonewall rebellion in late June of 1969, an action that argued for displacing the word "homosexual" with the word "gay," the use of "scientific" definitions of *homosexuality* did little to clarify understandings, especially for those with questions about their sexual orientation. Indeed, even for those who acknowledged a same-sex orientation, the volumes—published between 1948 and 1980—devoted to defining homosexuality appeared only to confuse.

More recent efforts at defining homosexuality have suggested that there may be anatomical differences in the brains of homosexuals and heterosexuals as well as a "gay gene." In August 1991, Simon LeVay reported that the hypothalamus, located in the forebrain and believed to regulate male sexual urges, was twice as large in men assumed to be heterosexual as it was in those who were homosexual (Angier 1991a, 1991b; Suplee 1991; Winslow 1991). Additionally, on July 16, 1993, the *New York Times* (Angier 1993:A1) reported "Report Suggests Homosexuality Is Linked to Genes," while *The Chronicle of Higher Education* similarly reported

"Study Suggests X Chromosome Is Linked to Homosexuality" (Wheeler 1993:A6). Both newspapers reported that scientists had discovered that "one or several genes located on the bottom half of the sausage-shaped X chromosome may play a role in predisposing some men toward homosexuality" (Angier 1993:A1).

Anatomical and genetic explanations do little, of course, to clarify social roles, and they may offer a false sense of control for parents who wish to determine the sexual orientation of their children. Indeed, LeVay, author of the hypothalamus study, has reported that anatomical brain differences may only be "one possible element predisposing" men to "homosexuality" (in Angier 1991a:D18). And Dr. Dean H. Hamer of the National Cancer Institute and the lead author of the genetic study, has reported, "Sexual orientation is too complex to be determined by a single gene. The main value of this work is that it opens a window into understanding how genes, the brain and the environment interact to mold human behavior" (in Angier 1993:C18).

Definitions can function as rhetorical strategies (Chesebro 1985). While perhaps not intended, the definitions produced by social scientists divided the concept of *homosexuality* into so many subcomponents that an overall meaning for the term was lost. The effect of these definitions has been disorientation, for those in same-sex relationships as well as for others who sought to understand the conceptions offered by social scientists. The definitions have not, for example, provided a reliable answer to the most basic question of how many homosexuals there are. As Cronin (1993:16E) has reported, "there is still no consensus as to how many homosexuals there are in America." Similarly, seeking to explain significant contradictory findings among various poll data, Humphrey Taylor, president of Louis Harris and Associates, has noted, "Whenever you get into measuring anything that is potentially awkward or embarrassing or might be construed as antisocial, people overreport socially desirable behavior and underreport behavior that might be considered antisocial" (in Barringer 1993:12). Rather than providing a commonly shared understanding, the definitions employed have created uncertainty and disorientation, if not social division, at virtually every level of society. Certainly, the definitions have done little to satisfy the preconditions for the development of a communication ethic. As noted at the outset of this essay, before a communication ethic can emerge, a social unit must possess a sense of its own social identity, a sense of its own cultural integrity, and a sense of its own history and future. The behavioral, psychological, anatomical, and genetic definitions of *homosexuali-*

ty posited by social and medical scientists simply bypassed these issues, and they ultimately detracted attention from the social and community issues required to develop a communication ethic.

The Paralyzing Effect of Divided Public Opinion

Public opinion surveys about homosexuality were first initiated by the Gallup Poll in 1977, and they have been consistently updated and reported since that time (Gallup Poll 1992b:59). Widely disseminated in the media, the results of these polls do little to foster and promote the development of a system of communication ethics among gay men and lesbians. As noted at the outset, a society can foster or inhibit the development of communication ethics, and in this case, the most readily available measure of the American society would seem to preclude the emergence of a communication ethic for gay males and lesbians.

These polls have consistently suggested that the larger society is divided in its attitude about but also in its understanding of homosexuality. In 1977, 43 percent of Americans favored "legalized gay relations," while 43 percent believed they should not be legalized (Gallup Poll 1992b:60). Some fifteen years later, in June 1992, Gallup Poll again reported that, "About half of Americans (48 percent) say that homosexual relations between consenting adults should be legal, but nearly as many Americans (44 percent) say gay sex should be illegal" (2). In April of 1993, following President Clinton's proposal to lift the ban on homosexuals in the military, the Gallup Poll (30) reported that attitudes toward homosexuality reflected people's understanding of homosexuality:

> Besides gender, the most important factor influencing people's attitudes toward gays is their opinion about what causes homosexuality.
>
> In the current poll, 31 percent say it is caused by "something that people are born with," nearly double what a *Los Angeles Times* poll reported ten years ago (16 percent). It is this group that displays the most tolerant attitudes toward gays. Two-thirds of them, for example, feel civil rights protection should be extended to gays, almost twice the support seen in the rest of the population. Similarly, 65 percent of this more tolerant group favor ending the ban against serving in the military, compared to just 34 percent among the rest of the population.

At the same time, 14 percent of Americans believe that homosexuality is "something that develops because of the way people are brought up" and 35 percent believe that homosexuality is a preference (i.e., "the way that some people prefer to live") (Gallup Poll 1993:31). For the majority of these two groups, homosexuals should not be given basic civil rights protection because homosexuals can and should change (Gallup Poll 1993:32–33; see also Turque et al. 1992). Accordingly, the Gallup Poll explicitly recognized that "public opinion" has been "divided on gay rights" (1992c:2) and is now "polarized on [the] gay issue" (1993:30).[5]

In all, such attitudes ultimately discourage the development of the preconditions required for the creation of a gay male/lesbian communication ethic. The surveys repeatedly imply—particularly on the question of the causes of homosexuality and whether or not homosexuals can change—that many Americans are fundamentally divided over the question of whether or not gay males and lesbians possess a legitimate social identity, cultural integrity, and a history or future. Insofar as a society possesses the power to foster the development of a system of communication ethics, the American public has denied a mandate for such action.

The Devastating Effects of AIDS

It might, of course, be possible for a minority to attempt to overcome the characterizations of social scientists and to change public opinion. Indeed, following the Stonewall riots of 1969, homosexuals did assume a new self-conception as *gay*, and they initiated a series of campaigns and confrontations designed to define their own social identity, develop a cultural integrity, and reconstruct their history and future. However, these persuasive efforts were ultimately to be short-lived (see, e.g., Chesebro 1982:162–65).

The emergences of AIDS in 1981 had devastating effects on the political aspirations of homosexuals, especially gay males. While it is true that only a minority of the gay male community is HIV positive or has contracted AIDS, nonetheless, the disease has affected the entire gay male community. AIDS kills, and it is an intimate killer, for friends and lovers are destroyed far before their time in a prolonged and painful death. In terms of priorities, physical existence precedes ethical questions—within the ongoing everyday activities of a community, immediate and biological life-sustaining efforts often take precedence over the development of a system of communication ethics.

But the AIDS epidemic has also had political consequences, particularly for gay males. Frequently identified as a "gay disease," in October of 1991 the Gallup Poll (62) reported that "Americans have grown less accepting of homosexuals. Three in five (61 percent) feel the tolerance of gay life in the 1960s and 1970s was a 'bad thing for our society.' Only 36 percent of adults today believe homosexual relations between consenting adults should be legal, a figure comparable to 1986 (33 percent), when it declined from the 43–45 percent level recorded between 1977 and 1985." Moreover, the Gallup Poll (1991:62) maintained that this reversal for homosexuals was linked to AIDS: " 'They were just beginning to get some of their rights and come out of the closet with their sexual habits, and then AIDS hits the scene' " (see also Gallup Poll 1992a). Moreover, as I have reported elsewhere (Chesebro 1994:79–80):

> Similarly, a 1991 New York Times/CBS News poll found that "only 39 percent said they have a lot or some sympathy for 'people who get AIDS from homosexuality activity,' about the same as the 36 percent who expressed such sentiment in 1988" [in Magay 1991]. Finally, it should be noted that many common AIDS educational programs apparently make people less tolerant of those with AIDS. Researchers at the Georgia Institute of Technology have found that workers who attended AIDS educations programs, "less than two hours long, were significantly less tolerant of people with AIDS than were workers who had received other forms of education, or none at all" [in "AIDS Talks" 1991]. In all, AIDS has altered how people respond to homosexuality, decisively altering the measured progress and quest for liberation which characterized the outcome of the discourse of gay males and lesbians in the 1960s and 1970s.[6]

In all, a communication ethics is unlikely to emerge when death occupies a central role in the lives of gay males. Related public opinion regarding AIDS-related deaths has functioned only to reinforce the negative and paralyzing effects that a divided public opinion had already exerted on efforts to develop a communication ethic.

The Potential Core of a Same-Sex Communication Ethic

Given the societal and political forces negating its development, a gay male/lesbian communication ethic can only be said to be in an embryonic stage. Yet, a foundation for this ethic can be detected in the word *gay*, which emerged as a self-defining conception for some homosexuals in the late 1960s. Since that time, additional dimensions appear to be emerging that contribute to and enrich the nature that a same-sex communication ethic may encompass.[7]

Gay as a New Foundation

Following the Stonewall riots of 1969, several homosexuals reconceived, redefined, relabeled, and reorganized themselves under the aus-
pices of the term *gay.* The term incorporated the traditional meaning of
being "keenly alive and exuberant," possessing "high spirits," and turning "from a sober traditional style to one more timely" (*Webster's* 1981:
472). However, the term also functioned as a foundation for a new
social identity and cultural integrity as well as a reconceived history and
self-determined future. Within this new framework, the term *gay* was to
function as a "meaning-centered, social, and multidimensional concept.
The word 'gay' identifies those who have adopted a particular *world view*
or perspective of reality which is *self-imposed* and a *self-defined* determi-
nant of the attitudes, beliefs, actions, and even the vocabulary affecting
human interactions. Thus, the word 'gay' specifies a kind of *consciousness* controlling personal identities, social predispositions, and anticipa-
tory orientations" (Chesebro 1980:138).

More specifically, "eight different dimensions are associated with the
word *gay*":

These dimensions are interrelated and mutually defining. Particularly, the word *gay* is associated with (1) a *preference* for same-sex
relationships, (2) an *affection* or mental and emotional inclination
involving loving, tender, and caring responses for members of the
same sex, (3) a respect for *diverse gay and lesbian life styles* or for a
community of unique individuals bonded by a similar preference
and affection, (4) a *positive self-image,* (5) a sense of *pride,* (6) a sense
of *power,* (7) the recognition that *confrontation* must be used if or
when others reject or deny the interpersonal and community significance of same-sex relationships, and (8) the human right to engage
in *sexual* relationships with those of the same sex. (Chesebro
1982:175)

Defined in these senses, *gay* provided at least a foundation for a communication ethic, for the term functioned as a self-definition of a group's
social identity, characterized the dimensions of the group's cultural integrity, and ultimately provided a symbolic framework for reconstruct-
ing a history and future for gay males and lesbians. Not all homosexuals
would ascribe to this conception, but for those who do, a base is established for a self-determined individual and collective identity, cultural
system, and a reconceived history and future.

Since the term *gay* emerged, additional dimensions appear to be emerging that contribute to and enrich the nature that a same-sex communication ethic may encompass. These dimensions include: (1) the use of tolerance as a unifying and divisive philosophy, (2) the development of an evolving, elaborated, and increasingly sophisticated sense of hedonics, and (3) the growing recognition of the paradoxical nature of same-sex relationships. As we shall see, these dimensions mutually influence and define each other, but each deserves individual attention.

Tolerance as a Unifying and Divisive Philosophy

Tolerance is a particularly complex yet intriguing label to adopt as a unifying theme for a social group and particularly as a perspective for defining those external to the social group. Indeed, *tolerance* possesses paradoxical or contradictory associations that, when recognized, enshroud the word in ambiguity. The vernacular, as provided by the dictionary, is an appropriate point of departure. *Webster's* (1981:1218) reports that *tolerance* encompasses a series of meanings such as the "ability to endure the effects" of an "insult," "the relative ability of an organism to grow or thrive when subjected to an unfavorable environmental factor," "the act of allowing something," and an "allowable deviation from a standard." In this context, a commitment to tolerance, as a dimension of a communication ethic, is a commitment on the part of gay males and lesbians to endure—but also to grow and thrive—in an oppressive society. Paradoxically, at the same time, tolerance also involves the recognition, if not a celebration, on the part of gay males and lesbians that they constitute an "allowable deviation" from the sociosexual and cultural "standards" that define the larger society. Finally, tolerance involves an element of withdrawal and rejection on the part of gay males and lesbians when dealing with the intolerable.

In his essay "Die Non: Gay Liberation and the Rhetoric of Pure Tolerance," James Darsey (1994) has provided one of the most articulate analyses of tolerance as a framework for the emerging gay male/lesbian rhetorical system and also as an ethical scheme that might allow gay males and lesbians to coexist within a world of multiple value systems. In Darsey's view, gay males and lesbians must decide that they live in, "A world where there is no center, where there is no division between the center and the periphery, . . . a world without the mystery and separation necessary to the sacred, and where there is no externalization of truth, there is no principle which commands assent except self interest, and there is thus no community" (48). Dismissing a world of "morality," for "only madmen talk to God," Darsey maintains that "the Second World War represents a very real change for sexual mores in general and for homosexuals in particular; the dereliction of natural law allowed for a new ethic of permissiveness. It is in this sense of permission that homophile liberation is best understood" (52). Indeed, rather than respond to specific legal and political institutions, the rhetoric of tolerance described by Darsey "is almost apolitical in that it addresses the multitude of a mass of individuals, not as a political unity; its appeal is not to *de cive* but to man the maker of his own destiny; it is a rhetoric of disengagement," for Darsey holds that, "The historical emphasis of gay rights rhetoric on difference and diversity is antithetical to the tendency to define, to order, to discipline, to regiment" (60). He concludes that, "There is no potential for radical commitment in such a discourse, for there is no clear locus for commitment, no compelling principle" (60).

Implicitly arguing for tolerance, in an earlier essay (1991), Darsey also invoked the more divisive sense of tolerance when he raised the possibility that AIDS may have created profound questions regarding the role, if any, of the homosexual within the moral scheme of the larger sociopolitical system. He reasoned:

> In recent years gays may have come to feel better about themselves as individuals than they did in the 1950s, but it appears that this may be tied to their ability to eschew stereotypes in their own lives and to emulate the surrounding straight culture; it appears that there remains very real reservations about homosexuality in general precisely in the degree that it fails to share the values of the larger society. . . .
>
> Perhaps this is the fundamental question for any movement for social reform, the question of how to define success. How much do *we* become like *them* in order to enjoy the fruits of what they call success, and how much do *we* make *them* acknowledge that there are alternatives that must be respected? (60)

Thus, as a philosophic concept, tolerance becomes a complex, if not paradoxical, symbol that can provide a unifying confidence for gay males and lesbians (i.e., casting gay males and lesbians as an allowable deviation from the standard), but it also possesses the simultaneous ability to separate gay males and lesbians from others (i.e., identifying gay males and lesbians as separate from others but capable of enduring pain as well as growing and thriving in an unfavorable environment).

"The Culture of Desire"

In 1982, I posited that "the gay culture is unlike any other cultural system that has ever existed," because "affection" functions as the "most nearly universal cultural variable unifying gay males and lesbians" (Chesebro 1982:177, 178). I specifically maintained: "The gay community gains its identity as a cultural system by virtue of this socially shared sense of affection or fondness and tender attachment among its members. The gay community is, in fact, the only cultural system unified by such a human socio-sexual emotion" (Chesebro 1982:178).[8] However, circumstances in the gay male/lesbian community have changed during the last ten years, and as a society we have also become increasingly explicit about how sex is discussed. In this context, while I continue to believe that affection has been and will continue to be a central and unifying element of the sociocultural system of gay males and lesbians, I now believe it is more appropriate to substitute *desire* for *affection* as a governing symbol of the gay male/lesbian community. More formally stated, I believe that an evolving, elaborated, and increasingly sophisticated sense of hedonics (i.e., the relationship of duty to pleasure) functions as a dimension of the communication ethic emerging in the gay male/lesbian community.

Reflecting the cluster of symbols that define this hedonic dimension, Frank Browning (1993) has coined the phrase "the culture of desire" to capture what he believes to be an overriding and unifying symbolic dimension of the gay male and lesbian culture. Browning has maintained: "Unlike any accepted culture, gaydom is a social world that none of us has inherited from our parents or families. Because the part of identity that is 'gay' emerges from the most powerful and universal of human drives—the imperative of desire—it is inextricably bound to the torments and the delicacies of taboo" (9). But Browning has also been clear to note that the culture of desire he describes includes more than the physical: the culture of desire is "an odyssey of personal and communal desire—desire not only in its limited physical sense, but desire for community, identity, and moral purpose" (9–10).

Employed in this larger sense, the discourses of the culture of desire reflect the struggle to achieve self-understanding and identity as a sexual entity, as a social agent within a community, and the historical and future role of the gay male/lesbian community. In some cases, these struggles are vivid, clearly sexual in nature, but in virtually all cases, they also reflect the quest to achieve a sense of individual and cultural identity as well as a place in time. Accordingly, there are significant ways in which the consciousness reflected in John Rechy's promiscuous experiences in *The Sexual Outlaw: A Documentary* (1977) constituted one of the first personal testimonies of this struggle. In a more contemporary vein, simultaneously reflecting the far wider range of individual differences but also the shared experiences that exist within the world of the gay male, is *Revelations: A Collection of Gay Male Coming Out Stories* (Curtis 1988). Yet, within all of these struggles to realize the culture of desire, there is an ever-present tension, an attempt to merge what the larger society has persistently viewed as contradictory elements.

The Paradox of Same-Sex Relationships

The discourse of gay males and lesbians would initially appear to deny the formation of a communication ethic. An ethic, as Nilsen has aptly reasoned, would require clear distinction between what is good and bad or right and wrong: "By ethics as a subject of study is meant systematic thinking and theorizing with respect to questions about good [and evil], right and wrong, and moral obligations" (1958:10). Yet, an ethic of communication might recast traditional distinctions, placing previously oppositional categories into a mutually defining relationship.

Perhaps the most paradoxical relationship explored in this essay is the fact that homosexuality and ethics are symbolically unified. *Homosexual ethics, gay ethics,* and *lesbian ethics* will seem to some to be totally contradictory constructions, nothing more than a semantic manipulation of the language, for homosexuality is perceived—by some—as inherently immoral, and within this context, it is reasoned that such an activity is incapable—in any form—of generating or being associated with a series of prescriptions for determining what is good or evil. Despite the prescriptions from the gay male/lesbian community outlined in this essay, there may be no way to persuade some that homosexuality and ethics can ever be linked. For this group, the concept of a *homosexual ethic* will forever remain an unresolved and mindless paradox. Yet, there is a sense in which the link between the words "homosexual" and "ethics" is more than appropriate, for many homosexuals have experienced the isolation, hatred, and oppression that allows them to understand vividly and personally the importance of developing a sense of what is good and what is evil.

But the paradoxical nature of homosexuality exists in many other forms. Within a gay male/lesbian community, traditional distinctions regarding sexuality are blurred, and concepts held to be contradictory become seamless. Hence, a male can be masculine and homosexual at the same time. And a female can be both a lesbian and feminine at the same time (see, for one of the first research reports describing these combinations, Terman and Miles 1936). Accordingly, *gay masculinity* and the lesbian as exemplar of the "woman identified as woman" function as meaningful objectives and symbolic reference points, frequently with identifiable referents or role models.

These paradoxes do, of course, redefine the objects placed in relationship to each other. Being a gay male exerts and redefines what is meant by being masculine, and being masculine redefines one's sense of what a gay male is. A gay male does not achieve masculinity by being emotionally and sexually indifferent to other men, and the meaning of the phrase "woman identified as woman" is not explained by defining a woman in terms of her relationship to males. In all, the categories of "masculine men," "masculine women," "feminine men," and "feminine women" begin to lose their explanatory power. The mix of masculine and feminine characteristics provides an opportunity to increase the range and kinds of strategies available for defining and responding to one's self, others, and circumstances. In this sense, the paradoxical nature of gay male and lesbian symbols increases the repertoire of communicative actions available for human interactions.

Conclusion

Political and societal forces have severely inhibited and restricted the development of the system of communication ethics that might govern same-sex relationships. Efforts to define homosexuality, popular attitudes about homosexuality, and AIDS have specifically hampered the development of a communication ethic for gay males and lesbians.

Despite this counterproductive environment, the potential for identifying a communication ethic for same-sex relationships seems to exist. The core of this ethic resides in the various meanings associated with the word *gay*, but this central term has been enhanced and elaborated by the addition of three concepts, *tolerance, desire,* and *paradox. Gay, tolerance, desire,* and *paradox* interact, and together they appear to be the primary dimensions of an ethic of communication.

A series of summative propositions emerge from the discussion we have conducted here that have the potential for characterizing a gay male and lesbian communication ethic. These propositions include: (1) moral condemnations themselves should first be examined self-reflectively before they are applied to others, (2) respect for differences should displace the need to determine and dominate, (3) sexual expression should be treated as a joyous and celebratory form of free speech, and (4) creativity should first be viewed to be a source of societal development before the disruptive elements of change are considered.[9]

These four propositions constitute a core for rendering ethical analyses and evaluations of discourse of both communicators external to and those within the gay male/lesbian community. A systematic research program should govern such assessments. Given the space limitations of this essay, I can only suggest how these four propositions might be used to isolate and formulate some ethical issues.

For communicators external to the gay male/lesbian community, discourses involving stereotypes can raise—among other reactions—ethical issues. Minimally, a stereotype is a standardized, oversimplified, and uncritical mental image attributed to all members of a group. The derogatory use of terminologies such as *faggot* and *dyke* constitute obvious examples of stereotyping. Yet stereotypes can be far more subtle, with far more destructive consequences. When used in its more elaborated forms, a stereotype can implicitly attribute a causal responsibility to a group by virtue of the concepts uncritically associated with the group.

Such is the case with AIDS stereotyping of gay males. When AIDS is defined as a "gay disease" (or identified as the "gay plague"), these more "sophisticated" forms of stereotyping occur. Particularly, when AIDS is defined or mentally conceived of as a "gay disease," the victims of the disease are implicitly understood as the cause of the disease. As Quadland and Shattls (1985:278) have concluded, "as with any sexually transmitted disease, it is important to recognize that certain sexual practices, and not sexual preference, are the critical factors in determining risk."

An alternative form of gay male AIDS stereotyping occurs when, for "educational" purposes, gay males are statistically identified as a "high-risk" AIDS group. Yet, as a matter of fact, after fifteen years, the majority of gay males are not HIV positive nor have the majority engaged in sexual behaviors that place them in the "high-risk" category.[10] And, throughout the world, 75 percent of AIDS victims are apparently heterosexual. Accordingly, rather than identifying gay males as a "high-risk" group, a more precise formulation of the "high-risk" category would single out those who engage in unprotected and uninformed promiscuous sex.[11] In all, the discourse of medical and social scientists can be as rhetorical as the discourse of any other group (see, e.g., Chesebro 1980).

Admittedly, gay male AIDS stereotyping may be unintended, and the severity of an ethical judgment might be tempered to reflect the use of uninformed terminologies. Nonetheless, in terms of the individual responsibility assumed when using symbols, and in terms of the consequences of using certain systems, ethical judgments of gay male AIDS stereotyping are appropriate. As already suggested earlier in this essay, the tendency to scapegoat gay males as a source of AIDS or to presume that a single kind of lifestyle characterizes all gay males has had "devastating effects" on the gay male/lesbian community.

AIDS stereotyping of gay males is a denial of all four of the ethical propositions developed here. Casting AIDS as a "gay disease" is a symbolic method of creating a political relationship between two classes, *hetereosexual* and *homosexual*. The phrase "gay disease" creates a distinction between the two classes, and given this distinction, it politically elevates heterosexuality insofar as it implicitly links and associates homosexuality with a deadly disease. In this sense, the phrase "gay disease" is a direct denial of the second proposition developed here that ethical communication should promote "respect for differences" and displaces "the need to determine and dominate" others. Moreover, as a scapegoating strategy, the phrase "gay disease" renders a moral condemnation of others without a corresponding self-reflective assessment. And, in a larger sense, the phrase "gay disease" invokes and establishes a perceptual frame of rejection for characterizing homosexuality that ultimately makes it impossible to consider how homosexuality can be treated as a form of "sexual expression" and "joyous and celebratory form of free speech" or how homosexuality can be cast as a form of "creativity" and as a "source of societal development before the disruptive elements of change are considered."

At the same time, these same four propositions also constitute a foundation for self-reflective ethical assessments of those within the gay male/lesbian community, especially when gay activists employ strategies such as "outing" closeted homosexuals who have developed a facade of heterosexuality. Tabloids may out any media personality in sensational ways on a relatively random basis, but gay activists have generally targeted closeted homosexuals in the public arena who are actively engaged in political efforts to promote anti-gay candidates and causes.

Accordingly, while the strategy itself is easily defined, outing requires more complex ethical considerations, for at least two sets of ethical standards are involved. On one hand, outing is consistent with ethical assessments emphasizing honesty, the denial of falsehoods, and standards of objectivity and truth. On the other hand, outing violates individual privacy, the right to define the self, and generates potentially negative consequences in terms of one's family, friends, and employment. Gross (1991) has aptly maintained that even this dichotomy conceals more complex ethical issues. He has suggested that one "hypothesize a continuum." At one extreme of the continuum, known homosexuals in the public domain who support anti-gay causes are outed. Characterizing outing at this end of the continuum, Gross has invoked the statement of openly gay Congressman Barney Frank's "oft-quoted remark, 'There's a right to privacy but not to hypocrisy'" (353). At the other extreme of the continuum, private citizens can also be outed, of which Gross has maintained, "Neither the mainstream press nor the militant gay activists who promote outing would endorse" (353). In Gross's view, cases in the middle of the continuum raise more controversial ethical questions: "In short, the real issue is not to decide *whether* outing is, by one view, always a violation of journalistic and human ethics, or, by the opposing view, a necessary political weapon of an oppressed minority whose pervasive invisibility fuels their oppression. For both sides would largely agree at the extremes of my imaginary continuum. The real question, therefore, is *where* in the middle one draws the line and *who* has the right to decide on which side of the line any particular instance falls" (353).

Given all of the particulars that need to be considered in each case, this issue cannot be resolved here. Moreover, if the context is interpersonal and involves friends in everyday situations, it is instructive to ask how the four propositions might be adapted to deal with outing:

1. While hypocrisy warrants moral condemnation, is the quest for truth and objectivity being applied to all equally?
2. Does outing generate respect for differences and eliminate dominance?
3. Does outing promote sexual expression as a joyous and celebratory form of free speech for those employing the strategy and for those who are outed?
4. Does outing establish a frame of creative social change or does it disrupt societal development?

Cast in these terms, in some circumstances, outing is an ethical, positive, and constructive strategy. In other circumstances, outing is ultimately destructive in both the short and long run. Most situations are complex, neither black nor white, and ethical judgments—regardless of the standards used—require that the analyst carefully determine the immediate and long-term consequences of an ethical assessment.

It is entirely appropriate to end this essay with such unresolved questions, for thoughtful ethical assessments should make us pause and recon-

sider our symbol-using practices, especially those that have been culturally transmitted—perhaps uncritically—from one generation to the next. As
is true of all symbol-using, but particularly in the case of ethical judgments
of communication practices, the objective of ethical assessments is ultimately to improve the quality of life for every individual. As we enter the twenty-first century, we should anticipate that a host of diverse ethical systems
will be proposed, and that each of these proposals will make us reconsider
our established and habitual symbol-using practices. This process will be
challenging, perhaps maddening, but it may also move us closer to our goal
of enhancing the quality of life for each of us.

Notes

The author acknowledges the useful feedback and suggestions provided by
Sheron J. Dailey, Donald G. Bonsall, Ronald C. Arnett, and Josina M.
Makau on an earlier draft of this essay.

1. This essay posits the emergence of a communication ethic for both
gay males and lesbians. There are powerful and decisive ways in which the
experiences, lifestyles, and communication and ethical systems of gay males
and lesbians differ (see, e.g., Blackwood 1985; Lockard 1985). At the same
time, there are times when gay males and lesbians are unified, even if temporarily, on certain issues such as securing basic legal and social rights, in
opposition to specific oppressive political actions or indifferences, and in
responding to tragedies such as AIDS. In this essay, it seems appropriate to
emphasize the unifying factors between gay males and lesbians. Because this
essay devotes its attention to the initial stages of an emerging same- sex communication ethic, the focus is necessarily upon fundamental commitments
to creating a discourse that argues for alternative options to traditional communication ethics. In this context, and given the four propositions identified
at the end of this essay, it seems reasonable to emphasize a link between gay
males and lesbians. Indeed, the basic orientation adopted here is reflected
in Adrienne Rich's observation that reconceptions in "poetry"—or, in the case
of this essay, "communication"—"can break open locked chambers of possibilities, restore numbed zones to feeling, [and] recharge desire" (quoted in
Flory 1993:7). Specifically, Rich has maintained that "sensual vitality is essential to the struggle for life," and that "we must use what we have to invent what we desire" (ibid.). For the purposes of this essay, Rich's statements
constitute an essential orientation to the communication ethic posited here.

2. The purpose of this essay is *not* to link the emerging gay male/lesbian
communication ethic to traditional conceptions used to describe communication ethics. I have a sustained interest in these traditional conceptions

(see, e.g., Chesebro 1969). However, gay male/lesbian communication ethics are now in an extremely dynamic and embryonic stage, and a placement
of this ethic against the ethical tradition of the discipline of communication
would be premature. Moreover, as the gay male/lesbian ethic develops, it may
ultimately offer a reconception of traditional systems of communication
ethics. In this view, I assume that all communication ethics are open-ended
systems that change and evolve over time. The communication and value
systems of groups identified as external to an "established" social system can
potentially exert influence upon and change traditional ethical systems.

3. For a view of the sociosexual factors motivating Foucault's intellectual analyses, see: Miller 1993 and de Courtivron 1993.

4. Some have read this observation to imply that the United States provides one of the harshest judgments of homosexuals. For some, this assessment of the United States is apt. Pomeroy (1969:4) has concluded that, "Our
own culture [in the United States] is plainly in the minority, not only in
rejecting homosexuality but also in rejecting male homosexuality more forcibly than female homosexuality. Among the religions of the world, the Judeo-
Christian system gives one of the harshest condemnations of homosexuality." In this regard, in a comparative study completed almost fifty years earlier,
Hock and Zubin (1949) also reported that of 193 world cultures, 28 percent accepted male homosexuality while only 14 percent, such as the United States, rejected it. In the remaining 58 percent, there was partial acceptance or some equivocation involved.

5. The causes of homophobia or the fear of homosexuals has not been
extensively examined, although there are indications that homophobia, especially in heterosexual males, may stem from two causes: (1) a need to "reassure themselves about their own sexuality," and (2) a "self-righteousness
in which homosexuals are perceived as contemptible threats to the moral
universe" (Goleman 1990).

6. More recently, in assessing the results of the National Leadership Coalition on AIDS survey of working Americans, Noble (1993:F25) has reported that an "apparent conflict" may be emerging between what people say in
public about AIDS ("what they were supposed to believe") and what people say in private about AIDS ("what they really believed"). Noble specifically reported that 78 percent of those surveyed said they would "treat a
person with AIDS like any other person with a serious disability or illness.
Even more—89 percent—said someone who is HIV positive should be treated like any other employee." At the same time, Noble also reported that two-
thirds of workers said they would not feel "comfortable working near someone who is HIV positive" and that one-third of workers "said they *should
not* feel comfortable. A third said the person would be dismissed or put on
disability at the first sign of illness, and a quarter said he or she should be
dismissed or put on disability."

7. For an example of the more recently emerging discourses illustrating this claim, see Osborn 1993.

8. Upon reflection, my own description of the gay disco in 1981 now appears to be a direct reflection of what Browning (1993) has called "the culture of desire"; see Chesebro and Klenk 1981:87–103.

9. Some have suggested that these same four standards might be applied to all communication rather than just by those inside and outside of the gay male and lesbian community in terms of homosexuality. Of course, there is a sense in which any construct could be applied to any social behavior. Generally, however, there should be a reason or need to apply a construct to a social behavior. The four standards posited here and applied to gay male and lesbian behaviors are responsive to the particular needs (i.e., definition as a strategy of disorientation, the paralyzing effect of divided public opinion, and the devastating effects of AIDS) as well as the specific sociocultural histories and evolutions of gay males and lesbians. Relevant analogies to related social groupings might be posited, and in these cases, the four standards might function as a scheme for understanding the behaviors of the related social groupings. However, it is largely anticipated that the number of groups possessing the same particular needs and similar sociocultural histories are likely to be few in number. Goffman (1963) may have provided some of the basic guidelines for such an endeavor.

10. The majority of gay males do not engage in what has been described as promiscuous sexual behavior. Employing a sample of one thousand males and lesbians in San Francisco, Bell and Weinberg (1978) identified five different sociosexual and cultural lifestyles within the gay male and lesbian communities. Of these five categories, compared to national norms, the majority had few sexual partners. Bell and Weinberg concluded: "Our hope is that, at the very least, it will become increasingly clear to the reader that there is no such thing as the homosexual (or the heterosexual, for that matter) and that statements of any kind which are made about human beings on the basis of their sexual orientation must always be highly qualified" (23). Additionally, in contrast to a related stereotype held by some, gay males and lesbians in "nonpromiscuous" relationships have also reported a higher satisfaction rate than those in "promiscuous" relationships. Kurdek and Schmitt (1985:95) have specifically concluded that gay males and lesbians in "closed" relationships (i.e., "sexually exclusive" in terms of a single partner) "reported higher relationship quality than did partners in open relationships."

11. Browning (1993:84) has more precisely identified four specific sexual practices required to avoid HIV infections: "1. Do not exchange bodily fluids. 2. Reduce the number of sexual partners. 3. Avoid anal intercourse (or, at least, use a condom). 4. Do not engage in fisting (anal penetration by the fist and, sometimes by the forearm as well) or rimming (oral-anal contact)."

References Cited

Adam, B. D. 1985. "Age, Structure, and Sexuality: Reflections on the Anthropological Evidence on Homosexual Relations." *Journal of Homosexuality* 11 (Summer):19–33.

"AIDS Talks in Study Hurts More Than Help." 1991. *New York Times,* May
28, p. C2.

Angier, N. 1991a. "Zone of Brain Linked to Men's Sexual Orientation." *New
York Times,* August 30, pp. A1, D18.

———. 1991b. "The Biology of What It Means to Be Gay." *New York Times,*
September 1, pp. 1E, 4E.

———. 1993. "Report Suggests Homosexuality Is Linked to Genes." *New
York Times,* July 16, pp. A1, C18.

Barringer, F. 1993. "Measuring Sexuality through Polls Can Be Shaky." *New
York Times,* April 25, p. 12.

Bell, A. P., and M. S. Weinberg. 1978. *Homosexualities: A Study of Diversity
among Men and Women.* New York: Simon and Schuster.

Blackwood, E. 1985. "Breaking the Mirror: The Construction of Lesbianism and the Anthropological Discourse on Homosexuality." *Journal of
Homosexuality* 11 (Summer):1–17.

Browning, F. 1993. *The Culture of Desire: Paradox and Perversity in Gay Lives
Today.* New York: Crown.

Carrier, J. 1992. "Miguel: Sexual Life History of a Gay Mexican American."
In *Gay Culture in Amerca: Essays from the Field.* Ed. G. Herdt. Pp. 202–
24. Boston: Beacon Press.

Chesebro, J. W. 1969. "A Construct for Assessing Ethics in Communication." *Central States Speech Journal* 20 (Summer):104–14.

———. 1973. "Cultures in Conflict: A Generic and Axiological View."
Today's Speech 21 (Spring):11–20.

———. 1980. "Paradoxical Views of 'Homosexuality' in the Rhetoric of
Social Scientists: A Fantasy Theme Analysis." *Quarterly Journal of Speech*
66:127–39.

———. 1982. "Homosexuality as a Communication Variable." In *Intercultural Communication: A Reader.* 3d ed. Ed. L. A. Samova and R. E. Porter. Pp. 162–85. Belmont, Calif.: Wadsworth.

———. 1985. "Definition as Rhetorical Strategy." *The Speech Communication Association of Pennsylvania Annual* 41:5–15.

———. 1994. "Reflections on Gay and Lesbian Rhetoric." In *Queer Words,
Queer Images: Communication and the Construction of Homosexuality.* Ed.
R. J. Ringer. Pp. 77–88. New York: New York University Press.

Chesebro, J. W, and K. L. Klenk. 1981. "Gay Masculinity in the Gay Disco." In *Gayspeak: Gay Male and Lesbian Communication.* Ed. J. W. Chesebro. Pp. 87–103. New York: Pilgrim Press.

Cronin, A. 1993. "Two Viewfinders, Two Pictures of Gay America." *New York Times,* July 27, p. 16E.

Curtis, W., ed. 1988. *Revelations: A Collection of Gay Male Coming Out Stories.* Boston: Alyson.

Darsey, J. 1991. "From 'Gay Is Good' to the Scourge of AIDS: The Evolution of Gay Liberation Rhetoric, 1977–1990." *Communication Studies* 42:43–66.

———. 1994. "Die Non: Gay Liberation and the Rhetoric of Pure Tolerance." In *Queer Words, Queer Images: Communication and the Construction of Homosexuality.* Ed. R. J. Ringer. Pp. 45–76. New York: New York University Press.

de Courtivron, I. 1993. "The Body Was His Battleground" [review of *The Passion of Michel Foucault,* by J. Miller]. *New York Times Book Review,* January 10, pp. 1, 29–30.

Flory, W. S. 1993. "Hidden Appetites: Adrienne Rich Examines the Power of Poetry to Help Us 'Invent What We Desire'" [review of *What Is Found There and Collected Early Poems,* by Adrienne Rich]. *New York Times Book Review,* November 7, p. 7.

Foucault, M. 1980 [1978]. *The History of Sexuality,* Vol. 1: *An Introduction.* New York: Vintage/Random House.

Freud, S. 1950 [1913]. *The Interpretation of Dreams.* Trans. A. A. Brill. New York: Modern Library.

Gallup Poll. 1991. "Sex in America." *Gallup Poll Monthly* 313 (October):62–70.

———. 1992a. *AIDS, 1983–1991: A Compilation of Gallup Poll Reports.* Princeton, N.J.: Gallup Poll.

———. 1992b. *Sex in the 20th Century, 1943–1991: A Compilation of Gallup Poll Reports.* Princeton, N.J.: Gallup Poll.

———. 1992c. "Public Opinion Divided on Gay Rights." *Gallup Poll Monthly* 321 (June):2–6.

———. 1993. "Public Polarized on Gay Issue." *Gallup Poll Monthly* 331 (April):30–34.

Goffman, E. 1963. *Stigma: Notes on the Management of Spoiled Identity.* Englewood Cliffs, N.J.: Prentice-Hall.

Goleman, D. 1990. "Homophobia: Scientists Find Clues to Its Roots." *New York Times,* July 10, pp. C1, C11.

Gross, L. 1991. "The Contested Closet: The Ethics and Politics of Outing." *Critical Studies in Mass Communication* 8 (September):352–88.

Hayes, J. J. 1981. "Lesbians, Gay Men, and Their 'Languages.'" In *Gayspeak: Gay Male and Lesbian Communication.* Ed. J. W. Chesebro. Pp. 28–42. New York: Pilgrim Press.

Herdt, G., and A. Boxer. 1992. "Introduction: Culture, History, and Life Course of Gay Men." In *Gay Culture in America: Essays from the Field.* Ed. G. Herdt. Pp. 1–28. Boston: Beacon Press.

Hock, P. H., and J. Zubin. 1949. *Psychosexual Development in Health and Disease.* New York: Grune and Stratton.

Hoffman, M. 1968. *The Gay World: Male Homosexuality and the Social Creation of Evil.* New York: Bantam Books.

Humphrey, L. 1970. *Tearoom Trade: Impersonal Sex in Public Places.* Chicago: Aldine.

Kinsey, A., W. Pomeroy, and C. Martin. 1948. *Sexual Behavior in the Human Male.* Philadelphia: W. B. Saunders.

Kurdek, L. A., and J. P. Schmitt. 1985. "Relationship Quality of Gay Men in Closed and Open Relationships." *Journal of Homosexuality* 12 (Winter):85–99.

Lockard, D. 1985. "The Lesbian Community: An Anthropological Approach." *Journal of Homosexuality* 11 (Summer):83–95.

Magay, M. R. 1991. "Poll Finds AIDS Causes Single People to Alter Behavior." *New York Times,* June 18, p. C3.

Masters, W. H., and V. E. Johnson. 1979. *Homosexuality in Perspective.* Boston: Little, Brown.

Miller, J. 1993. *The Passion of Michel Foucault.* New York: Simon and Schuster.

Morin, S. F. 1977. "Heterosexual Bias in Psychological Research on Lesbianism and Male Homosexuality." *American Psychologist* 32 (August):629–37.

Nilsen, T. R. 1958. "Free Speech, Persuasion, and the Democratic Process." *Quarterly Journal of Speech* 44:235–43.

Noble, B. P. 1993. "Attitudes Clash on Jobs and AIDS." *New York Times,* November 7, p. F25.

Osborn, T. 1993. "America without Closets" [editorial]. *New York Times,* November 29, p. A15.

Pomeroy, W. B. 1969. "Homosexuality." In *The Same Sex: An Appraisal of Homosexuality.* Ed. R. W. Weltge. Philadelphia: Pilgrim Press.

Quadland, M., and W. D. Shattls. 1987. "AIDS, Sexuality, and Sexual Control." *Journal of Homosexuality* 14:277–98.

Rechy, J. 1977. *The Sexual Outlaw: A Documentary.* New York: Dell.

Suplee, C. 1991. "Brain May Determine Sexuality: Node Seen as Key to Gay Orientation." *Washington Post,* August 30, pp. A1, A13.

Terman, L. M., and C. C. Miles. 1968 [1936]. *Sex and Personality: Studies in Masculinity and Femininity.* Rev. ed. New York: Russell and Russell.

Turque, B., C. Friday, J. Gordon, D. Glick, P. Annin, F. Chideya, J. Duignan-Cabera, and P. Rogers. 1992. "Gays under Fire." *Newsweek* 120 (September 14):35–40.

Webster's New Collegiate Dictionary. 1981. Springfield, Mass.: G. and C. Merriam.

Wheeler, D. L. 1993. "Study Suggests X Chromosome Is Linked to Homosexuality." *Chronicle of Higher Education,* July 21, p. A6.

Winslow, R. 1991. "Study Raises Issue of Biological Basis of Homosexuality." *Wall Street Journal,* August 30, pp. B1, B2.

PART 3

Technology, Diversity, and Responsibility

Introduction

While the authors in Parts 1 and 2 focus primarily on issues associated with group and individual identities, the authors in Part 3 explore communication ethics and diversity in the worlds of popular culture, media, commerce, and over the Internet.

Richard L. Johannesen's essay, "Diversity, Freedom, and Responsibility in Tension," moves inside and out of the world of commerce to examine inevitable tensions between freedom and responsibility in contemporary speech contexts. Johannesen provides insights into three different, but related, contexts: rap music lyrics, pornography, and hate speech. He underscores the importance of identifying means for fostering ethical communication without succumbing to calls for regulations and laws. He stresses the importance of understanding and tolerance of diversity in ethical systems, and calls for the promotion of morality through conduct and attitudes.

Clifford G. Christians's essay, "Social Ethics and Mass Media Practice," moves from popular culture to a broader rubric. He assesses technological structures of the mass media in terms of global diversity. His essay focuses in particular on the emerging interactive electronic highway and mergers of computers, telephones, and video. Christians argues that we have reconstructed our social institutions in terms of efficiency. *La technique* precludes moral judgment. Even those who remain committed to a moral base have confused the aggregate of individual goods with the common good. Christians's solution is a reordering of media systems around communitarian ethics. He is careful to note, however, that this perspective must give priority to the voiceless along the fringes. Christians proposes reciprocity, inclusiveness, and empowerment as key ingredients to ethical media systems.

James A. Jaksa and Michael S. Pritchard move to an assessment of a different, but related, set of communication contexts. In "Communication in High-Risk Technologies: Global and Local Concerns," they attempt to identify ethical standards of communication for the export of high-risk products. They seek to apply the standard of informed consent associated with medical ethics to cross-cultural distribution of potentially dangerous products. While stressing respect for persons and the importance of autonomy, Jaksa and Pritchard also acknowledge a role for social norms.

Jana Kramer and Cheris Kramarae's essay, "Gendered Ethics on the

Internet," closes the volume with a critical look at emerging Internet ethics. Through the lens of the Internet's impact on and consideration of girls and women, these authors assess the four themes dominating these early days of Internet communications. Their analysis shows that, rather than enhance the likelihood of directing this new communication medium to the fulfillment of its promise, these four themes actually exacerbate the problem of gender bias and inequity. They propose an alternate approach that borrows from recent feminist work.

The essays in this section represent starkly different philosophical centers and foci. Included are an integrative, a communitarian, an individualized but socially normative universalist, and finally a feminist perspective. Diversity is viewed differently in each of the essays, revealing the complexity of this concept. As with the other essays in this volume, the authors in Part Three struggle to develop concrete, viable help for those who seek answers to the complex issues they raise.

The essays in this section offer different views of the relationship of diversity to communication ethics. One calls for tolerance, another for understanding, still others for inclusiveness. Despite these differences, the essays all prescribe a major role for responsibility. Whether considering commercial speech, popular cultural lyrics, media structural development, or communication over the Internet, the authors in this section admonish practitioners to identify and practice personal and professional responsibility.

Also noteworthy is the role that individualist versus communitarian roots play in the development of each of the authors' perspectives. The authors' stances on this issue inform not only the theoretical perspectives advanced in the essays, but also the specific proposals made for addressing perceived problems.

Despite sharp differences on several key issues, most of the authors share with those represented in Parts 1 and 2 commitments to reciprocity, inclusiveness, truthfulness, authenticity, and empowerment. Some would suggest that these shared elements provide meaningful grounds for cross-contextual norms for ethical communication in an age of diversity. Whether this is so remains to be seen. We would note ironically, however, that the answer may well depend upon our ability to embrace these very norms of cross-cultural communication. Only through open, reciprocal, engaged, authentic, respectful dialogue across difference can we hope to discover and embrace a meaningful communicative ethic for the twenty-first century. The authors in this volume have sought to contribute to this dialogue.

8   Diversity, Freedom, and Responsibility in Tension

Richard L. Johannesen

Congress shall make no law respecting an establishment of religion, or prohibiting the free exercise thereof; or abridging the freedom of speech, or of the press; or the right of the people peaceably to assemble, and to petition the Government for a redress of grievances.

Thus reads the First Amendment to the Constitution of the United States of America. Nowhere in this amendment that protects a citizen's freedom of communication is there guidance concerning the ethically responsible exercise of that freedom. In our culture norms for ethical communication are embodied and enforced less by governmental law and constitutional interpretation than they are through more informal means. This chapter will explore some of the ways in which free speech and ethical communication often are found in tension, sometimes in opposition, with each other. What is the appropriate balance, on the one hand, of First Amendment rights of freedom of expression, and, on the other hand, of the ethically responsible use of that freedom? I will examine some specific areas of tension that illustrate difficult issues of communication ethics. Also, I will suggest ways in which, short of law and court interpretation, communication ethics may be developed, exert influence, and to some degree be institutionalized.

Rooted in British law and custom and codified in the First Amendment, the American tradition of free speech has evolved and expanded through Supreme Court interpretation of federal and state laws and regulations.

Excellent histories of the cases and controversies constituting this evolution are found in such works as Thomas Tedford, *Freedom of Speech in the United States* (1993), and Kent Middleton and Bill Chamberlin, *The Law of Public Communication* (1994). In their histories, Tedford (1993:374, 378) and Middleton and Chamberlin (1994:24–30; see also Cohen 1993:223–30) succinctly summarize the major arguments for maximum freedom of expression that have been offered by various theorists such as Mill (1947), Emerson (1970), and others. The absolute wording of the First Amendment provides one argument. In the view of Justice Hugo Black, the declaration that "Congress shall make no law . . . abridging freedom of speech . . ." is a categorical and absolute prohibition. No law means no law. But differences of opinion exist, as we shall see, concerning to what types of "speech" that language refers. Second, freedom of expression is a necessary condition for fulfillment of each individual's intellectual and psychological potential. Freedom of speech promotes human self-actualization and restriction and censorship thwarts personality growth. Third, the high-quality public decisions necessary for a healthy representative democracy are best achieved in full and open presentation of diverse ideas, values, arguments, and programs. Effective decision-making presupposes free access to all relevant information.

Fourth, freedom of expression vitally aids the search for truth in a society, especially political and social truths. Ideas or information censored or suppressed may actually be true and thus society is deprived of the benefit of that truth. The "truth" on some issues often proves to be an amalgam or synthesis of the best features of a number of diverse positions. And, in Mill's view (1947), we reassure ourselves of the adequacy of our own position, our own truth, by having that truth withstand the test of the opposing views and arguments of others. Fifth, freedom of speech promotes healthy societal change; it fosters a balance of stability and change. Suppression only fosters an unhealthy neglect of problems. And suppression drives dissent underground where it may turn to apathy or where it may rigidify, intensify, and ultimately erupt in violence. In the words of the African-American poet Langston Hughes, "a dream deferred" too long may "dry up like a raisin in the sun" or it may "explode." Maximum freedom of speech affords a vital societal safety valve. Sixth, and finally, freedom of speech, and the press, provide necessary checks on or exposure of abuses of power by elected or appointed government officials. Freedom of speech and of the press serve a "watchdog" function.

On the other hand, a number of arguments have been offered supporting significant degrees of restriction or control on communication.

First, there are other values that should take precedence, in general or in specific cases, over freedom of speech, despite the supposed "preferred position" of First Amendment rights. Among such competing values, even "higher" values, are maintenance of national security (especially in wartime), maintenance of civil order to protect internal governmental processes, protection of public morality, protection of the right of privacy, and the right of equal protection under the law specified by the Fourteenth Amendment. Second, only the enlightened or educated should be allowed freedom of speech. Even the free speech advocate John Stuart Mill (1947), the nineteenth-century English utilitarian philosopher, limited the right to those "persons in mature possession of their faculties." Third, anti-democratic groups that advocate (violent) overthrow of representative democracy forfeit their free speech rights. At this point some liberals might advocate censoring the speech of neo-Nazis, while some conservatives might advocate censorship of the speech of communists. (Concerning this argument see the refutation by Emerson 1970:46–53.) Fourth, and finally, the First Amendment has become in some respects outdated. While applicable in earlier centuries, twentieth-century economic conditions and technology have changed so drastically that there is not, in fact, a workable "marketplace" of ideas. The government actually may need to intervene through law to guarantee such a marketplace through restrictions on some communication institutions in order to facilitate freedom of speech for a wider spectrum of citizens (see Graber 1991; Sunstein 1993).

The Supreme Court typically has held that not all "speech" is free. Or to put it another way, communication that is fully protected speech should be differentiated from speech deserving only partial protection and from "worthless" speech or "non-speech" that merits no protection. The Supreme Court holds that "political speech" very broadly defined merits the strongest First Amendment protection. No matter how extremely divergent from mainstream views it may be, communication on political, social, religious, and cultural issues may very rarely be restrained in advance and seldom punished after the fact. This protected communication encompasses, for example, forms of speech and writing, film and broadcasting, slogans and symbols, arm bands and political advertising, and even the burning of the American flag in protest. A unanimous Supreme Court in *Brandenburg v. Ohio*, 395 U.S. 444 (1969), declared that the First Amendment only allows governmental prohibition and punishment when advocacy of the use of force or of violation of law "is directed to inciting or producing imminent lawless action and is likely to incite or produce such action." This is an extension of the so-called clear and present danger test.

The Supreme Court holds that other types of "speech" merit some degree of First Amendment protection but not full protection. This category includes speech intertwined with action (such as protest marches), some commercial advertising, and the speech of public secondary school students, employees of private businesses, military personnel, and prisoners. The Supreme Court holds that communication categorized as "worthless non-speech" warrants no First Amendment protection at all. Such worthless speech lacks ideas and redeeming social value. In this unprotected category usually are libel and slander, obscenity, false advertising, and so-called fighting words that are spoken directly to an individual, face-to-face, one-on-one. While the Supreme Court does allow government to regulate the time, place, and manner of protected and partially protected speech to facilitate public order, such regulation must not be used to restrict or censor controversial or repugnant ideas. I turn now to consider how the tradition of free speech often collides with the ethical obligation to communicate responsibly

Ethical Responsibility in Tension

While some philosophers draw distinctions between ethics and morals as concepts, other philosophers use the terms ethics and morals more or less interchangeably—as will be done in this chapter. Ethics involves issues and standards concerning degrees of right and wrong, of virtue and vice, and of obligation in human behavior.

As communicators our ethical responsibilities may stem from a position or role we have earned or been granted, from commitments (promises, pledges, agreements) we have made, from established ethical principles, from relationships we have formed, or from consequences (effects, impacts) of our communication on others. Responsibility includes the elements of fulfilling duties and obligations, of being held accountable to other individuals or groups, of being accountable as evaluated by agreed-upon standards, and of being accountable to our own conscience. But an essential element of responsible communication, for both sender and receiver, is the exercise of thoughtful and caring judgment. That is, the responsible communicator reflectively analyzes claims, soundly assesses probable consequences, and conscientiously considers relevant values (both abstract principles and personal relationships). In a sense, a responsible communicator is *response-able*. She or he exercises the ability to respond (is responsive) to the needs and communication of others in sensitive, thoughtful, fitting ways (Johannesen 1990:9).

The tension between freedom and responsibility seems to be an inherent aspect of the human condition. The psychiatrist Thomas Szasz eloquently captures the interrelated nature of freedom and responsibility.

> The crucial moral characteristic of the human condition is the dual experience of freedom of the will and personal responsibility. Since freedom and responsibility are two aspects of the same phenomenon, they invite comparison with the proverbial knife that cuts both ways. One of its edges implies options: we call it freedom. The other implies obligations: we call it responsibility. People like freedom because it gives them mastery over things and people. They dislike responsibility because it constrains them from satisfying their wants. That is why one of the things that characterizes history is the unceasing human effort to maximize freedom and minimize responsibility. But to no avail, for each real increase in human freedom . . . brings with it a proportionate increase in responsibility. (1977: xiii)

The continuing tension between freedom and responsibility emerges not only in public communication but also in intimate interpersonal communication. "For there to be *freedom* to converse intimately with another person," contends William Rawlins (1983), "each party must take *responsibility* for communication behavior." Rawlins also believes that "disclosing personal thoughts and feelings and speaking freely in a relationship are *rights,* not *obligations.* To allow viable associations to develop, intimates should acknowledge limits on their communication and respect each other's separateness." He urges that "the tension between candor and restraint must be managed consciously in responsible relational communication" (153).

In the public arena of communication, notes Tedford (1993:390), "freedom to speak does not always result in thoughtful, 'responsible' discourse—abuses of the liberty of speech inevitably occur." I turn now to a discussion of the freedom-responsibility tension as it relates to diversity.

Diversity, Freedom, and Responsibility

Issues of freedom of communication, of ethically responsible communication, and of diversity in gender, race and ethnicity, culture, religion, and affectional orientation often intersect in contemporary American society. For example, based upon traditions and theories of maximum freedom of expression, advocates would use the First Amendment to guarantee that a wide diversity of citizens and views be allowed to enter the public debate on controversial topics, no matter how extreme or distasteful the arguments or opinions might be. "The First Amendment teaches an important lesson: we must restrain the impulse to silence what is threatening or strange, and thus acknowledge our diversity as a community" (Public Agenda Foundation 1992:33–34). On the other hand, advocates who see free speech simply as one among a number of competing societal values might urge degrees of governmental or institutional restriction on communication in order to promote ethically responsible communication that respects rather than denigrates or threatens diverse individuals or groups. On this view, too often difference becomes equated with inferiority. In the next sections of this chapter, I will discuss three contemporary types of communication that illustrate how issues of freedom, responsibility, and diversity intersect to spark controversy: rock and rap music lyrics; pornography; and "hate speech" on college campuses (see, for example, Leone 1994:71–223).

Rock and Rap Music Lyrics

In June 1990, a U.S. District judge in Ft. Lauderdale, Florida, declared obscene the album, *As Nasty As They Wanna Be,* by the 2 Live Crew rap group. But in a local trial in Florida in October of 1990, three members of 2 Live Crew were acquitted of obscenity charges for performing the songs. These incidents are part of a larger controversy concerning lyrics for music and rap songs that explicitly depict the sexual and violent abuse and debasement of women and that verbally attack ethnic groups.

Exactly what kind of lyrics were at issue in the above cases? Here is a sample (modestly sanitized) from "The F—k Shop" on the *Nasty* album:

> Whole lotta suckin and f—kin' at the F—k Shop
> Please come inside and make yourself at home
> I want to f—k 'cause my d—k's gone to bone
> You little whore behind closed doors
> You would drink my c—m and nothing more
> Now spread your wings and open for the flight
> Let me fill you up with somethin' milky and white
> 'Cause I'm gonna slay you rough and painful
> You innocent bitch, don't be shameful.

Another song on the album celebrates the busting of women's vaginal walls, forcing women to have anal sex, and forcing them to lick feces (Will 1990). By one count, the song "S and M" contains 117 explicit references to male genitals and eighty-seven to oral sex. "Bitch" is used over one hundred times and "f—k" 226 times. The album is also explicit about urination, incest, group sex, and violent sex (Public Agenda Foundation 1992:5).

Examples from other rock and rap groups further illustrate the controversy (Gore 1987:83–88; Gore 1990; Public Agenda Foundation 1992:11; Matsuda et al. 1993:122; see also Stanley 1992). In "Eat Me Alive," Judas Priest describes "squealing in passion as the rod of steel injects." In "On Your Knees," Great White proclaims: "Gonna drive my love inside you / Gonna nail you to the floor." The rapper Ice-T, in "Iceberg," describes how "Evil E was out cooling with a freak one night / F—ked the bitch with a flashlight / Pulled it out, left the batteries in / So he could get a charge when he begins." In their song, "Anything Goes," Guns 'N' Roses describe "Panties 'round your knees / With your ass in debris / Doin' that grind with a push and a squeeze / Tied up, tied down, up against the wall / Be my rubbermade baby / An' we can do it all." And bigotry surfaces in Guns 'N' Roses' song, "One in a Million":

> Police and Niggers that's right, get outta my way
> Don't need to buy none of your gold chains today
> Now don't need no bracelets clamped in front of my back
> Immigrants and faggots, they make no sense to me
> They come to our country and think they'll do as they please
> Like start some mini-Iran or spread some f—kin' disease.

The tension at the heart of the controversy over rock and rap lyrics is captured by the Public Agenda Foundation in their booklet, *The Boundaries of Free Speech* (1992:8–9). "How can we honor a commitment to free speech without doing injury to other things we value, such as our commitment to diversity and tolerance? . . . In the case of 2 Live Crew, for example . . . what is an appropriate response that is consistent with our commitment to free speech?" In a 1990 survey of American citizens, 61 percent of those interviewed said that recordings dealing with sexual acts should not receive any First Amendment protection whatever, while 24 percent favored protection sometimes and 13 percent favored protection all the time (Wyatt 1991:17, 29). Often, states and cities have enacted laws and ordinances prohibiting obscene communication and these laws often have been applied to allegedly obscene ·

rap lyrics. Such laws must conform with the attempts of the U.S. Supreme Court to define "obscene" visual and verbal material in *Miller v. California,* 413 U.S. 15 (1973) and in *Pope v. Illinois,* 481 U.S. 497 (1987). The average person, using contemporary state or local standards, must find that the material taken as a whole appeals to prurient (lustful or lascivious) interests and must find that the material depicts sexual conduct in obviously offensive ways as specified by the law. In addition, a reasonable person (perhaps a critic, scholar, or other expert) must judge that the material, taken as a whole, lacks serious literary, artistic, political, or scientific value.

As we will see in the next section on pornography, the view of pornography as actionable under civil law rather than criminal law and as explicit sexual debasement of women (rather than pornography as obscenity) also has potential for application to rock and rap lyrics. Nevertheless, that the types of rock and rap lyrics cited above are unethical, even if at times not illegal, seems obvious. Such lyrics debase and dehumanize women, trivialize and depersonalize them, and celebrate sexual violence against them. Other lyrics encourage hatred toward ethnic groups and toward gays and lesbians and reinforce denigrating stereotypes. Whether ethical perspectives would be rooted in assumptions about the essence of human nature, in Martin Buber's philosophy of dialogue, or in feminist ethical perspectives, such ethical perspectives clearly would support the judgment that such lyrics are ethically irresponsible (Johannesen 1990:41–77, 128–32).

Without relying on state or local legislation and on Supreme Court interpretations of obscenity, the citizen action organization called the Parents' Music Resource Center voices its moral outrage and works to develop "ethical boundaries" in the production of recorded music. The center alerts parents and children to lyrics describing explicit sex, violence, substance abuse, and the occult. The center promotes a Media Watch program for parents to monitor electronic media and to mount persuasive campaigns of complaint to radio and television stations, recording companies, program sponsors, and government officials. (For specific suggested strategies, see Gore 1987:161–63, 167–74.)

A specific effort of the Parents' Music Resource Center (PMRC), and of one of its founders, Tipper Gore, was a persuasive campaign to pressure the Recording Industry of America (RIAA) into a type of self-regulation (Gore 1987:15–38). Originally the PMRC wanted the RIAA to create a uniform definition of what constituted blatant, explicit lyric content, to provide printed lyrics to accompany albums, cassettes, and compact discs, and to put a label or symbol on the album to warn consumers about explicit lyrics. With the aid of the National Parents and Teachers Association, in 1985 the PMRC secured an agreement from RIAA to place warning labels on albums and tapes. In monitoring the system, however, PMRC found it to be ineffective during the years 1986 to 1990 because labels were applied inconsistently. Prompted in part by the furor over the 2 Live Crew *Nasty* album, more than a dozen state legislatures started debating laws to require detailed and visible warning labels. In March 1990, the RIAA announced a new voluntary policy of affixing visible and uniform labels to offensive recordings: "Explicit Lyrics—Parental Advisory" (Public Agenda Foundation 1992:22).

Tipper Gore and the PMRC make it quite clear that they oppose governmental censorship legislation that would prohibit the production or sale of objectionable music. They are very sensitive to protecting citizen First Amendment freedoms. "Our approach was the direct opposite of censorship," says Tipper Gore. "We called for more information, not less. We did not advocate a ban on even the most offensive albums or tapes. . . . The PMRC proposal does *not* infringe on the First Amendment. It does *not* raise a constitutional issue. But it *does* seek to reform marketing practices by asking for better and more informative packaging." Gore recognizes the societal tension between freedom and responsibility. "The dilemma for society is how to preserve personal and family values in a nation of diverse tastes." Gore contends: "Censorship is not the answer. In the long run, our only hope is for more information and awareness, so that citizens and communities can fight back against market exploitation and find practical means for restoring individual choice and control. As parents and consumers, we have the right and the power to pressure the entertainment industry to respond to our needs" (Gore 1987:12–13, 22, 26–27, 37–38, 100).

Pornography

The issue of pornography also illustrates the freedom versus responsibility tension in contemporary American society, particularly as that tension affects women (Linz and Malamuth 1993). Typically, states and cities have attempted to combat the rising tide of pornography by applying laws and ordinances based on the Supreme Court definition of obscenity outlined in the *Miller* and *Pope* decisions. On the whole, such efforts have not been very successful (Tedford 1993:145–60; Middleton and Chamberlin 1991:371–88).

But feminist scholar Andrea Dworkin (1981) and feminist lawyer Catharine MacKinnon (1987, 1988, 1989, 1993), both separately and together, strive to shift the debate on pornography from the realm of obscenity law to that of civil rights law and from the realm of the First Amendment to that of the Fourteenth Amendment (see also Sunstein 1993:210–26). Indeed, MacKinnon (1987:147) argues the *difference* between obscenity and pornography: "Obscenity law is concerned with morality, specifically morals from the male point of view, meaning the standpoint of male dominance. The feminist critique of pornography is a politics, specifically politics from women's point of view, meaning the standpoint of the subordination of women to men. Morality here means good and evil; politics means power and powerlessness. Obscenity is a moral idea; pornography is a political practice." She further argues: "Nudity, explicitness, excess of candor, arousal or excitement, prurience, unnaturalness—these qualities bother the obscenity law when sex is depicted or portrayed. . . . Sex forced on real women; women's bodies trussed and maimed and raped and made into things to be hurt or obtained or accessed, and this presented as the nature of women; the coercion that is visible and the coercion that has become invisible—this and more bothers feminists about pornography" (see also MacKinnon 1988: 261). American obscenity law is an inadequate tool to fight pornography as defined by MacKinnon because it ignores the fact that pornography "hurts women and their equality." Indeed, she claims, obscenity law ignores the "rape, sexual abuse of children, battering, sexual harassment, prostitution, or sexual murder in pornography" (1993:88–91).

"First Amendment speech and Fourteenth Amendment equality have never contended on constitutional terrain," believes MacKinnon. She argues that there "never has been a fair fight in the United States between equality and speech as two constitutional values" and that the "law of equality and the law of freedom are on a collision course in this country" (1993:71, 73, 85). Often constitutional doctrines and court decisions concerning freedom of speech and concerning equality of protection under the law have developed largely independently of each other. "More precisely, the First Amendment has grown," says MacKinnon, "as if a commitment to free speech were no part of a commitment to equality and as if a commitment to equality has no implications for the law of speech" (1993:71). Typically, when free speech and equality rights have clashed, the situation is seen not as a problem of "balance between two cherished constitutional goals" but rather as "whether the right of speech is infringed acceptably or unacceptably" (1993:73). Only recently have some equal protection under the law cases (such as sexual harassment cases) indicated that equality might contend fairly and might take precedence over free speech in certain instances. "In other words, expressive means of practicing inequality can be prohibited" (1993:107–8).

Pornography, in this view, is a form of forced sex and institutionalized gender inequality, and it should be civilly actionable in court as sex discrimination and a violation of civil rights (MacKinnon 1987:148; 1988:261). MacKinnon and Dworkin define pornography as "the graphic sexually explicit subordination of women through pictures or words that also includes women dehumanized as sexual objects, things, or commodities; enjoying pain or humiliation or rape; being tied up, cut up, mutilated, bruised, or physically hurt; in positions of sexual submission or servility or display; reduced to body parts, penetrated by objects or animals, or presented in scenarios of degradation, injury, or torture; shown as inferior, filthy, bleeding, bruised, or hurt in a context that makes these conditions sexual" (MacKinnon 1987:176, 201, 262). If men, children, or transsexuals are used in place of women, that, too, is pornography. Subordination involves the active practice of making a person unequal and may include objectification, hierarchy, forced submission, and violence. In contrast, erotica "might be sexually explicit materials premised on equality" (MacKinnon 1988:263).

Pornography laws modeled on this view would involve civil law, not criminal law, and would have individual citizens bring civil suit concerning alleged civil rights harms, not government prosecutors enforcing interpretations of obscenity law. "Victims of four activities only—coercion into pornography, forcing pornography on a person, assault, and trafficking (which is production, sale, exhibition, and distribution)—can sue" (MacKinnon 1988:263). For example, a woman could sue a film producer for coercing her to perform in a pornographic video, sue a publisher or book seller of a pornographic magazine that contributed to an identifiable harm to the woman (such as assault or rape), or sue a man (even her husband) for forcing her to view or read pornography in order to force her to "do this."

MacKinnon sees no violation of First Amendment free speech protections under the civil rights approach to pornography (see also Longino 1986:172–74). The definition's specificity reduces any significant "chilling effect" or hesitancy to communicate due to vagueness about what is publishable. The approach does not involve prior restraint of communication. In fact MacKinnon argues that pornography actually undermines four traditional goals of freedom of expression, in this case freedom of expression for women: individual self-fulfillment; facilitation of consensus; participation in civic life; and facilitation of change. Moreover, MacKinnon contends that other societal values (such as gender equality) should compete with free speech and at times take precedence (1987:177, 203, 210).

In 1984 the Indianapolis city council passed an ordinance based on the civil rights approach. Eventually it was ruled unconstitutional by a U.S. Court of Appeals, and that ruling was upheld, without comment, by the U.S. Supreme Court in 1986. The Appeals Court faulted the ordinance for not including the necessary definitional elements of obscenity outlined in the *Miller* decision and because an ordinance allowing depiction of women in situations only of equality, no matter how vivid the sexual content, constituted "thought control" by establishing a single approved view of women, of how they should react in sexual encounters, and how the sexes should relate to each other (Middleton and Chamberlin 1994:356–57). Needless to say, MacKinnon responded with a scathing attack on the Appeals Court decision, and judged the Indianapolis case to be the "*Dred Scott* of the women's movement" (MacKinnon 1987:210–13; 1993:91–97).

In contrast, other feminists have serious reservations about the civil rights approach (Burstyn 1985; see also Cohen 1993:242–44; Strossen 1995). A report of the Feminist Anti-Censorship Task Force argues: "Removing sexually explicit materials would not stop violence against women. Such ordinances would give enormous power to the courts to interpret and rule on a wide variety of sexual images. These laws could be used to attack and limit feminist self-expression. This ordinance attempts to enforce, with the power of the state, one view of pornography. But many feminists believe that the law represents a dangerous and misguided strategy." The feminist attorney Wendy Kaminer contends that feminists "cannot look to the government to rid us of pornography. The feminist movement against pornography must remain an anti-defamation movement involved in education and consciousness-raising. Legislative and judicial control of pornography is simply not possible without breaking down the legal principles and procedures that are essential to our own right to speak" (both quoted in Public Agenda Foundation 1992:20–35). Here, too, MacKinnon responds harshly to such stances by feminist lawyers (1987:198–205).

Despite the fact that MacKinnon does not believe pornography should be condemned primarily on traditional humanistic ethical grounds (1987:158–60), and no matter whether law is used to control pornography, feminist ethicists do pinpoint the ethical bases for objecting to por-nography (Assiter 1988). Longino (1986:168–70) defines immoral behav-ior as that which "causes injury to or violation of another person or peo-ple. Such injury may be physical or psychological. To cause pain to another, to lie to another, to hinder another in the exercise of his or her rights, to exploit another, to degrade another, to misrepresent and slander another are instances of immoral behavior." Beyond pornography's degrading and dehumanizing depiction of women, to accomplish its purposes pornogra-phy must lie about women. She contends that pornography lies by saying women's sexual life is or ought to be subordinate to men, that women are depraved, that women's pleasure consists of pleasure for men not themselves, and that women are appropriate victims for rape, torture, bondage, or murder. "Pornography lies explicitly about women's sexuality," stresses Longino, "and through such lies fosters more lies about our humanity, our dignity, and our personhood" (1986:170–72).

Jacqueline MacGregor Davies (1988:137–38, 142–43) takes a post-liberal feminist position that condemns pornography as both politically and ethically objectionable. The assault, coercion, exploitation, sexual objectification, and dehumanization fostered by pornography "threaten the consensual process of articulating what it is to be human." In por-nography "women are no longer present as human subjects who can gen-erate signs. . . . They are spoken through." Pornography functions to deny women their status as members "of the community of subjects."

Hate Speech on College Campuses

The issue of "hate speech" on both public and private college and university campuses further illustrates the tension between the right of freedom of speech and the ethically responsible exercise of that right. Supreme Court interpretations of the First Amendment clearly allow officials to place more restrictions on student communication in high schools and private colleges and universities than in public higher edu-cation. Hate speech is a broad label "that has come to embrace the use of speech attacks based on race, ethnicity, religion, and sexual orienta-tion or preference" (Smolla 1992:152; see also Walker 1994). Examples of hate speech from the late 1980s and early 1990s typify the kinds of communication at issue. Eight Asian-American students on their way to a dance at the University of Connecticut were harassed for almost an hour by a group of football players who called them "Oriental faggots," spat on them, and challenged them to a fight. At the University of Arizona at

Tempe, a fight broke out and police were called to restore order after some white fraternity members harassed a black student by chanting "Coon," "Nigger," and "Porchmonkey" (Tedford 1992:183). At the University of Pennsylvania, a white male freshman was charged under the school's speech code with racial harassment for calling five black female students "water buffaloes" (*Chicago Tribune,* May 25, 1993, sec. 1, p. 6).

In response to such controversies, by 1992 over one hundred American colleges and universities had instituted speech codes to deal with hateful and offensive public messages (Public Agenda Foundation 1992:23, 25; see also Korwar 1994). In a survey of American citizens, improper speech offensive to different racial or ethnic groups should be protected all the time in the view of 30 percent of the respondents, sometimes in the view of 36 percent, and *not at all* in the view of 34 percent (Wyatt 1991:19, 24). Indeed, these survey results lead the survey researchers to conclude that increasingly many Americans believe that they have a new right, "the right not to be offended" (Wyatt 1991:21, 55, 87; also Rauch 1993:4–6, 18, 22–24; Will 1993). This new right, although not mentioned in the Constitution or Bill of Rights, would allow suppression of offensive, distasteful, disagreeable, or objectionable communication.

Examples of university speech codes reflect the fact that most of them address use of "fighting words," or creation of emotional distress, or creation of a hostile and intimidating environment (Public Agenda Foundation 1992:25–26; Tedford 1992:183–84). Among the varied forms of expression that are punishable at various schools are: use of derogatory names, inappropriately directed laughter, inconsiderate jokes, and conspicuous exclusion of another person from conversation; language that stigmatizes or victimizes individuals or that creates an intimidating or offensive environment; face-to-face use of epithets, obscenities, and other forms of expression that by accepted community standards degrade, victimize, stigmatize, or pejoratively depict persons based on their personal, intellectual, or cultural diversity; extreme or outrageous acts or communications intended to harass, intimidate, or humiliate a student on the basis of race, color, or national origin thus reasonably causing him or her severe emotional distress.

The 1988 University of Michigan code, in part, banned behavior, "verbal or physical, that stigmatizes or victimizes an individual on the basis of race, ethnicity, religion, sex, sexual orientation, creed, national origin, ancestry, age, marital status, handicap or Vietnam-era veteran status." The University of Michigan Office of Affirmative Action issued a guide describing some of the kinds of prohibited speech: distribution in dormitories of flyers containing racist threats; writing racist graffiti on an Asian woman's study carrel; a male creating a hostile learning environment by remarking in a class that "women just aren't as good in this field as men"; telling jokes about gay men and women; sponsoring a comedian who slurs Hispanics; and displaying a confederate flag on a dorm room door.

When the constitutionality of some of the codes has been tested in court, typically they have been overturned as invasions of First Amendment protections. The codes both at the University of Michigan and at the University of Wisconsin, for example, were found to be *vague and overbroad*. Vagueness means that language in the codes, such as *stigmatize* and *victimize*, is so unclear and imprecise that a person would not know in advance whether his or her message was punishable. Overbreadth means that the code, while punishing some behaviors that do lack First Amendment protection, goes too far and includes types of communication that clearly warrant First Amendment protection (Middleton and Chamberlin 1994:33, 42–44; Tedford 1993:184).

A number of arguments have been levied against the use of campus speech codes as ineffective or inappropriate responses to "hate speech." In summary, the main ones are: (1) "By driving speech underground, we miss the message, making it harder to combat the underlying attitudes"; (2) "Since campus rules on permissible speech are vague, they tend to be unevenly enforced, thus inviting the arbitrary exercise of power"; (3) "Speech codes are a constricting intellectual influence on campus, where open-mindedness and freedom of expression should be paramount values"; and (4) "Codes focus on symptoms, rather than the underlying problem of prejudice and insensitivity" (Public Agenda Foundation 1992:29–30; also Haiman 1993:32–34, 84). An American Civil Liberties Union policy statement on "Free Speech and Bias on College Campuses" condemns most codes as unconstitutionally vague and overbroad. Rather, the ACLU says that only conduct should be punishable that is directed at a specific person or persons and that intends to "frighten, coerce, or unreasonably harry or intrude upon the target." Such prohibitable behavior would include a threatening phone call to a minority student's dorm room and threats of attack, extortion, or blackmail (Tedford 1993:185–86).

Those who want to restrict hate speech through state laws or campus codes frequently argue that racist, sexist, and homophobic epithets and phrases are not ideas at all and thus make no useful contribution to the marketplace of ideas. Others, such as First Amendment scholar Franklyn Haiman (1991c), insist that hate speech does contain ideas and that it is precisely because such speech communicates horrible and repugnant ideas "that anyone even wants to suppress it." Those who favor restriction of hate speech also argue that such speech is primarily lacerating and venomous emotion more than cognitive ideas (Fish 1992:240–41). It must be remembered, however, that the Supreme Court declared in *Cohen v. California*, 403 U.S. 15 (1971), that the First Amendment protects both the cognitive and emotional dimensions of messages. In that decision, Justice Harlan observed "that words often are chosen as much for their emotive as their cognitive force. *We cannot sanction the view that the Constitution, while solicitous of the cognitive content of individual speech, has little or no regard for that emotive function which, practically speaking, may often be the more important element of the overall message sought to be communicated* " (emphasis in original).

Because courts typically overturn campus speech codes on constitutional grounds as being vague and overbroad, many schools adapt the "fighting words" doctrine to their campus situation and deem such words as the equivalent to a "slap in the face" (Public Agenda Foundation 1992:24). After an earlier code did not survive a court test, for example, the University of Connecticut banned the "face-to-face use of 'fighting words' by students to harass any person(s) on university property." The revised code explained that the words must be used in a way that is "likely to provoke an immediate violent reaction" and the words must be "widely recognized to be derogatory references to race, ethnicity, religion, sex, sexual orientation, disability, and other personal characteristics" (Tedford 1993:185; see also Hentoff 1992a:221).

A problem even with this narrower approach is that words considered as "fighting" by one person or group may not be by others. Is there any real degree of societal consensus (the Supreme Court asks for judgment by the "average" person) as to what words are "fighting" words and in what contexts (Fish 1992:241)? Furthermore, the "fighting words" doctrine, first promulgated in *Chaplinsky v. New Hampshire*, 315 U.S. 568 (1942), in over fifty years has never been used by the Supreme Court to uphold the conviction of persons in alleged "fighting words" cases (Gates 1993:39; Gunther 1994:77). Haiman (1993) rejects the "slap in the face" and words as "triggers" to action metaphors as valid reinforcement for the "fighting words" doctrine. Such metaphors mistakenly assume "that human beings . . . are inanimate objects that have no consciousness, make no decisions, and react mechanically to stimuli" (23–29). Hate speech need not uniformly or inevitably result in automatic responses. Humans are capable, even if for split seconds, of reflectively and consciously choosing how to respond (see also Haiman 1981:277–78, 425–26).

In the hate speech controversy, the value of First Amendment protection competes with other societal values (Cohen 1993:220–22, 262). Some, like Stanley Fish (1992:238–43; also Fish 1994), contend that the First Amendment cannot automatically be assumed as the preeminent value in educational settings. It must be weighed against other political and educational values in the context of higher education. The president of Yale University, Benno Schmidt, notes that civility and community have been proposed at some universities "as paramount values of the university, even to the extent of superseding freedom of expression." But such a view, argues Schmidt, could prove "disastrous to freedom of thought" (in Hentoff 1992:222–23). Franklyn Haiman (1991b:100–101) rejects attempts to make the choice one of equality of educational opportunity versus one of freedom of speech. "Freedom of speech and equality of opportunity are, and always have been, allies, not enemies." "Where reason breaks down," Haiman believes, "is in the leap to the conclusion that it is freedom of *speech* which is in conflict with equality, rather than the racist and sexist *behaviors* and *practices* that underlie the verbal expression of racial and sexual bigotry."

In contrast to Haiman's analysis, Catharine MacKinnon and Charles Lawrence believe that the Fourteenth Amendment protection of equality under the law should be a constitutional value of equal importance with free speech in hate speech cases. MacKinnon laments that no one, to her knowledge, has proposed that Congress control hate speech in order to actualize protection of equality under the law. In the hate speech controversies, the First Amendment reigns supreme and equality interests seldom are mentioned (1993:83, 870.) The traditional civil liberties position, argues Lawrence, "does not take into account important values expressed elsewhere in the Constitution." He urges that a balance "must be struck between our concerns for racial equality and freedom of expression" (Matsuda et al. 1993:58, 71–72, 81). And in narrowly worded speech codes based on the "fighting words" doctrine, Lawrence contends that racial harms should outweigh free speech interests (ibid.:53–88; also Smolla 1992:157–58, 161–62; Sunstein 1993:203–4; Cohen 1993:253–62).

In the Supreme Court decision in *Whitney v. California,* 274 U.S. 357 (1927), Justice Brandeis proposed the "more speech" remedy as antidote to distasteful and inflammatory speech: "If there be time to expose through discussion the falsehood and fallacies, to avert the evil by the process of education, the remedy to be applied is more speech, not enforced silence." But proponents of restrictions on campus hate speech, such as Fish (1992:240–41), argue that more speech is ineffective in offsetting the "lacerating" emotional harms that hate speech can inflict. Other advocates of restrictions seem to believe that female and ethnic minority students need to be protected from emotional trauma for their own good. Nevertheless, defenders of free speech on campus, even members of minority groups, could well view such an attitude as patronizing and condescending; those subjected to hate speech can learn to handle it through exercise of their own counter-persuasion (Hentoff 1992a:219, 224; Haiman 1991c; Rauch 1993:158–59; see also Hentoff 1992b).

Hentoff firmly believes that targeted students can learn to "demystify language, to strip it of its ability to demonize and stigmatize" them, and to answer bigoted language "with more and better language" of their own (1992a:221; also Hentoff 1992b). Barbara Ehrenreich condemns administration-enforced speech codes as ineffective in combating sexist, racist, and homophobic attitudes: "It is not a problem you turn over to the police, to the administration, or anybody else. The only route is through persuasion, education, and organizing" (1992:335). Uniformly, the "more speech" alternative is preferred by Haiman (1993:34; see also Haiman 1991a). "People who are insulted and denigrated," Haiman argues, "find the strength within themselves, or in concert with others, to talk back, to insist on being respected, to demand their rights" (1991b:102). "Only when people are directly and immediately threatened with immediate harm do they need the law to protect them, and there are adequate legal remedies available for intimidation of any kind. Special protections are not needed against racist, sexist, or homophobic verbal threats" (1991c).

But advocates of regulation of hate speech (especially that analogous to "fighting words") through laws and speech codes believe that hate speech inhibits rather than protects freedom of speech (Matsuda et al. 1993:68–70, 79, 95). Given the power differential typical between the hate speaker and the target, who often is relatively powerless and marginal, hate speech has a potent "chilling effect" on most targeted minorities, homosexuals, and women. Usually they do not physically "fight" back against the verbal slap in the face. Rather the hate speech functions as a "preemptive strike" that silences any target verbal response, certainly any verbal response that attempts to discuss ideas. Assaultive racist speech, according to the advocates of control, produces defensive psychological reactions of rage, shock, fear, and flight that disrupt potential reasoned responses. And the target literally may feel that *any* words of response would be inadequate. Or "many victims do not find words of response until well after the assault, when the cowardly assaulter has departed" (Matsuda et al. 1993:68; also Cohen 1993:256).

However, Haiman (1993) would limit control of hate speech to much more concretely specified power differential contexts, such as a boss or teacher regularly directing racist or sexist remarks at "members of target groups under his or her supervision." In contrast, "when it comes to interpersonal communication between peers or to messages promulgated to the public at large," speech codes clearly are problematic (30–31). Haiman contends that hate speech should lose its First Amendment protection *only* "*if* there is a persistent pattern of abusive words, gestures, or other symbols directed at specifically targeted individuals in situations from which they cannot, as a practical matter, escape; *if* fair warning has been given that the communication is unwelcome and inappropriate; and *if* the effect on the victims is to interfere demonstrably with their ability to function effectively in that environment" (60).

To deal with hate speech beyond the college campus in society at large, some legal scholars, such as Greenwalt (1989:301; Greenwalt 1995) and Matsuda (Matsuda et al. 1993:17–52), urge adoption of narrowly defined laws that criminalize the most blatant forms of such speech. For our purposes in exploring the relation between free speech and ethical responsibility, a very interesting proposal is that of R. George Wright in his book, *The Future of Free Speech Law* (1990). In his view, the use of the "fighting words" doctrine or the adoption of group libel laws are not appropriate or effective solutions (61, 75–76). However, because he believes that hate speech does not convey "ideas" as protected by the First Amendment, he does favor the legal suppression of hate speech. Wright proposes adoption of either a tort law or a criminal law both because of the psychological harms he believes stem from such speech and, more importantly, because of community agreement that the "use of racial epithets involves a clear and fundamental moral wrong." Wright rests his view firmly on the "sheer moral disvalue of racist speech." Hate speech is fundamentally a "deontic moral wrong" (58–59, 69, 73–76). In other words, hate speech is, in his view, by its very nature unethical; it is unethical in and of itself; it never is ethically justifiable. Wright thus seeks use of legal enforcement of a primarily ethical judgment.

Altman (1993) favors narrowly worded regulations against hate speech because such speech is a fundamental moral wrong. In his view, the reason for regulating hate speech is not because of the psychological harm it may cause, not because it contains virtually no ideas of value to society, but because it is a type of speech act (illocutionary) that by its very utterance treats someone as a moral subordinate—as having inferior moral standing. Haiman (1993) objects to "speech act theory" as a sound basis for free speech law because it blurs necessary distinctions between speech and action (10–20; see also Bracken 1994).

"Treating persons as moral subordinates," argues Altman, "means treating them in a way that takes their interests to be intrinsically less important, and their lives inherently less valuable" than those of others. Epithets such as "kike," "faggot," "spic," or "nigger" are "verbal instruments of subordination" and degradation that not only express hatred and contempt for persons but also "put them in their place" as "having inferior moral standing" (310). Altman roots his ethical judgment in the belief that "wrongs of subordination based on such characteristics as race, gender, and sexual preference . . . are among the principal wrongs that have prevented—and continue to prevent—Western liberal democracies from living up to their ideals and principles" (312).

Regardless of whether societal laws or campus codes are involved, hate speech clearly should be condemned on ethical grounds that broadly have been labeled as human nature, dialogical, or feminist perspectives (Johannesen 1990:41–77, 128–32). Hate speech reinforces demeaning stereotypes, dismisses taking serious account of the targets as persons deserving of respect as humans, or even dismisses people as citizens entitled to participate in public discourse. Hate speech dehumanizes by undermining and circumventing the distinctively human capacities for symbol-use and reasonable thought. Hate speech reflects a depersonalized, superior, exploitative attitude of one human toward another, thus hindering equal opportunity for self-fulfillment. On all of these grounds, hate speech should be condemned as ethically irresponsible by individual students, by activist groups mounting campaigns of education and counter-persuasion, and by campus administrators through taking an official public position on such speech. What are some alternatives to censorship through law for implementing negative ethical judgments against objectionable rap and rock lyrics, against pornography, and against campus hate speech?

Alternatives to Government Enforcement

In general, I believe that approaches short of local, state, or federal law should be found to address problems of communication ethics (see also

Haiman 1993:81–86). When faced with a significant crisis in public communication ethics, citizens often feel caught in the tension between two old but seemingly contrary sayings: "There ought to be a law!" and "You can't legislate morality." In siding with the second view in the context of journalistic practice, Chief Justice Warren Burger spoke for a unanimous Supreme Court in the case of *Miami Herald v. Tornillo*, 418 U.S. 241 (1974): "A responsible press is an undoubtedly desirable good, but press responsibility is not mandated by the Constitution and like many other virtues it cannot be legislated." In the more general context of speaking about "The Spirit of Liberty" to an audience in 1944, the respected judge Learned Hand mused: "I wonder whether we do not rest our hopes too much on constitutions, upon laws, and upon the courts" (in Tedford 1993:393).

In this section I will suggest some alternatives for fostering ethical communication other than government enforcement through law, regulation, and court interpretation. *Educational programs and campaigns of counter-persuasion* are one route for combating ethically irresponsible communication (Smolla 1992:169). The American Civil Liberties Union's policy statement on "Free Speech and Bias on College Campuses" recommends a number of efforts: the administration, faculty, and students should organize to publicize the school's commitment to understanding and tolerance; workshops, programs, and counseling about bias can be conducted; administrators and student leaders can formulate a plan for rapid public response to incidents of harassment and discrimination; schools should more actively recruit minorities as faculty, administrators, and students; courses on the various manifestations of prejudice can be offered (Tedford 1993:186). Bad speech requires not censorship but "moral censure"—efforts at counter-persuasion through cogent criticism (Public Agenda Foundation 1992:9). The fostering of freedom of speech requires not only tolerance for expression of disagreeable views but also combating those views "clearly and strongly" through argument against and exposure of the "folly and meanness" of the disagreeable speech ("Free Speech and the Campuses" 1993; Public Agenda Foundation 1992:37). A *Washington Post* editorial concludes: "The distinction that will matter on campuses is not between left and right but between those who—hearing something that goes against cherished American principles of tolerance and civility and sense—reach reflexively for the nearest rule and those who take on what has been said or done and show it up for what it is. That is the way of education" ("Free Speech and the Campuses" 1993).

Another avenue for education and counter-persuasion is through citizen action groups and citizen watchdog groups such as the previously described Parents' Music Resource Center. In Chicago during local political campaigns, the Committee on Decent and Unbiased Campaign Tactics (CONDUCT), a nonpartisan citizen watchdog organization, fought campaign tactics that were "morally wrong, that undermine the community peace and subvert the political process." CONDUCT urged candidates to pledge to observe a seven-point Code of Fair Campaign Practice. If a complaint was substantiated and the irresponsible remark, statement, or action was not repudiated publicly by the offender, CONDUCT publicized both the refusal and the findings on the complaint (*Chicago Tribune,* February 25, 1989, pp. A1, A6; also Johannesen 1990:186).

Formal codes of ethics, whether adopted by colleges and universities, corporations, or professional associations, are a potential but controversial means to deal with unethical communication short of invoking law, regulation, or court interpretation. The strengths and weaknesses of formal codes of communication ethics depend in part on how clearly worded they are, on whether effective mechanisms for enforcement are desired or not, and on the degree of participation in their formulation by all of the affected parties (Johannesen 1990:169–73). (A number of the objections to campus speech codes were summarized previously in this chapter.)

One useful function of a soundly drawn code, even without enforcement provisions, is as a framework for argument, a framework of standards for use by advocates and critics of particular communication practices on campuses, in politics, and in business. Communication practices can be examined, justified, or condemned in light of the code's standards and a number of argumentative strategies may flow from the nature of the code (Johannesen 1990:173–74). Codes also provide one way of debating and clarifying *institutional* responsibilities and policies for communication ethics; individual decisions on communication ethics are not enough (ibid.:17–18, 265–78).

In response to ethically irresponsible communication, people should *exercise their own right of free speech to publicly condemn communication practices that dehumanize persons,* especially women, ethnic groups, and others who traditionally have been trivialized and marginalized by mainstream communication. The grounds for condemning dehumanizing communication can stem from perspectives rooted in the essence of human nature, in the conception of human communication as dialogue, or in feminist ethical perspectives (Johannesen 1990:41–77, 128–32; Jaggar 1992; Manning 1992). For example, racist, sexist, and homophobic communication dehumanizes—makes a person less than human—by demeaning other people through embodying unfair negative value judgments concerning traits, capacities, or accomplishments. Communication that dehumanizes reinforces stereotypes, conveys inaccurate depictions of people, dismisses taking serious account of people, or even makes them invisible for purposes of decision or policy. Communication that dehumanizes undermines or subverts the human capacities for symbol-use and reasonableness. Communication that dehumanizes reflects a superior, exploitative, inhumane attitude of one person toward others, thus hindering equal opportunity for self-fulfillment. Communication that dehumanizes views others not as persons inherently worthy of respect but as things or objects to be manipulated for the communicator's pleasure or selfish gain. Communication that dehumanizes may place sole emphasis on cold, abstract, rationality and on individual rights without the counterbalance of an ethic of caring, of responsibilities stemming from relationships, and of emotion as a legitimate part of human experience and decision-making.

Another nonlegalistic approach to promoting ethically responsible communication is through early education to foster *formed ethical character*. Sound ethical character may be of significant value in prompting mature reaction and communication when freedom and responsibility come into tension or conflict.

An emphasis on duties, obligations, rules, principles, and the resolution of complex ethical dilemmas has dominated the contemporary philosophy of ethics. The past several decades, however, have witnessed a growing interest among ethicists in a largely ignored tradition that goes back at least as far as Plato's and Aristotle's philosophies of ethics. This largely bypassed tradition typically is called "virtue ethics" or "character ethics" (Sherman 1989). Most ethicists of virtue or character see that perspective as a crucial compliment to the current dominant ethical theories. Ethicists describe virtues variously as deep-rooted dispositions, habits, skills, or traits of character that incline persons to perceive, feel, and act in ethically right and sensitive ways. They also describe virtues as learned, acquired, cultivated, reinforced, capable of modification, capable of conflicting, and ideally coalesced into a harmonious cluster.

Communication sometimes is not simply a series of careful and reflective decisions, instance by instance, to communicate in ethically responsible ways (Johannesen 1990:11–15; Johannesen 1991). Deliberate application of ethical rules sometimes is not possible. Pressure may be so great for a decision that there is not time for careful deliberation. We may be unsure what ethical criteria are relevant or how they apply. The situation may seem unique and thus applicable criteria do not come readily to mind. In such times of crisis or uncertainty, our actions concerning ethical communication (both our own and that of others) stems less from deliberation than from our "character." Our ethical character influences the terms with which we describe a situation and whether we believe the situation even contains ethical implications.

In Judeo-Christian or Western cultures, good moral character usually is associated with the habitual embodiment of such virtues as courage, temperance, prudence (or practical wisdom), justice, fairness, generosity, patience, truthfulness, and trustworthiness. Martin Buber's dimensions of genuine dialogue might be viewed as virtues of character: authenticity, inclusion, confirmation, and presentness (Johannesen 1990:57–77). Other cultures or ethnic groups may praise additional or different virtues that they believe constitute good ethical character. Instilled in us as habitual dispositions to feel, see, and act, the virtues guide the ethics of our communication when careful or clear deliberation is not possible.

Early formal education in the development of moral character is possible (Carr 1991; Lickona 1991; Noddings 1984). And we can develop good ethical character through emulating models or moral exemplars. We may encounter such models directly, for example, in interpersonal relationships, business, or public life (Cooper and Wright 1992; Williams and Houck 1992). Or we may encounter the models indirectly through stories or narratives we read or are told (Booth 1988:8–15, 179, 230–40; Bellah et al. 1985:153).

Finally, in fostering ethical communication through approaches short of governmental law, regulation, and court interpretation, we should *practice and preach efforts at understanding and tolerance (without necessarily approving) of diversity in ethical systems* rooted in diverse ethnic, gender, and cultural systems. Thus we can show respect for persons even if we disagree with their ideas. We should at least understand the other person's ethical view so that we are able to better ground and argue our own ethical assessment.

Here are several examples of efforts to broaden our ethical understanding and tolerance. Some feminist scholars examine an Ethic of Care rooted in relationships, interdependence of self and others, compassion and nurturance, and concrete responsibilities as an equal compliment to the presently dominant Ethic of Justice rooted in individual autonomy, impartial and abstract rules, rights, and a logic of equality and fairness (Manning 1992; Noddings 1984; Tronto 1993; Wood 1994).

We should consider carefully the perspective developed by Anthony Cortese in his book, *Ethnic Ethics: The Restructuring of Moral Theory* (1990). He argues at length that "morality must be bound to a particular culture or sociocultural context. Morality contains no intrinsic laws of development. Its validity has no ultimate basis. Instead, moral systems prosper or fail within specific cultural and historical settings" (41). In Cortese's judgment, traditional "moral principles that aze allegedly universal are viewed as the highest good." But he takes the position that "people are more important than principles, that relationships are more crucial than conceptions of justice, and that subcultural moral systems are more relevant than universal standards of ethics" (91).

"The key to morality is in social relations," contends Cortese, "not in abstract rational principles." "Ethnic background, gender, role demands, and socioeconomic status" are key factors (1–6). And yet the "structures of moral reasoning used by Western middle-to-upper-middle-class white males appear to be taken to be everyone's ideal type by many researchers. Similarly the norms of the dominant culture are taken as the model for the entire society" (94). Cortese takes seriously "the possibility that ethnic groups have different moral structures, each adequate to the reproduction of the social life-world found in each ethnic group." "One must consider," he believes, "the possibility that the 'scientific findings' on moral development are more appropriately viewed as ideology that sets the Western European life-world as the model for all people in all places" (107).

I do not believe, however, that the moral pluralism view developed by Cortese necessarily must lead to a radical cultural relativism wherein whatever ethical standards "work" for an ethnic group or culture uniformly are acceptable. Rather what Emmet (1966:89–109) terms "soft" moral relativism, what Benhabib (1992:1–19, 153) labels "interactive universalism," and what Gutmann (1993:193–200) calls "deliberative universalism" open up for examination the possibility that cultural variation in certain moral principles between cultures or within a culture does not preclude moral judgments of better or worse between or within those cultures. Lack of commitment solely to a complete set of invariable or universalizable principles does not mean impossibility of a minimum set of ethical norms that are or should be transcultural. I would suggest for consideration such potential transcultural ethical standards as humaneness, truthfulness, promise-keeping, nonviolence, and caring relationships. Other ethical standards within a culture or subculture properly may be more relative to specific cultural, ethnic, class, or gender factors. And some of these more relativistic standards may be critiqued in light of the transcultural norms. The Josephson Institute of Ethics, for instance, has proposed six "core consensus ethical values that transcend cultural, ethnic and socio-economic differences": trustworthiness; respect; responsibility; justice and fairness; caring; and civic virtue and citizenship. But the institute also recognizes that there are additional ethical values that properly vary among cultures, ethnic groups, religions, and political philosophies (Josephson 1993:1–10.)

Conclusion

Clearly, the tension between freedom and responsibility, between constitutional rights of free speech and the ethically responsible exercise of that freedom, is a tension that pervades American society. Freedom and responsibility are in tension in varied communication arenas, in public and private spheres, and between persons at the centers and those at the margins of power. Any precise balancing between freedom and responsibility is problematic for almost any communication transaction. Perhaps the best we can expect in a given instance is not to "resolve" the tension in some ultimate sense but to "manage" the tension in humane and fair ways.

As guides to assist in the management of this tension, we would do well to bear in mind the words of two respected Supreme Court justices. In delivering the majority opinion in *Terminiello v. Chicago,* 337 U.S. 1 (1949), Justice William Douglas argued: "Accordingly a function of free speech under our system of government is to invite dispute. It may indeed best serve its high purpose when it induces a condition of unrest, creates dissatisfaction with things as they are, or even stirs people to anger." Douglas continued: "That is why freedom of speech, though not absolute . . . is nevertheless protected against censorship or punishment, unless shown likely to produce a clear and present danger of a serious substantive evil that rises far above public inconvenience, annoyance, or unrest." In his dissent in *Abrams v. United States,* 250 U.S. 616 (1919), Justice Oliver Wendell Holmes contended that "the ultimate good desired is better reached by free trade in ideas,—that the best test of truth is the power of the thought to get itself accepted in the competition of the market."

The current state of affairs is that while government has the authority to enforce ethical standards in a few areas of public communication, such as false advertising or private libel, in "religious, social, and political discourse in general, the First Amendment provides that individuals make decisions about communication ethics for themselves" (Tedford 1993:391). "Freedom is a good thing," believes syndicated political columnist Stephen Chapman (1990), "and it requires letting people make their own choices about morality. But it doesn't require pretending that all choices are morally equal. The less we rely on our rulers to enforce morality by law, the greater our duty to promote it through our own conduct and attitudes" (25).

References Cited

Altman, A. 1993. "Liberalism and Campus Hate Speech: A Philosophical Examination." *Ethics* 103 (January):302–17.

Assiter, A. 1988. "Autonomy and Pornography." In *Feminist Perspectives in Philosophy.* Ed. M. Griffiths and M. Whitford. Pp. 58–71. Bloomington: Indiana University Press.

Bellah, R. N., R. Madsen, W. M. Sullivan, A. Swidler, and S. M. Tipton. 1985. *Habits of the Heart: Individualism and Commitment in American Life.* Berkeley: University of California Press.

Benhabib, S. 1992. *Situating the Self: Gender, Community, and Postmodernism in Contemporary Ethics.* New York: Routledge.

Booth, W. C. 1988. *The Company We Keep: An Ethics of Fiction.* Berkeley: University of California Press.

Bracken, H. M. 1994. *Freedom of Speech: Words Are Not Deeds.* Westport, Conn.: Praeger.

Burstyn, V., ed. 1985. *Women against Censorship.* Vancouver: Douglas and McIntyre.

Carr, D. 1991. *Educating the Virtues: An Essay on the Philosophical Psychology of Moral Development and Education.* New York: Routledge, Chapman, and Hall.

Chapman, S. 1990. "Jimmy Breslin and the Limits of Offensiveness." *Chicago Tribune,* May 10, sec. 1, p. 25.

Cohen, J. 1993. "Freedom of Expression." *Philosophy and Public Affairs* 22 (Summer):207–62.

Cooper, T. L., and N. D. Wright, eds. 1992. *Exemplary Public Administrators.* San Francisco: Jossey-Bass.

Cortese, A. 1990. *Ethnic Ethics: The Restructuring of Moral Theory.* Albany: State University of New York Press.

Davies, J. M. 1988. "Pornographic Harms." In *Feminist Perspectives: Philosophical Essays on Method and Morals*. Ed. L. Code, S. Mullett, and C. Overall. Pp. 127–45. Toronto: University of Toronto Press.

Dworkin, A. 1981. *Pornography: Men Possessing Women*. New York: Perigee.

Ehrenreich, B. 1992. "The Challenge of the Left." In *Debating P.C.: The Controversy over Political Correctness on College Campuses*. Ed. P. Berman. Pp. 333–38. New York: Laurel.

Emerson, T. I. 1970. *The System of Freedom of Expression*. New York: Random House.

Emmet, D. M. 1966. *Rules, Roles, and Relations*. New York: St. Martin's.

Fish, S. 1992. "There's No Such Thing as Free Speech and It's a Good Thing, Too." In *Debating P.C.: The Controversy over Political Correctness on College Campuses*. Ed. P. Berman. Pp. 231–45. New York: Laurel.

———. 1994. *There's No Such Thing as Free Speech, and It's a Good Thing, Too*. New York: Oxford University Press.

"Free Speech and the Campuses." 1993. *Washington Post* (National Weekly Edition), May 24–30, p. 26.

Gates, H. L., Jr. 1993. "Let Them Talk: Why Civil Liberties Pose No Threat to Civil Rights." *New Republic*, September 20–27, pp. 37–49.

Gore, T. 1987. *Raising PG Kids in an X-Rated Society*. Nashville: Abingdon.

———. 1990. "Raising PG Kids in an X-Rated Society." Speech delivered at a meeting of the Junior League of Greenville, S.C., September 25.

Graber, M. A. 1991. *Transforming Free Speech: The Ambiguous Legacy of Civil Libertarianism*. Berkeley: University of California Press.

Greenwalt, K. 1989. *Speech, Crime, and the Use of Language*. New York: Oxford University Press.

———. 1995. *Fighting Words: Individuals, Communities, and Liberties of Speech*. Princeton: Princeton University Press.

Gunther, G. 1994. "All Speech Should Be Unrestricted on College Campuses." In *Free Speech*. Ed. B. Leone, Pp. 75–79. San Diego: Greenhaven.

Gutmann, A. 1993. "The Challenge of Multiculturalism in Political Ethics." *Philosophy and Public Affairs* 22 (Summer):171–206.

Haiman, F. S. 1981. *Speech and Law in a Free Society*. Chicago: University of Chicago Press.

———. 1991a. *First Amendment Hazards: Tinkering with the Boundaries between Speech and Action, Morality and Law*. Minneapolis: Silha Center for the Study of Media Ethics and Law, School of Journalism and Mass Communication, University of Minnesota.

———. 1991b. "Majorities versus the First Amendment: Rationality on Trial." In *Representative American Speeches, 1990–1991*. Ed. O. Peterson. Pp. 93–105. New York: H. W. Wilson.

———. 1991c. "Why Hate Speech Must Be Heard." *Chicago Tribune*, October 30, sec. 1, p. 19.

―――. 1993. *"Speech Acts" and the First Amendment.* Carbondale: Southern Illinois University Press.

Hentoff, N. 1992a. "'Speech Codes' on the Campus and Problems of Free Speech." In *Debating P.C.: The Controversy over Political Correctness on College Campuses.* Ed. P. Berman. Pp. 215–24. New York: Laurel.

―――. 1992b. *Free Speech for Me—But Not for Thee.* New York: Harper-Collins.

Jaggar, A. M. 1992. "Feminist Ethics." In *Encyclopedia of Ethics.* Ed. L. C. Becker and C. B. Becker. Pp. 361–70. New York: Garland.

Johannesen, Richard L. 1990. *Ethics in Human Communication.* 3d ed. Prospect Heights, Ill.: Waveland.

―――. 1991. "Virtue Ethics, Character, and Political Communication." In *Ethical Dimensions of Political Communication.* Ed. R. E. Denton, Jr. Pp. 69–90. New York: Praeger.

Josephson, M. 1993. *Making Ethical Decisions.* 2d ed. Marina del Rey, Calif.: Josephson Institute of Ethics.

Korwar, A. R. 1994. *War of Words: Speech Codes at Public Colleges and Universities.* Nashville: Freedom Forum First Amendment Center.

Leone, B., ed. 1994. *Free Speech.* San Diego: Greenhaven.

Lickona, T. 1991. *Educating for Character: How Our Schools Can Teach Respect and Responsibility.* New York: Bantam.

Linz, D., and N. Malamuth. 1993. *Pornography.* Newbury Park, Calif.: Sage.

Longino, H. E. 1986. "Pornography, Oppression, and Freedom: A Closer Look." In *Women and Values: Readings in Recent Feminist Philosophy.* Ed. M. Pearsall. Pp. 167–76. Belmont, Calif.: Wadsworth.

MacKinnon, C. A. 1987. *Feminism Unmodified: Discourses on Life and Law.* Cambridge: Harvard University Press.

―――. 1988. "The Civil Rights Approach to Pornography." In *Contemporary American Speeches.* 6th ed. Ed. R. L. Johannesen, R. R. Allen, and W. A. Linkugel. Pp. 259–65. Dubuque: Kendall-Hunt.

―――. 1989. *Toward a Feminist Theory of the State.* Cambridge: Harvard University Press.

―――. 1993. *Only Words.* Cambridge: Harvard University Press.

Manning, R. C. 1992. *Speaking from the Heart: A Feminist Perspective on Ethics.* Lanham, Md.: Rowman and Littlefield.

Matsuda, M. J., C. R. Lawrence III, R. Delgado, and K. W. Crenshaw. 1993. *Words That Wound: Critical Race Theory, Assaultive Speech, and the First Amendment.* Boulder: Westview.

Middleton, K. R., and B. F. Chamberlin. 1994. *The Law of Public Communication.* 3d ed. New York: Longman.

Mill, J. S. 1947. *On Liberty.* New York: Appleton-Century-Crofts.

Noddings, N. 1984. *Caring: A Feminine Approach to Ethics and Moral Education.* Berkeley: University of California Press.

Public Agenda Foundation. 1992. *The Boundaries of Free Speech: How Free Is Too Free?* New York: McGraw-Hill.

Rauch, J. 1993. *Kindly Inquisitors: The New Attacks on Free Thought.* Chicago: University of Chicago Press.

Rawlins, W. K. 1983. "Individual Responsibility in Relational Communication." In *Communications in Transition.* Ed. M. S. Mander. Pp. 152–67. New York: Praeger.

Sherman, N. 1989. *The Fabric of Character: Aristotle's Theory of Virtue.* New York: Oxford University Press.

Smolla, R. A. 1992. *Free Speech in an Open Society.* New York: Knopf.

Stanley, L., ed. 1992. *Rap: The Lyrics.* New York: Penguin Books.

Strossen, N. 1995. *Defending Pornography: Free Speech, Sex, and the Fight for Women's Rights.* New York: Scribner.

Sunstein, C. R. 1993. *Democracy and the Problem of Free Speech.* New York: Free Press.

Szasz, T. 1977. *The Theology of Medicine.* Baton Rouge: Louisiana State University Press.

Tedford, T. L. 1993. *Freedom of Speech in the United States.* 2d ed. New York: McGraw-Hill.

Tronto, J. C. 1993. *Moral Boundaries: A Political Argument for an Ethic of Care.* New York: Routledge.

Walker, S. 1994. *Hate Speech: The History of an American Controversy.* Lincoln: University of Nebraska Press.

Will, G. F. 1990. "America's Slide into the Sewer." *Newsweek,* July 30, p. 64.

———. 1993. "'Compassion' on Campus." *Newsweek,* May 31, p. 66.

Williams, O. F., and J. W. Houck, eds. 1992. *A Virtuous Life in Business.* Lanham, Md.: Rowman and Littlefield.

Wood, J. T. 1994. *Who Cares? Women, Care, and Culture.* Carbondale: Southern Illinois University Press.

Wright, R. G. 1990. *The Future of Free Speech Law.* New York: Quorum.

Wyatt, R. O. 1991. *Free Expression and the American Public: A Survey Commemorating the 200th Anniversary of the First Amendment.* Washington, D.C.: American Society of Newspaper Editors.

9 Social Ethics and Mass Media Practice

Clifford G. Christians

Political entities born of war are no longer compelling. Global information systems are creating their own economic and social orders outside national boundaries. Indigenous languages and ethnicity have come into their own. Sects and religious fundamentalists insist on recognition. Country is less salient these days than culture.

Chechen defiance of the Russian military is of historic proportions. Muslim immigrants are the fastest-growing segment of France's population and longstanding policies of assimilation have not been credible.[1] Debates over language and history embroil the Portuguese colony of Macao in the Pearl River delta on the eve of its reverting to China in 1999. Thirty thousand Navajos live in Los Angeles isolated from their native nation and culture. Macedonia in the former Yugoslavia is not at war, but the fear of anarchy or repression stifles free expression and cripples self-identity. Though the Mapuche Indians in the Southern region of Chile have deep historic roots in this territory below Santiago, revitalizing their culture under desperate socioeconomic conditions may not succeed (Colle 1992:127–48). The nomadic Fulani search for good pasture throughout sub–Saharan West Africa, held together by clan fidelity but their political future hanging in the balance. Hasidic Jews in the

Williamsburg area of Brooklyn, New York, live under constant threats to their safety.

Daniel Moynihan's recent book on ethnicity in international relations is appropriately titled *Pandaemonium* (1993). With identity politics the dominant issue in world affairs after the cold war, he worries that societies are becoming ungovernable. Moynihan is horrified at the prospect of ethnically based politics, and he hopes that self-determination will not always lead to full independence.

Though sometimes flawed and ambiguous, *Pandaemonium* correctly identifies ethnicity as an elemental force in the upcoming global order. Can ethnic self-consciousness be a source of pride and social vitality? If so, do the public media have a special obligation to channel ethnic struggles toward a healthy cultural pluralism? Have the new world information systems and the electronic superhighway arrived just in time—with hundreds of channels and dazzling speed to shuttle every ethnic inflection from one end of the planet to the other? Given all the technological breakthroughs of late, are the media now complex and sophisticated enough to empower ethnic subcultures to speak with their own voice? This essay assesses the current technological structure of the mass media in terms of cultural pluralism.

Information Highway

Through the electronic highway, American industry presumes it can be a world leader in information hardware and software. Superhighways direct speeding traffic toward an appropriate destination. "Put plainly by Rupert Murdoch, the information age is like a steamroller: One must either get on board for the ride or become part of the pavement" (Calabrese and Wasko 1992:122). The label also reinvents an administrative achievement—Eisenhower's interstate expressway project integrating the United States geographically through a nationwide transportation system.

This technologically advanced communication network combines the storage capacity of data banks with the transmission prowess of advanced cable systems, and video imaging with the routing capabilities of cellular telephones. "Just punch up what you want, and it appears when you want it. Welcome to the information highway" (Elmer-Dewitt 1993:50–51).

This merger of computers, telephones, and video is driven by recent technological breakthroughs: (1) audio and video communications turned into digital information; (2) fiber optic channels with nearly limitless capacity; (3) over-the-air telephony that eliminates rewiring. Blue-chip corporations are furiously launching pilot projects. They are investing and reorganizing to take advantage of what they see as an unprecedented opportunity—Bell Atlantic merging with TCI, Microsoft and McCaw Cellular creating a global satellite network, and MCI investing in the wireless network Nextel. For Vice President Albert Gore, "'This is by all odds the most important and lucrative marketplace of the 21st century. . . .' Apple Computer chairman John Sculley estimates that the revenue generated by this megaindustry could reach $3.5 trillion worldwide by the year 2001" (Elmer-Dewitt 1993:52–53).[2]

Time Warner Merger

Is the media megasystem the answer? Granted it provides virtually unlimited transmission capacity. Is a technological solution to cultural diversity at hand? Can groups demanding recognition be given a voice electronically?

In order to make the analysis more concrete, examine one merger of media giants out of the hundreds that together make up the information highway. Time Warner is a case study of the process currently unfolding. The merger of these two companies illustrates the direction in which convergent technologies are undoubtedly headed.

In June 1989, Time Inc. acquired Warner Communications for $13 billion. "The first stretch of the information superhighway was laid" (Dennis and Pease 1994:xvi). The result was hailed as a business feat made in heaven.

When Time Inc. was separate, its magazines included *Time, Southern Living, Sports Illustrated, Fortune, Life, Money,* and *People.* The magazine division had long been wonderfully profitable. In fact, Time Inc. controlled nearly one-fourth of all U.S. magazine advertising revenue. However, Time's investment bankers could no longer project more than 6 percent annual growth. The corporate strategy began to focus on video investment, but the company was underdeveloped there, given today's explosion in visual technologies. Since the early sixties, Time Inc. had diversified into cable and book publishing in order to expand its potential. And most of these ventures had become household words—Book-of-the-Month Club, HBO Video, Home Box Office, Time-Life Books, and Scott-Foresman. But none of those achievements compared with Warner. Its records-and-music division had been wildly successful. It owned 2,200 films—including *Batman* and *Lethal Weapon*—1,500 popular cartoons, and 23,000 television programs. Warner's production capabilities and extensive overseas marketing made a merger attractive. During the acquisition process management argued that combining their assets would jumpstart the merged corporation into a growth cycle neither one could experience separately.

Henry Luce III of Time Inc.'s board of directors, and former editor-in-chief Hedley Donovan, objected to the deal then and continue to do so now. They argue that Time is primarily a journalistic enterprise. They are deeply suspicious of Warner's organizational culture embedded in entertainment. However, the supporters of acquisition have turned the independence of the news-editorial component into one of Time's weaknesses. Video and print were never integrated, they said; putting the swimsuit issue of *Sports Illustrated* into video format had been one of Time's few meager attempts to exploit the company's resources. Warner's dazzling electronic expertise should overcome that "deficiency" forever.

Critics have charged that executives from both companies have been more interested in padding their income than in serving either stockholders or the public. According to *Fortune* magazine (Saporito 1989:165), Steve Ross of Warner orchestrated a compensation package for himself, "so abundant in dollars that, should the oilman fail to show this winter, Ross can shovel money into his furnace and have plenty left over in the spring." In addition to multi-million dollar salary and pension packages, Ross received $193 million in cash and stock. In fact, these early warning signals about Ross dogged his career until he died of cancer in December 1992, the company in a positive cash flow but still staggering under $15 billion in debt and $1.2 billion in annual debt service.

In terms of the media's capacity for cultural diversity, two issues are obvious: the welfare of independent producers and cultural imperialism.

First, in spite of Time Inc.'s corporate luster, it owned few important copyrights in the video sector of its business. Time's cable operations gave it a distribution system, but software had to be purchased in the open market where prices continued to climb. Thus Time concluded: "In the media and entertainment business of the future, the winners will own the copyrights to creative products, as well as avenues of distribution. We intend to increase our ownership of both" (Thiesen and Beckwith 1989:B7).

In order to secure copyrights without violating the law, Time needed to control more creative talent. And with the merger, its copyright capabilities expanded one-hundredfold. But, in the process, Time Warner no longer has been motivated to draw upon independent writers and producers, especially those from subcultures of limited size. Time Warner has solved its copyright problem by cutting itself off from a diverse pool of ideas, in favor of a creative staff that generally conforms to the values of the mainstream media oriented to majority values. This is "repression by the bottom line," in which strengthening a corporation's financial position ironically diminishes the quality, flexibility, independence, and variety of the very programming it is designed to market. When the history of independent producers is written, June 1989 will mean one more nail in the coffin of diversity in popular art.

Second, in addition to putting a squeeze on the creative sector at home, Time Warner views the international audience in a way that destroys rather than fosters cultural diversity. At a time when global markets offer the greatest opportunities, only 10 percent of Time Inc.'s revenues had come from overseas. Warner Communications, however, had been a stunning financial success worldwide, with 40 percent of its profits outside the United States.

Under Warner's synergistic communications strategy, articles are spun off domestically as books, movies, TV shows, paraphernalia, and toys, and then sold abroad through an international network. There are displays of movie heroes in the department stores of Manila identical to those in downtown Chicago. Warner's flair for marketing *Batman* and *Superman* recommended it to Time executives as the standard when the merger was first discussed. Since then they have been able to compete in marketing strategies with Sony of Japan, Bertelsmann of Germany, Pearson PLC of England, and the handful of communications companies that operate on the world scene.

But in the process the international audience is reduced to an exploitable resource. Driven by instrumentalism, the merger has paid no attention to indigenous programming and local talent. This one-way notion of information flow maintains the colonialism and paternalism no longer acceptable in politics or international business. Standardized cultural products give no voice to the voiceless along the sidelines. The objections leveled against cultural imperialism in general are apropos to Time Warner as well.[3]

Monopoly Contradicts Diversity

Imagine standing on a riverbank, observing the waves and water patterns on the surface. In what direction is the current actually flowing underneath?

In historical terms, Time Warner represents a profoundly unsettling conundrum in our technological culture. Ten years ago, fifty corporations controlled the majority of U.S. media, whereas twenty-five firms—including Time Warner—now hold that distinction. If the present trends continue—driven to a frenzy over market share in the global information order—the mass media will be largely owned before the next century by a dozen major companies (Bagdikian 1990). And the disturbing structural questions are obvious for democratic nations that prize in principle diversity of opinion and access to the marketplace of ideas. In classical liberal theory, information is equal to education in grounding public opinion; for democracy to thrive, citizens need their minds educated in schools, but also in up-to-date information as well. When the media fail in their mission, civic life is stymied. Time Warner manufactures social resources, not something secondary such as silver doorknobs for Corvettes or swimming pools for the world's Hollywood stars.

But media conglomeration is symptomatic of something deeper. Oligopolies mask a juggernaut made obvious in the philosophy of technology. The Frankfurt School since Herbert Marcuse has demonstrated compellingly that modern technology, far from being neutral, embodies values incompatible with democracy's core commitments. Martin Heidegger's (1977) seminal essay "What Is Technology?" contends that a technological society is at odds with human freedom. And Jacques Ellul develops these ruminations into a full-scale critique of technology's deep-structure. He demonstrates that its efficiency breeds normlessness. The overwhelming power of means buries a consideration of ends. The critical challenge is not the immoral decisions of corporate leaders, but amorality in our culture.

In Ellul's view, industrialized civilizations have their own *geist* or characteristic consciousness. He calls it *la technique*. This ethos of efficiency appears everywhere—in agriculture, business, the church, and medicine. The technological phenomenon is decisive in defining twentieth-century culture (Ellul 1980, 1981). The spirit of efficiency leads an early theorist of the information order, Buckminster Fuller, into a rhapsody for communication satellites—at $\frac{1}{700,000}$ the weight of the transatlantic cable, they quadruple our information capacity. We are so beguiled by machine productivity that we almost unconsciously reconstruct our social institutions in terms of efficiency. And, for Fuller, technological modes of thought even determine our self-understanding:

> Man is a self-balancing, 28-jointed adapter-base biped, an electrochemical reduction plant, integral with the segregated stowages of special energy extracts in storage batteries, for subsequent actuation

of thousands of hydraulic and pneumatic pumps, with motors attached; 62,000 miles of capillaries, millions of warning-signals,
railroad, and conveyer systems; crushers and cranes . . . and a universally distributed telephone system needing no service for 70 years
if well managed; the whole, extraordinarily complex mechanism
guided with exquisite precision from a turret in which are located
telescopic and microscopic self-registering and recording range
finders, a spectroscope, et cetera. (Mumford 1970:56)

In the technicized world, moral values are precluded, in principle. *La
technique* and judgments about rightness or wrongness are mutually exclusive. *La technique* acts as a spiritual guillotine, decapitating other values. Civilizations engrossed in means eliminate all moral obstructions to
their ascendancy, as "in ancient days we put out the eyes of nightingales
in order to make them sing better" (Ellul 1967:75). The information
system subtly adjusts the citizenry to accept the efficiency motif, even to
welcome it eagerly. A surfeit of data, far from permitting people to make
judgments and form opinions, actually paralyzes them.

Moral purpose is ravaged by the spirit of machineness. The self-aug-
menting process of the technological imperative is alien to moral imperatives. Thus our conundrum: Whatever we gain in transmission, we lose
in ethics. In the process of fabricating Time Warner colossi, we build a
world sanitized of ends. Efficiency and a moral commitment to cultural
diversity are a contradiction in terms.

The natural environment no longer dominates; rather, a milieu of
technological products is the contrivance in which we live. Technology
constitutes an engulfing universe; we find ourselves in it as in a cocoon.
In Ellul's framework, communications media represent the meaning-edge
of the technological system. Information media thus incarnate the prop-
erties of technical artifacts, while serving as the agent for interpreting the
meaning of the very phenomenon they embody. As the media sketch out
our world for us, organize our conversations, determine our decisions,
and influence our self-identity, they do so with a technological cadence,
massaging in our soul a mechanized rhythm and predisposition.

The conundrum is obvious, at least in its starkest terms. Global realities demand global communications. In these heady days of transition
from the Industrial Age to the Information Age, Time Warner has no
choice but to position itself for competition with AT&T, Viacom, CBS,
Gannett, Xerox, Turner Enterprises, Australia's News Corporation, Asia's
STAR-TV, Mexico's Grupo Financiero Banamex-Accival, Walt Disney,

and IBM. Global information is a social necessity for today's worldwide system where national boundaries are increasingly tenuous. But as we expand the power and speed of media transmission we are thereby undermining a normative base that is more needed now than ever. While endeavoring to form a new order of international understanding through technically efficient communications, we simultaneously build a mechanistic world where ethical principles carry little resonance. Time Warner's merger produced twelve thousand pages of sworn testimony, and social responsibility or ethics appears almost nowhere. The information empire has no clothes.

Guerilla Warfare

And wherein the revolution if information structures are being shaped by self-augmentation rather than the common good? The media giants organize themselves at will in a culture of silence, in a moral vacuum without resistance. The challenge is creating pockets of critical consciousness, a mosaic of principled pluralism, that reinvents the moral discourse of cultural diversity in a technological artifice stripped clean. Since supercharged, centralized information systems are the problem, the solution must radically redesign the technological form in which cultural life is delivered. Communication superhighways carry standardized and homogenized information; to invigorate ethnic diversity we need wellworn footpaths within subcultures and among them.

Time Warner savages the independent producer at home and indigenous popular art abroad. Solidarity with the freelancer and the native initiates a counterattack. While battling the behemoths and seeking a legislative overhaul, a strategy of empowerment is the only genuine hope of revolution. Representing ethnicity within the major media must remain an urgent political concern in multi-ethnic democratic societies; but meanwhile participation in media production, appraisal, and distribution by members of minority communities themselves have the most explosive potential (Husband 1994:1–19). Participatory models view "ordinary people as agents of change. . . . Local cultures are respected and brought to bear in the work of social change. . . . In essence, participatory development involves the strengthening of democratic processes and institutions at the community level and in this way it propels the devolving of social, economic, and even political power to the grassroots level" (Arnaldo and Servaes 1995:7; cf. Mayo and Servaes 1994). And illustrations of such revolutionary media practice can be found on every continent.

Rural newspapers in Zambia help local areas determine what kind of development they want and how it should be achieved. Papers published in metropolitan centers and shipped to the countryside are "tainted with an urbanized vision or outlook" (Kasoma 1994:405); but those following the participatory model insist that all sectors of the community originate copy themselves, aided by an editorial staff that reports on activities and polemics as they occur in everyday life. This model does not make the staff less responsible, but its "gatekeeping role is carried out with care and taste" (Kasoma 1994:410) on behalf of the locale it is meant to serve. Writing skills are developed where necessary and the print medium passes along interpersonal voices and ritual drama as effectively as possible. In their strongest versions, these newspapers are cooperatively owned by pooling resources together from as many local sources as possible. Regarding development issues, they "not only set the agenda for the community but also set the agenda for the central government" (Kasoma 1994:412). Enlightened government officials in Africa recognize "that development planning must start with the people" (412); these newspapers play a pivotal role in identifying policies that have widespread support.

In Bolivia, a barrio in the northern section of urban El Alto is the focal point of Aymara migration from the surrounding countryside. The thirty thousand people in this community live in critical poverty and put most of their energy into strategies of survival. Since women play a central role in managing subsistence resources, the Gregoria Apaza Center for the Advancement of Women (CPMGA) launched a communication project in 1984 that enables women to defend their rights against political repression, develop collaborative projects, enhance their status, and educate their community in health and safety.

The centerpiece of this effort is the radio program *La vaz de las Kantutas.* Radio is a strategic medium because it "corresponds to a strong oral tradition in Andean cultures" (Ruíz 1994:166), has played an important role in other Bolivian political movements, uses the native language, and fits everyday schedules. In developing a radio magazine, and through serious work in radio drama, women have become "active broadcasters of their own discourse" (Ruíz 1994:167) and have provided an open forum for public discussion. As a side benefit, a network of trained women reporters are now highly respected news analysts and social commentators beyond the barrio and in other media.

In Toronto, collaborative video projects funded by community organizations are an important tool for immigrants settling into a new way of life in Canada. In *Video Stories,* for example, refugee and immigrant teenagers struggle with the transition from their Caribbean homeland. Familiar with popular theater movements and with media resistance efforts in Latin America, participatory video enables them to communicate among themselves and to the broader public. Videos produced and distributed by the immigrants on their own encourage the cultural authenticity that is marginalized by the corporate and technological constraints of the traditional media. Shown in schools, community forums, churches, and occasionally on standard outlets, these videos on various themes "build a sense of community and collectivity that tries to unify without homogenizing"; they challenge "social and political agendas that segregate and separate" (Kawaja 1994:135) by enriching people's understanding of heterogeneity in the Canadian context. "The power of this type of videotape rests with its capacity to extend people's responsibility over their own lives by giving them direct access to the experiences of others like themselves. This in turn can facilitate political mobilization" (Kawaja 1994:146).[4]

Is this revolutionary praxis? Obviously there are debatable issues involved when mobilizing citizens through participatory media into a revolutionary movement. But ask Shah Mohammed Reza Pahlavi of Iran why his massive technological fortress crumbled in 1979 before video cassettes, copy machines, small group meetings, direct-dial telephones, posters, and pamphlets (Ganley 1992:13–24; Sreberny-Mohammadi and Mohammadi 1994). In June 1989, the government of the People's Republic of China brutally crushed the student-led pro-democracy movement at Tianamen Square. The government slapped restrictions on the foreign reporters in China for the Sino-Soviet Summit, and issued massive disinformation. But Chinese students within the country and abroad set the record straight by using personal electronic media—fax, personal computers (some of them tied into the academic computer network), audiotapes, instamatic cameras, and videotapes. "Occurring just ten years apart, the Iranian revolution and the student uprising bracketed a decade of collection, creation, copying, and communication of politically useful information by individuals on a scale without historical precedent" (Ganley 1992:1). When Romania exploded in mid-December 1989, and the Ceausescus were executed, video cassettes and underground VCR's formed the backbone of the information system (Ganley 1992:50–51).

Since expensive and sophisticated media are ordinarily stitched into systems of political and economic power, radical ruptures are often needed in media's technological structure before an alternative voice can be heard. Since the late 1970s, "mediated culture has become . . . central to the revolutionary process" (Sreberny-Mohammadi and Mohammadi 1994: 19). In situations where people are not allowed to assemble or demonstrate, "small media can help foster an imaginative social solidarity, often as the precursor for actual physical mobilization" (24). Nurturing cultural identity among various groups typically requires what Ivan Illich (1973) calls "tools for conviviality," and personal tools of resistance are vital resources for emancipation from authoritarian regimes.

Communitarian Ethics

But political activism at the interstices can only be sustained theoretically if an individualistic morality of rights is given up for a social ethics of the common good. The catalyst for permanent change consists of reordering media systems around communitarian ethics.[5] A commitment to cultural pluralism makes sense when the community is understood to be axiologically and ontologically prior to persons. Human beings do not disappear into the tribe or state, but their identity is constituted organically; persons depend on and live through the social realm. In the communitarian perspective, our selfhood is not fashioned out of thin air. We are born into a sociocultural universe where values, moral commitments, and existential meanings are either presumed or negotiated (Schutz 1967:chap. 2). The Aristotelian *polis* is prior to its members. Social systems precede their occupants and endure after them. Indeed, Socrates argued playfully that he could not be responsible for ruining the *polis* or free to save it because the *polis* educated him.

In communitarian ethics, morally appropriate action intends community. Unless my freedom is used to help others flourish, my own well-being is negated. Fulfillment is never achieved in isolation, but only through human bonding at the epicenter of social formation. Contrary to the eighteenth-century dualism between thinker and agent, reason and will, we know ourselves primarily as whole beings in relation. Martin Buber made the in-between inescapable, the reciprocal bond cannot be decomposed into simpler elements without destroying it. There are no singular selves split into mind and body pursuing an isolated identity across time. Humans survive and develop through interaction with others and not from isolated introspection or private experience.

A streamlined and efficient technological system flourishes without contradiction in an individualistic ethics based on merit. There are several variants of this laissez faire approach, but all of them judge on the basis of someone's conduct or achievement, rather than in terms of communal mutuality. Thus, the argument goes, those who have expended the most energy or taken the greatest risk or suffered the most pain deserve the highest reward. Though not all differences among people result from varying amounts of their own effort or accomplishment, in this view, ability to pay is considered a reasonable basis for determining who obtains the service. A prominent canon is whether consumers are at liberty to express preferences, to fulfill their desires, and to receive a fair return on their expenditures. The information structure would be unjust only to the degree that supply and demand or honest dealings are abrogated.

Such free competition among goods and services has been the historical rationale for mass media practice. Individual autonomy infects Western politics and culture to its core, including its dominant ethical and technological systems. On this model, we can better admit from the beginning that some people will always be shortchanged in a technological revolution. Companies are not charitable organizations. "Just as we have poor people today, just as we have homeless people today, just as we have jobless people today, we will have information-rich and the information poor" (Grady 1993:A13). In his book, *Multiculturalism and the Politics of Recognition,* Charles Taylor (1992:25–73) turns the issue into a conundrum for democratic politics generally. Can a democratic society treat all members as individually equal and at the same time recognize specific cultural identities as essential to someone's dignity? Must a democracy ensure the survival of particular cultural groups, and, if so, on what grounds?

As long as the mass media's individualistic orientation continues unchallenged, they are accomplishing as much as can be reasonably expected. Since the 1920s, an ethics of individual rights and personal decision-making in terms of a day-by-day orientation has controlled the press's agenda. Despite the conceptual baggage of the atomistic paradigm, a few practitioners and media outlets have risen to the occasion in some instances; but this classical liberal commitment has not yielded a comprehensive approach to the age of diversity. Because the social nature of human life has been underdeveloped in liberal theory, it "lacks the theoretical resources" to form a multicultural society. "A new philosophy framed in terms central to community must be constructed for this task" (Daly 1994:xix). We need a sophisticated ethics commensurate with today's complicated social order.

Contrary to individualistic rationalism, communitarianism represents a radical alternative. It rejects Enlightenment atomism by making the social primary and irreducible. For communitarians, political liberalism confuses an aggregate of individual pursuits with the common good. In a communitarian world view, "our social commitments and community ties . . . in a large measure constitute" us as persons (Daly 1994:xxi). Moral agents need such a context for assessing what is valuable. What is worth preserving cannot be self-determined in isolation, but ascertained only within specific social situations where human identity is nurtured. The public sphere is conceived as a mosaic of particular communities, a pluralism of ethnic identities and world views intersecting to form a social bond but each seriously held and competitive as well.

In placing community values at the heart of political theory, communitarians move them out of the private sphere of traditional liberalism. "More is lost through the eclipse of community than a sense of belonging and secure identity. Citizenship itself disappears from view" (Evans and Boyte 1992:185). Alexis de Tocqueville observed in the 1840s a sharp divide in American culture between liberty in the public sphere of business and politics, and moral values in the private sphere of family and peers. At its origin three centuries ago, liberal political philosophy found traditional communities unproblematic and saw the intellectual challenge in defining individual autonomy. Thus while coming to grips with liberty and expanding its scope conceptually and governmentally, liberal societies have tended to rely on "the public sphere of involved citizens who learned community values in their families, schools and religions" (Daly 1994:xiii). Rather than pay lip service to the social nature of the self while presuming a dualism of two orders, communitarianism interlocks liberty and communal well-being. The common good is the axis around which communities and politics become a social organism.

For linking communal values with the political ideals of freedom and equality, only democratic models of community are appropriate. Some forms of association are authoritarian and gender biased. Church communities and extended families may be hierarchical. Occupational groups or fans supporting a local baseball team are not communities in the sense that one's self-identity is derived from the whole. The Ku Klux Klan is driven by racial supremacy. Thus Carole Pateman advocates participatory democracy as the normative core of community formation. Only through participation are we obligated. In her perspective, social contract theory from John Locke to Rawls argues for voluntary consent, but actually demands acquiescence. Liberal arguments for freely created obligation obscure the nature of the political obedience involved, for otherwise "it would strip the liberal democratic state of a major portion of its ideological mantle" (Pateman 1989:70). As Rousseau understood most clearly, only participatory or self-managing democracy lives up to the liberal ideal. And likewise in community formation. "A community is composed of a limited set of people who are bound together in networks of relationships, . . . share a set of beliefs and values, . . . and demonstrate solidarity with one another" (Daly 1994:xv).[6] Civil associations of that kind are only possible through active participation in articulating the common good and mutuality in implementing it. The goal in a participatory model is interaction and involvement that achieve moral equity.

Language is the catalyst of community. Persons are displayed, made accessible, nurtured, and integrated into social units through symbol, myth, and metaphor. The meaning of words derives from an interpretive, historical context humans themselves supply. Our constitutive relations as human beings are linguistic.[7] The lingual variables that produce ethnic identity by defining outlook and lifestyle are inherently value-centered. Therefore, the goal lies in achieving moral equity in everyday affairs by winning the endorsement of the various parties involved.[8] Language from the communitarian perspective is the matrix of humanity; it is not privately nurtured and made problematic as it enters the public sphere. The social and individual dimensions of language are weaved into a unified whole. We are ransomed from John Locke's (1690: Book 3) unproductive question, "How can private and isolated minds engage one another?" Communitarian ethics takes back our language and makes it inescapably communal, the agent through which human identity is realized and the common good understood.

For the communitarian paradigm, universal human solidarity is the totalizing alternative to individual autonomy. Both terms ought to be stood on their head—universal for individual and solidarity for autonomy. The ultimate trump of all individualism is global oneness. Universalism contradicts individualism at its roots. Human beings have certain inescapable claims on one another that cannot be renounced except at the cost of their humanity. As Helmut Peukert (1981:10) concludes: "Universal solidarity is the basic principle of ethics and . . . the normative core of all human communication." Thus the staying power of UNESCO's version—the 1948 Universal Human Rights Declaration: every child, woman, and man is worthy of dignity and sacred status, without exception.[9]

But if language is the matrix of community, universal norms such as human dignity can only be recovered locally. Language situates them in history. As the examples above from Zambia to Canada demonstrate, master-norms are of the first order conceptually speaking, yet human beings enter them only through that second-order reality known as ethnicity, geography, and ideology. We distinguish between the first and second orders as with a windowpane—knowing there is a decisive break, yet both realms are transparent to each other as well. Thus a bona fide community in a normative sense must meet the human solidarity test. And the most convincing proof of a subculture's authenticity is its willingness to include toward a common citizenship those most alienated from communal oneness. A stringent condition of its own legitimacy is whether a community's institutions—schools, churches, and the press, for example—move beyond tokenism and give priority to the voiceless along the fringes. Rather than insist on individual autonomy, ethicists who concentrate on communal formations that are morally appropriate emphasize reciprocity, inclusiveness, and empowerment for all—including the restless culture groups locked outside the social mainstream and seeking a place in the civic sunshine.

Conclusion

The enemy is not mass media technology per se, but technicism, the technological imperative, the worship of machineness as sovereign god. And our task is schooling in its broadest sense—taking back the language from its technological metaphors, desacralizing the cult of efficiency, building dialogic communication models as alternatives to monologic theory, establishing participatory media conceptually, fashioning a moral consensus around universal human solidarity, reinventing power in terms of local empowerment.[10] In today's "highly mobile, nomadic, restless" world, new theorizing is needed to explode the "either-or logic of the older models" and to account for the growth of "multiple media products" and the "complexity of cultural" formation (Sreberny-Mohammadi and Mohammadi 1994:6–7).

Ethicists should start at home. We may have largely frittered away our birthright, given our penchant for miniscule ethics that fails to encompass the complicated nature of social structures as a tapestry of communities nurturing their identity by controlling their language. In an ironic twist on our commonplaces about cultural diversity, an identity politics borne along by interactive technologies is the opening shot in a revolution heard round the world. In fact, self-righteous tribalism can always overwhelm the public order; but, on balance, ethnic identity is a destructive force only when it is trivialized, stolen, or repressed. When indigeneity prospers, humans resonate cross-culturally through a species oneness grounded in human dignity. A communitarian philosophy of communication provides a rationale for democratized media in which ethnicity and citizenship are integrated. Our common moral imagination rather than electronic networks are the sinews holding the public sphere together.

Notes

1. Boucaud and Stubbs (1994:85–105) outline the current practical and conceptual conundrums in French immigration policy, given its unitarian notion of citizenship (see also Cheval 1992:165–95).

2. For a detailed critical analysis by experts inside and outside the university, see Williams and Pavlik 1994.

3. The ethical issues involved in this merger and other high-tech information systems are developed further in Christians et al. (1995:31–50, 52–55, 94–97, 216–22, 252–57).

4. Jennifer Kawaja, a Caribbean writer and video film producer in Toronto, recommends Vidéazimut, an organization in Montreal working with alternative media practitioners "from every continent" (Kawaja 1994:147–48). For nearly two decades, *Media Development* (Journal of the World Association of Christian Communication) has promoted participatory media.

5. Communitarianism is understood in this essay as a social philosophy developed by Charles Taylor, Michael Sandel, Carole Pateman, and others as an alternative to egalitarian democracy (such as Richard Rorty's version). When Amitai Etzioni uses the term for a political movement, it bears the same discontinuity with communitarian political theory as the democratic party does with the term "democracy."

6. This definition represents the legacy of *Gemeinshaft* in social theory— "close-knit communities where people live in multidimensional relations with one another" (Evans and Boyte 1992:184).

7. H. Richard Niebuhr (1963) anchors *The Responsible Self* in the "nature and role of symbolic forms" (151). By a schematic of persons accountable to one another in community, Niebuhr establishes the distinctiveness of communitarian theory and releases us from the deontological-teleological debate in ethics. Through his commitment to language as the marrow of our humanness, Niebuhr demonstrates the centrality of normative language for nurturing moral integrity within subcultures, in an age of fragmented lives and alienation within society as a whole. Following Gadamer's hermeneutics, Alejandro (1993:35) also presumes that social entities are "fundamentally and essentially linguistic." But in developing "the textual character of citizenship," Alejandro seeks to encompass both "the principle of individuality and the value

of communal pursuits" (6) instead of following Niebuhr in opting for communication.

8. This value-centered theory of communication that aims at endorsement from participants, differs conceptually from Jurgen Habermas's communicative rationality. Habermas's ideal speech conditions and universal pragmatics stand outside everyday public communications, whereas in communitarian understandings of language moral equity emerges within the lingual process itself. Obviously, to be intelligible this perspective must presume that cultural diversity does not prohibit the development of universal moral standards and that some moral claims bear truth value. (For precisely such arguments without Kantianism or divine command theory, see Paul et al. 1994, esp. pp. 1–21, 139–58.) Within the symbolic domain, humans exercise their moral imagination by maintaining boundaries between the self and our roles, moral objects and actual behavior, the intentional and inevitable (Wuthnow 1987:71–75). We establish a moral order within our cultural constructions because humans not only process information about reality, but commit themselves to a particular course of behavior (66).

9. It should be obvious that appealing to human solidarity differs in kind from modernist universals driven by reason—Kant's formal law systems and R. M. Hare's universalizability criterion, for instance. These claims to universalism presume that a foundational order can exist independently of historical contingency. In contrast, human solidarity in this essay is understood as a universal value across space, but does not claim to be an absolute over time. It seeks to embed norms in history rather than locate them transcendentally above it.

10. For an elaboration of the way communitarian ethics restructures our understanding of high-tech news reporting and large-scale media organizations, see Christians et al. 1993, chaps. 4–5.

References Cited

Alejandro, R. 1993. *Hermeneutics, Citizenship, and the Public Sphere.* Albany: State University of New York Press.

Arnaldo, C., and J. Servaes. 1995. "UNESCO-IAMCR Roundtable, Seoul 1994." *Newsletter of the International Association for Mass Communication Research,* March, pp. 7–9.

Bagdikian, B. 1990. *Media Monopoly.* 3d ed. Boston: Beacon Press.

Boucaud, P., and P. Stubbs. 1994. "Access to the Media and the Challenge to Cultural Racism in France." In *A Richer Version: The Development of Ethnic Minority Media in Western Democracies.* Ed. C. Husband. Pp. 85–105. London: John Libbey.

Calabrese, A., and J. Wasko. 1992. "All Wired Up and No Place to Go: The Search for Public Space in U.S. Cable Development." *Gazette* 49:121–51.

Cheval, J.-J. 1992. "Local Radio and Regional Languages in Southwestern France." In *Ethnic Minority Media: An International Perspective.* Ed. S. H. Riggins. Pp. 127–48. Newbury Park, Calif.: Sage.

Christians, C., M. Fackler, and K. Rotzoll. 1995. *Media Ethics: Cases and Moral Reasoning.* 4th ed. New York: Longman.

Christians, C., J. Ferré, and M. Fackler. 1993. *Good News: Social Ethics and the Press.* New York: Oxford University Press.

Colle, R. "A Radio for the Mapuches of Chile: From Popular Education to Political Awareness." 1992. In *Ethnic Minority Media: An International Perspective.* Ed. W. H. Riggins. Pp. 127–48. Newbury Park, Calif.: Sage.

Daly, M. 1994. *Communitarianism: A New Public Ethics.* Belmont, Calif.: Wadsworth.

Dennis, E. E., and E. C. Pease. 1994. "The Race of Content." *Media Studies Journal* 8(1):xi–xxiii.

Ellul, J. 1967. *Presence of the Kingdom.* New York: Seabury Press.

———. 1980. *The Technological System.* Trans. J. Neugroschel. New York: Continuum.

———. 1981. *Perspectives on Our Age.* Trans. J. Neugroschel. New York: Seabury Press.

Elmer-Dewitt, P. 1993. "Take a Trip into the Future on the Electronic Superhighway." *Time,* April 12, pp. 50–58.

Evans, S. M., and H. C. Boyte. 1992. *Free Spaces: The Sources of Democratic Change in America.* Chicago: University of Chicago Press.

Ganley, G. D. 1992. *The Exploding Political Power of Personal Media.* Norwood, N.J.: Ablex.

Grady, W. 1993. "FCC Member: Electronic Highway to Bypass Poor." *Chicago Tribune,* November 5, sec. 1, p. 13.

Heidegger, M. 1977. *The Question concerning Technology and Other Essays.* Trans. W. Lovitt. New York: Harper and Row.

Husband, C., ed. 1994. *A Richer Vision: The Development of Ethnic Minority Media in Western Democracies.* London: John Libbey.

Illich, I. 1973. *Tools for Conviviality.* New York: Harper Colophon.

Kasoma, F. P. 1994. "Participatory Newspapers as Agents of Development: A Reciprocal Agenda-Setting Model." In *Participatory Communication: Working for Change and Development.* Ed. S. A. White, K. S. Nair, and J. Ascroft. Pp. 400–419. New Delhi: Sage Publications India.

Kawaja, J. 1994. "Process Video: Self-Reference and Social Change." In *Women in Grassroots Communication: Furthering Social Change.* Ed. P. Riaño. Pp. 131–48. Thousand Oaks, Calif.: Sage.

Locke, J. 1894 [1690]. *An Essay concerning Human Understanding.* Vol. 2. Oxford: Clarendon Press.

Mayo, J., and J. Servaes, eds. 1994. *Approaches to Development Communication.* Paris: Unesco.

Moynihan, D. P. 1993. *Pandaemonium: Ethnicity in International Politics.* New York: Oxford University Press.

Mumford, L. 1970. *Myth of the Machine: The Pentagon of Power.* Vol. 2. New York: Harcourt Brace Jovanovich.

Niebuhr, H. R. 1963. *The Responsible Self.* New York: Harper and Row.

Pateman, C. 1989. *The Disorder of Women: Democracy, Feminism, and Political Theory.* Stanford: Stanford University Press.

Paul, E. F., F. Miller, and J. Paul, eds. 1994. *Cultural Pluralism and Moral Knowledge.* Cambridge: Cambridge University Press.

Peukert, H. 1981. "Universal Solidarity as Goal of Communication." *Media Development* 28(4):10–12.

Ruíz, C. 1994. "Losing Fear: Video and Radio Productions of Native Aymara Women in Bolivia." In *Women in Grassroots Communication: Furthering Social Change.* Ed. P. Riaño. Pp. 161–78. Thousand Oaks, Calif.: Sage.

Sandel, M. J. 1982. *Liberalism and the Limits of Justice.* Cambridge: Cambridge University Press.

Saporito, B. 1989. "The Inside Story of Time Warner." *Fortune,* November 20, pp. 164–85.

Schutz, A. 1967 [1932]. *The Phenomenology of the Social World.* Evanston: Northwestern University Press.

Sreberny-Mohammadi, A., and A. Mohammadi. 1994. *Small Media, Big Revolution: Communication, Culture, and the Iranian Revolution.* Minneapolis: University of Minnesota Press.

Taylor, C. 1992. *Multiculturalism and the Politics of Recognition.* Princeton: Princeton University Press.

Thiesen, C., and B. Beckwith. 1989. "Marketplace of Creative Ideas May Now Go to the Highest Bidder." *Los Angeles Times,* November 20, p. B7.

Williams, F., and J. V. Pavlik. 1994. *The People's Right to Know: Media, Democracy, and the Information Highway.* Hillsdale, N.J.: Lawrence Erlbaum.

Wuthnow, R. 1987. *Meaning and Moral Order: Explorations in Cultural Analysis.* Berkeley: University of California Press.

10   Communication in High-Risk Technologies: Global and Local Concerns

James A. Jaksa and Michael S. Pritchard

Technological developments often place people at high risk. These risks may be global (the Chernobyl nuclear disaster), international (the exportation of hazardous materials or high-risk technologies to Third World countries), or local (safety concerns in the workplace and surrounding community). These risks may be voluntarily incurred (when purchasing a mountain bike), or they may be incurred without either one's consent or knowledge (when workers are not informed about workplace risks). In this chapter we will explore ethical concerns about communication in the context of such areas of significant risk.

Unfortunately, those placed at highest risk (often the poor, minorities, or indigenous peoples in Third World countries) may have little say about whether or not they will be exposed to such risks. Further, they are often, through no fault of their own, ill-informed about the nature and consequences of risks to which they are exposed. For example, dangerous pesticides may be exported to Third World countries and used by farmers who have no knowledge of the harm the pesticides might cause to the local environment, to those who ultimately consume the products, or to those who do not handle them properly.

In recent years, within the United States we have seen a rise in *right to know* legislation intended to protect consumers and workers. However, it is obvious that technological developments in one society can also have a profound impact on the lives of those in other societies, especially in less industrialized societies, many of whom have very different cultural traditions. From a legal point of view, safety standards and regulations vary widely internationally. The United States is a particularly litigious society. It places a high premium on legally enforceable rights and responsibilities, backed with the threat of fines and punishment. Even so, it is clear that far more harms to United States citizens result from advancing technology than is desirable. Even more, these harms are rather unevenly distributed, with minorities, the poor, and the less educated bearing a disproportionately large share of the burdens of risk.

Citizens of other countries fare no better at the hands of U.S. supported industry. High-risk ventures may be undertaken by multinational corporations without careful regard for how these ventures might affect the environment or indigenous people (as illustrated by the devastation of the Amazon rainforests). Admittedly, multinational corporations are not simply U.S. operations, and ventures are undertaken with the cooperation of host governments. Nevertheless, we need to ask whether, for example, a case can really be made for exporting products that are banned or untested in the U.S. to other countries, particularly less technologically developed countries that are much less knowledgeable about the potentially harmful effects of these products. Does our acceptance of this practice imply that we believe human life in other countries is less worthy of respect and concern than in our own? Or is this simply a matter of not being willing to impose our standards on others and letting them decide for themselves? If the latter is the case, then we must ask what responsibilities we have to ensure that others' decisions are, nevertheless, well-informed about known risks. At the same time, we must ask whether the zealous pursuit of new markets shows appropriate regard for the often very different cultural beliefs, practices, and traditions of less technologically developed societies.

These are complex and troubling questions. It is tempting to turn to law for answers. However, it seems unacceptable to assume that ethical considerations are exhausted by matters of law. Ascertaining that something is legally acceptable is seldom sufficient to ascertain that it is also ethically or morally acceptable. This is so within any particular society. It seems equally so at the international level, although some might claim that, in the absence of a relevant body of international law, no ethical standards are sustainable. We disagree. One of our special concerns in this chapter will be to explore the extent to which, even in the absence of international law, ethical standards of communication can be formulated to deal with the risks to which technological developments expose us—globally, as well as nationally and locally.

We are reminded daily of the global reach of modern technology.[1] Technological developments in communication themselves play a critical role in this. Thanks to telephones, radios, televisions, satellite communication systems, computers, fax machines, and the like, we are brought in touch with events thousands of miles away at virtually the moment they are occurring. Billions of people around the globe can watch a soccer game on television—*live*. Natural disasters, warfare, industrial accidents, and political revolutions are witnessed in our living rooms.

The high technology required for the kinds of communication that we have quickly come to take for granted obviously has the potential for good and ill. Rapid, accurate communication can save lives (for example, a phone call warning a community to take cover because a tornado has been sighted a few miles away), vastly improve the efficiency and reliability of services we depend on, expedite beneficial business transactions, and so on. At the same time, communication systems driven by high technology can place us at high risk, especially when combined with other products of high technology (such as military facilities that house launch-ready nuclear weapons). If the wrong message is sent, or if a communication system itself suffers a breakdown, the consequences can be disastrous. And abuses are possible (for example, invasions of privacy by tapping telephones, unauthorized merging of confidential files, raiding of computer files, and even computer theft of money).

So communication systems that are driven by high technology can put us at serious risk, either locally or globally. But there are many other kinds of technological developments that have vital communication dimensions even though the technological developments are not themselves inherently concerned with communication. Television is a communication medium. Communication is an inherent aspect of the technology itself. In contrast, pesticides are the result of the use of high technology in biochemistry. Neither the technology nor its products have inherent communication aspects in the way television does. The same is true of nuclear power. Yet, the risks associated with the development and use of pesticides and nuclear power raise communication issues of vital importance. We will focus on some of these communication issues, too, rather than restricting ourselves to communication technology as such.

"Making a Mountain Out of a Mole Hill": A Simple Example

We begin with a fictional story, but one that raises large questions about how far one's responsibilities reach. Joe has a mole problem, but he does not want to harm the moles tunneling around his backyard. A mechanical engineer by day and a tinkerer by night, Joe devises a trap that captures moles without harming them. He then transports them to a nearby forest preserve and releases them. One day a hiker, Tom, observes Joe releasing moles. Since Tom, too, has a mole problem, he asks Joe about his traps. Impressed by Joe's traps, Tom asks Joe if he will construct a few for him. They agree on a price, and Joe builds several traps for Tom.

The traps are set in the ground and made to blend in with the surrounding environment. So, an inattentive person could quite easily step into a trap. When Joe sets his own traps, he places a marker beside each one so that he will not inadvertently step into one and injure his foot. The triggering mechanism is rather sensitive. This is no problem for moles, since they are small enough that they are entirely within the trap when the mechanism slams the trap door shut. But the feet and hands of people can easily get caught, and the force of the trap door shutting is sufficient to cause serious harm.

Should Joe warn Tom about possible injury? Should he advise Tom that markers should be placed beside the traps? Joe has made the traps, and he is in a better position than Tom to determine the risks. The potential harm is avoidable, but only if one knows the risks and how they might be minimized. A basic ethical consideration is that such knowledge is power, and that power carries responsibility with it.[2] Another basic ethical consideration is that we should not cause avoidable harm. A third is that we should prevent harm, at least when this can be done at little cost or risk to ourselves.[3] All three considerations strongly suggest that Joe ought to warn Tom. The idea of reversibility might make this apparent to Joe if he needs any coaching.[4] Suppose the roles were reversed. Would Joe expect Tom to warn him if Tom knew about the dangers?

How far does Joe's responsibility extend? Suppose he advises Tom, but he learns that Tom is ignoring the advice. He learns this from a friend who works in the emergency room of the local hospital. He reports that a child from Tom's neighborhood was treated for a broken hand from a mole trap. Now Tom comes to Joe and asks him to build another trap for him (to replace the one damaged by the child). When Joe asks Tom what he is going to do to prevent other children from being injured, Tom says, "That's not my problem. I don't have any kids. Besides kids don't have any business running through my backyard. It's up to their parents to keep them where they belong."

Or, suppose Tom comes to Joe after the accident and asks Joe to build some traps that he wants to sell to someone else. Can Joe deny all responsibility for any harms that might come to the ultimate users?

In the United States we tend to rely on the law to answer these questions for us. As a highly litigious society, we may assume that the injured have opportunities for legal remedy and that manufacturers and distributors have the good sense to avoid expensive lawsuits. However, even if legal avenues for remedy are available, only those who know about this and can afford representation are likely to benefit. Furthermore, whatever legal avenues exist now have evolved over time. (The slow development of workman's compensation law in Wisconsin, its birthplace, is a good illustration of this.) Existing regulations typically lag behind the need for constraints—at least some suffer before regulations are enacted.

To complete this fictional example, let us suppose that Joe finds out about the child with the broken hand because she is *Joe's* daughter, who was playing at a friend's home—which, unknown to Joe, is in Tom's neighborhood. No doubt Joe is now upset with Tom's indifference to the harms that might befall children. Is he also upset with himself? If so, this is the entering wedge that might awaken Joe to the responsibility he bears for the ultimate use of his traps—unless his concern is restricted to what happens to his own child. We can hope, however, that his daughter's injury will finally lead him to reflect in a more general way on the question of responsibility: His daughter could have been *any* child not wanting or deserving harm, and he could have been *any* parent concerned about his child's well being.

Unfortunately, as we shall see, our moral concerns tend not to stray far from our own neighborhood, even though it would seem that reflection on the mole trap example should lead us to more universal considerations.

"What Goes Around Comes Around": A Circle of Poison

Joe's mole trap is, by today's standards, an example of low technology. Yet, even such a simple example can raise far-reaching ethical questions. Similar questions can be raised about high technology. Dibromochloropropane (DBCP) is a pesticide whose domestic use is banned in the United States.[5] Not even a partial ban was imposed until it was learned in 1977 that several workers became sterile as a result of working with DBCP at the Occidental Chemical Plant in Lathrop, California. Evidence that DBCP might be associated with related problems surfaced in the late 1950s. But companies financing the research concerning the effects of exposure to DBCP were reluctant to share the results with their competitors. Although Dow Chemical and Shell Oil reported the results of their studies to the federal government (and allowed the joint results of their studies to be published in the *Journal of Toxicology and Applied Pharmacology*), Dow asked the government to treat the results as a trade secret that should not be shared with competing companies. Dow's rationale? "The cost of registration of pesticides has become so immense that some protection of our competitive position is essential if the pesticide industry in this country is to continue its investment in the research necessary to develop safer and more effective pesticides."[6]

Despite evidence of degeneration of the testes of rats exposed to DBCP, neither Shell nor Dow conducted sperm tests on employees between 1955 and 1977. This was considered to be a sensitive matter "because of social difficulties that people may have, because of church attitudes."[7] This raises an interesting ethical issue about communication. How could company officials know that some workers would prefer being shielded from this information rather than hear something that might offend their religious sensitivities? But even if some would, it seems unlikely that all, or even most, workers would. Here it seems that sensitivity to the "church attitudes" of some was used as a basis for shielding all workers from vital information. Even if some would prefer not to know, what justifies imposing this preference on those with different sensitivities?

Manuel Velasquez asks, simply, why the workers were not informed of the test results and given the chance to decide for themselves whether to have sperm tests.[8] A Dow spokesperson claimed that at that time blood sampling and sperm tests were not a part of "routine physical examination."[9] Why the researchers' advice that DBCP workers be kept under close observation was interpreted as calling only for routine physical examination is not explained. In any case, apparently the only warning given Dow workers at the time was: "Warning. Harmful liquid and vapor; causes skin irritation and blisters on prolonged contact; avoid breathing vapor; avoid contact with eyes, skin, and clothing; do not take internally; and use only with adequate ventilation."[10]

Hindsight tells us that it would have been better for the workers if companies producing DBCP had taken an aggressive posture in testing out the effects of DBCP in the workplace. But there is another possible line of resistance, one voiced by workers themselves. Several years ago it was reported in the *New York Times* (November 20, 1985) that a Tacoma, Washington, company received an EPA ruling that it could place an estimated two of one hundred workers at risk of eventually dying from arsenic in the workplace. Interviewed workers said they found the risk acceptable. But some said that they would prefer not knowing about the risk. Since they planned to work there anyway, why add worry to the unavoidable risk?

Essentially, this is a request by some workers that they be treated paternalistically by management. Management's responsibility, presumably, is to provide as safe a workplace as reasonably possible (consistent with the company's legitimate ends). But, from a paternalistic perspective, only management is to worry about the likelihood of two workers in one hundred being poisoned to death by arsenic. This raises an important ethical concern about communication between management and employees. A comparison with recent developments in medical practice in the United States is instructive. Physicians are now expected to treat their patients as autonomous decision-makers even in the face of bad news. Respect for persons, it is urged, requires avoiding paternalistic intervention in areas related to a patient's fundamental values. The range of "doctor knows best" has considerably shrunk. Physicians have discovered that patients typically (though not always) prefer to decide for themselves rather than have the physician decide for them. This requires being presented with bad news as well as good. Respect for autonomy requires presenting information to patients that will enable them to make informed choices. So we find that informed consent is replacing paternalism as the norm from which departures must be justified, rather than the reverse.

At the same time, patients cannot acquire the information they need on their own. They lack medical knowledge and expertise. Further, presenting patients with information is no simple matter. It must be done in ways that can be understood, both in terms of what medical problems are present and what alternative ways of addressing these problems are available (along with the likely consequences). And the information must be presented in ways that are sensitive to values and likely emotional responses of patients.[11] So, medical professionals play an essential role in finding the best ways to communicate important information to patients so that they can exercise their right to informed consent. Patient autonomy is not to be confused with simply leaving patients to their own devices.

However, suppose a patient wants to be treated paternalistically by medical professionals, at least in regard to some matters? This complicates matters. But even if paternalism-by-consent is acceptable in some circumstances in the physician/patient relationship, adopting this practice in the workplace is problematic. Withholding high risk information from those workers who do not want to know is unlikely to work unless it is withheld from all, or nearly all, workers. Once the word gets out to some, it can be expected to spread rapidly—even to those who do not want to hear it. So, again, we must ask how the desire of some for paternalistic treatment justifies withholding information from those who desire it.

The workplace analogue to informed consent in medical practice is the right to know. Even if some workers wish to waive their own right to know, they cannot do this for others. Furthermore, it would seem (especially today) that the presumption is in favor of respecting the right to know rather than the wish of some not to know. Correlative to the right to know are certain responsibilities on the part of employers to make relevant risk information available, and to do what it reasonably can to minimize those risks. Providing information itself can reduce risks. Those who know, through their medical or personal history, that they are at higher risk than others can decide whether to continue employment at the company or modify their health-related behavior both at home and in the workplace. (For example, information about risks to those working with asbestos would be very helpful to smokers, who are at much higher risk than nonsmokers.) Others can explore ways of reducing their risks in the workplace. Employers might be expected to welcome the shift of some of the responsibility to workers themselves; but this shift can be accomplished only if information is provided to them.

A particular worry about the availability of information about health risks is that it will be used in discriminatory ways against workers. For example, an employer might attempt to bar women who could become pregnant from working in areas that might adversely affect the fetus. This is apparently what prompted five women at the Willow Island plant of the American Cyanamid Corporation to subject themselves to sterilization in 1979. This, they claimed, was the only way they could avoid being shifted to lower paying jobs.[12] Aside from presenting women with dire choices in order to have jobs as high paying as men, another troubling feature of policies like American Cyanamid's is that much more research has been done on hazards to women than men. Yet, as the DBCP case illustrates, what men are exposed to could have a detrimental affect on the fetus, too.

In sharp contrast to today's emphasis on the right of workers to know workplace risks is the view of one of Johns-Manville's medical directors in 1949:[13]

> It must be remembered that although these men have the X-ray evidence of asbestosis, they are working today and definitely are not disabled from asbestosis. They have not been told of this diagnosis, for it is felt that as long as the man feels well, is happy at home and at work, and his physical condition remains good, nothing should be said. When he becomes disabled and sick, then the diagnosis should be made and the claim submitted by the Company. The fibrosis of this disease is irreversible and permanent so that eventually compensation will be paid to each of these men. But as long as the man is not disabled, it is felt that he should not be told of his condition so that he can live and work in peace and the company can benefit by his many years of experience. Should the man be told of his condition today there is a very definite possibility that he would become mentally and physically ill, simply through the knowledge that he has asbestosis.

This wait-and-see paternalism apparently prevailed until the early 1970s—a time that coincided with the establishment of the Occupational Safety and Health Administration (OSHA).[14]

Returning to DBCP, Dow and Shell got out of the DBCP business entirely when they learned of the sterilized workers. They decided that the cost of protecting workers would be too severe for the marketing of DBCP to be profitable. DBCP, like many other pesticides, had also come under criticism from the perspective of health risks to the consumer, and from a more general ecological perspective. In 1979 the EPA banned all uses of DBCP domestically except on Hawaiian pineapples because of evidence that it is carcinogenic.[15] However, the American Vanguard Corporation (Amvac) continued to export DBCP. Its 1979 10-K report states, "Notwithstanding all the publicity and notoriety surrounding DBCP it was [our] opinion that a vacuum existed in the marketplace that [we] could temporarily occupy. [We] further believed that with the addition of DBCP, sales might be sufficient to reach a profitable level."[16]

It should be noted that Amvac's exportation of DBCP was not illegal. In June 1990 the U.S. Senate Agriculture Committee supported legislation barring U.S. chemical companies from exporting pesticides that are banned in the United States.[17] This was known as the "circle of poison" amendment, as one of its major purposes was to prevent banned pesticides from returning to the United States in goods imported from countries using the pesticides. However, by October 1990 this amendment was dropped by a joint U.S. Senate and House committee.[18] The amendment was originally introduced by Senator Patrick Leahy of Vermont. He withdrew it when a proposal by Senator Richard Lugar of Indiana threatened to weaken it. Lugar's proposal was to allow the export of any chemicals registered in an Organization for Economic Cooperation and Development (OECD) country. Apparently at stake in the debate was how many U.S. jobs would be lost if Leahy's proposal were passed. In any case, both proposals failed.[19]

There are two basic arguments that might be advanced to defend the exportation of at least some banned pesticides. Both, however, need to address important communication concerns.

First, it might be argued that our standards are overly restrictive—either because the evidence is inconclusive about the actual level of risk or because we may be less willing than others to take risks in certain areas. Not everyone has the same standard of acceptable risk—which, after all, is a normative, not just a scientific, standard. What gives us the right to universalize our standard—especially given its controversial standing here?

Second, although a pesticide might be harmful or unnecessary here, it may be needed elsewhere, where climates are different, health conditions are different, and economic development is different. DDT may be harmful here, and unnecessary because we do not have a problem with malaria. Elsewhere, particularly in malaria infested countries, it may be otherwise. Other countries may want to raise their standard of living through technological development; but they may not be able to afford their workers the kind of protection provided by more affluent countries. Trade-offs must be made; and, the argument goes, we should not condemn the economic progress of other countries by employing the safety standards only affluent countries can afford.

Communication is critical to both arguments at two levels. First, even granting that our standards may not be right for other countries, the principles of respect for persons and not causing others avoidable harm do have universal application. Failing to pass on all the relevant information we have about the pesticides in question violates principles on the international level just as much as it does domestically. Taking these principles seriously at the international level may be even more vital ethically since the legal remedies available within the United States do not apply. That is, consumers in the international market are much more vulnerable to harm without recourse than U.S. citizens are.

We might not need to paternalistically protect other countries from the pesticides we produce if we provide them with the same information we use in making our decisions about their use. However, even this matter is more complicated than it might at first seem. What assurance is there that the information we pass on to officials in other countries will reach those who may need it most—the farmers and consumers? A PBS documentary, "For Export Only," raises serious doubts.[20] Several U.S. banned pesticides, including DBCP, are shown in use in Third World countries. The level of regulation portrayed is woefully inadequate. Dangerous products are shown sold over the counter without warning labels or only in the language of the exporting country, products are sold under different labels, or with no labels at all, and workers are shown spraying fields without protective clothing and liberally brushing chemicals on trees without worry about getting them on their skin. A government official in charge of overseeing the distribution of imported pesticides is asked about a U.S. banned pesticide and says he has no knowledge of its being banned in the U.S.

A chemical that can cause uncontrolled muscle contractions, liver disease, and worse is shown contaminating and diminishing the supply of fish in a lake. The fish in this lake are the main source of food and trade for a small village. The villagers themselves poured the chemical into the lake— but without any information about the risks involved. It might be objected that the high level of illiteracy in the village makes the problem unmanageable. However, effective communication does not necessarily require the written word. Later in the film, informed village leaders convey the dangers of the product to other villagers by putting on a play that graphically (and humorously) depicts what can happen to those who eat chemically fed fish. This highly imaginative way of communicating a vital message provides an instructive model for highly industrialized societies that tend to rely more on bland warnings written in small print on product labels.

Obviously, communication is necessary at a variety of levels if reasonably safe use of the pesticides is to be possible. One complicating factor is that not everyone has the same concerns in the process. Companies in foreign countries may have no more concern for the health and well-being of their workers than U.S. firms. And just as providing protection for workers costs U.S. firms money, it costs foreign firms money. Government officials may be less interested in the health and well-being of the workers and consumers of their countries than in making money themselves. In short, there is no reason to think that those in positions of authority and power are any more concerned about the welfare of others than those in the U.S. are. We have a rather long history in this country of technological developments that expose workers and consumers to unreasonable and (to them, at least) unknown risks.

Recent controversies concerning the production and marketing tactics of the tobacco industry provide little reason to believe that this history is taking a positive turn. First, there is the question of whether the tobacco industry has been fully candid with U.S. consumers about smoking risks (ranging from concerns about habituation to disease). Second, there are questions about whether the tobacco industry is targeting more exploitable U.S. populations (e.g., children, the poor, and the less educated) as more informed populations decrease their smoking.

Finally, there are questions about exploiting foreign markets. As the U.S. market is shrinking, Asian markets are increasing. A recent *New York Times* feature article describes the trends.[21] Author Philip Shenon points out that Asian cultures that have previously frowned on women smoking are rapidly changing. While U.S. tobacco companies claim that they are simply trying to compete in already established markets rather than accelerating change, Shenon casts doubt on this and closes his article with this disturbing observation:

> But some of the industry's advertising in Asia would suggest otherwise. Only about 2 percent of women in Hong Kong under the age of 40 smoke, so logic would suggest that a tobacco company interested only in encouraging smokers to switch brands would not introduce a cigarette there marketed specifically for women—it is just too small a market. Yet that is precisely what Philip Morris did in Hong Kong several years ago by introducing Virginia Slims. As in the United States, the cigarettes were sold in Hong Kong with an advertising slogan that linked smoking to the liberation of women: "You've come a long way, baby."[22]

The U.S. government is not an innocent bystander in these developments. According to Shenon, U.S. government trade negotiators worked very hard to open foreign tobacco markets. Since entering the Japanese market in 1980, U.S. cigarettes have captured 20 percent of that market. Since the mid-1980s, South Korea, Taiwan, and Thailand have opened up to the U.S. China is the latest target, with a 7 percent annual increase in adult smokers and estimated 300 million smokers consuming 1.6 trillion cigarettes a year.

What are the health implications of increased smoking in Asia? Shenon writes:

Physicians say the health implications of the tobacco boom in Asia are nothing less than terrifying, and there are frequent comparisons here to the Opium War of the mid-19th Century, when the British went to war to force the Chinese to accept imports of a dangerous addictive drug—opium, an important cash crop for British merchants.

Richard Peto, an Oxford University epidemiologist has estimated that because of increasing tobacco consumption in Asia, the annual worldwide death toll from tobacco-related illnesses will more than triple over the next two or three decades, from about 3 million a year to 10 million a year, a fifth of them in China. His calculations suggest that 50 million Chinese children alive today will eventually die from diseases linked to cigarette smoking.

"If you look at the number of deaths, the tobacco problem in Asia is going to dwarf tuberculosis, it's going to dwarf malaria and it's going to dwarf AIDS, yet it's being totally ignored," said Judith Mackay, a British physician who is a consultant to the Chinese Government in developing an anti-smoking campaign.[23]

It seems to fall to governments both to permit and at the same time develop effective campaigns against smoking. As advertising campaigns for tobacco products accelerate, what countermeasures might offer some resistance? It is clear that cigarettes themselves will not be banned (at least not in the foreseeable future). The real communication challenge is to devise effective counter-advertising. Taking a cue from the Clinton Administration's plan to supplement the costs of health care reform with cigarette taxes, perhaps foreign governments could use some of their tax revenues to support counter-advertising (perhaps supplemented by U.S. Government contributions!).

Even seemingly benign products can pose serious risks. The marketing of infant formula milk is a case in point. Properly prepared and used, infant formula does not present serious health problems (although many advise that breast feeding is preferable). However, if the formula is diluted or the water is not sterilized, the consequences are quite terrible—as is all too evident in many Third World countries.[24] Largely through the efforts of the World Health Organization (WHO) and vigorous campaigns by religious organizations and groups of citizens, the aggressive marketing tactics of infant formula producers such as Nestle have stopped. This story illustrates the dangers that even potentially health-promoting products can pose when insufficient attention is paid to the actual circumstances and needs of the ultimate consumer.

It might be replied that responsibility must stop somewhere. Indeed, it does. But will it do to say that, as long as information is provided to appropriate officials in another country, the rest is up to them—and U.S. companies bear no responsibility for what happens next? Much depends on how the information is presented. Thomas Donaldson offers an example that shows how problematic this can be.[25] He observes that in 1987 five European ships unloaded dangerous toxic waste in Nigeria. Workers in shorts unloaded the barrels for $2.50 per day and placed them in a dirt lot in residential Kiko. They were not told about the contents of the barrels (e.g., polychlorinated biphenyls and PCBs). The ships, says Donaldson, unloaded under an import permit for "non-explosive, non-radiative and non-self-combusting chemicals." Technically, the poisonous chemicals satisfied these criteria, but the Nigerian government neither knew it was accepting, nor intended to accept, toxic wastes; and it demanded the removal of the barrels. Donaldson draws an important conclusion about responsibility for communication: "This example reveals the difficulty many developing countries have in formulating the sophisticated language and regulatory procedures necessary to control high-technology hazards. It seems reasonable in such instances, then, to place the responsibility not upon a single class of agents, but upon a broad collection of them, including governments, corporate executives, host country companies and officials, and international organizations."[26] Donaldson's point is that responsibility for respecting the rights of Nigerians is shared by all whose actions might contribute to harming them.

Further, responsibility does not necessarily end when clearly stated and understood information is passed on to the next level. To conclude that it does would imply that Joe has no further responsibility once he informs Tom about the dangers of his mole trap—even when he learns that Tom is not concerned about others being harmed by the traps. Responsibility is not simply transferred to the next party in cases like this. What must be rejected is a zero-sum view of responsibility.

Tom does have a responsibility to alert others to the dangers of his mole traps. But Joe may also have some responsibility should he learn that Tom is not meeting his.

Unfortunately, moral lessons are often learned only the hard way. Joe may see things differently when it is his daughter who is harmed. The "circle of poison" debate pivots around the discovering of significant traces of the pesticides we have banned on foods we import from the countries to whom we export those pesticides. What goes around comes around. However, depending on this for our moral lessons has two serious shortcomings. First, it may take a very long time for things to come around—and we often settle for short-run gains, especially when the long-run harms take a long time to surface. (Asbestosis may take twenty or more years to show up.) Also, the senders may be long gone by the time their descendants are presented with the returns. So there is a strong temptation to believe that things will not come around again; and perhaps not everything does—thus leaving everything in the laps of the victims.

The second shortcoming is that relying on the maxim "What goes around comes around" avoids the fundamental moral reason for being concerned about the harms we cause others. The victims, particularly those in Third World countries, typically are defenseless, though not inherently so. They are defenseless because they are poor, unrepresented, and technologically unsophisticated. Henry Shue observes:

> Where technically sophisticated firms are hiring technically unsophisticated—often, in fact, illiterate—workers, the inequality of power to be overcome is considerable. It is absurd to act as if an unschooled peasant who fails to reinvent biochemistry deserves whatever befalls him or her. Such a fight is extremely unfair. It is no insult to an intelligent former peasant to think that he or she will sometimes be outsmarted by someone backed by a research department filled with scientists who have enjoyed twenty years more education than the new recruit in the labor force.[27]

However, Shue adds, "given minimal information, they (the workers) can often be counted upon to defend themselves vigorously."[28] The same, it would seem, can be said of consumers in other countries.

But, *why,* one might ask, should one be concerned about defenseless human beings? Shue answers: "Because they are human beings and they are defenseless." That is, Shue grounds our responsibility in the humanity and vulnerability of others—not in the worry that what goes around comes around. Respect for the dignity and autonomy of others, and concern not to bear responsibility for causing or not preventing avoidable harm to others are Shue's ground-level appeals—not self-interest. We should not have to eat our own poison in order to see why we should not send it to others in the first place.

Mechanisms for Change

In the U.S. we typically resort to government and the legal system to force change. To some extent this reflects prior failure at the level of moral appeal—if people will not avoid harming others and violating their rights on their own, a coercive mechanism may be necessary. To some extent reliance on government and law reflects a recognition that some problems require institutionalized, collective action. There is no governmental or legal mechanism comparable at the international level. Still, there are international bodies and organizations that have some effect.[29] The United Nations's Declaration of Human Rights provides a framework for addressing moral problems at the international level. The World Health Organization has effectively intervened in many instances, as have various international religious organizations.

The magnitude of some of the problems we are now facing may eventually do much to bring about global cooperation. Concerns about global warming, damage to the ozone layer, the destruction of rain forests, and other ecological matters are not merely local. Technological developments in regard to nuclear energy raise urgent concerns as well. As the 1986 Chernobyl nuclear facility accident has graphically illustrated, these concerns are not confined to the threat of nuclear weapons. Nuclear power facilities intended entirely for peaceful purposes put all of us at serious risk should accidents occur. The Soviet handling of the Chernobyl accident was widely criticized.[30] But as critical questions were raised about safety standards and procedures at facilities around the world, the answers were not comforting. Although efforts to address these concerns were quickly undertaken, clearly the work has just begun.

What can we expect at the level of corporate behavior? Richard De-George comments:

> Ideally, there should be international agreements on minimally acceptable standards of safety in industry. In the absence of such standards moral sense and pressure must function until law can equalize the position of the workers vis-a-vis the employer. But moral sense and pressure seem to play little role in the policies of many international corporations. . . . But American companies who are operating abroad and wish to be moral should not ignore the moral dimensions of these actions; they should not simply follow the letter of the law in the countries in which they operate. . . .
>
> If moral restraints are ineffective, then the restraints on such activity must be international restraints. The abuses of multinationals underscore the need for effective international controls—controls, however, which the present international climate has not strongly fostered.[31]

So, it is probably too optimistic to think that most corporations will comply with reasonable standards of international morality without some external pressure. If we wait for what goes around to come around to corporate leaders and management, we will likely miss many opportunities to minimize harms. So we should be actively looking for constructive ways of addressing these problems earlier rather than later.

Evidence that U.S. courts may be willing to provide assistance is found in the 1990 Texas Supreme Court decision in *Dow Chemical Company and Shell Oil Company, v. Domingo Castro Alfaro et al.*[32] In this case the Texas Supreme court upheld the right of more than eighty Costa Rican workers to sue Dow and Shell for injuries alleged to have resulted from exposure to DBCP after its use in the U.S. was banned. In his concurring opinion, Judge Doggett said:

> The dissenters are insistent that a jury of Texans be denied the opportunity to evaluate the conduct of a Texas corporation concerning decisions it made in Texas because the only ones allegedly hurt are foreigners. Fortunately Texans are not so provincial and narrow-minded as these dissenters presume. Our citizenry recognizes that a wrong does not fade away because its immediate consequences are first felt far away rather than close to home. Never have we been required to forfeit our membership in the human race in order to maintain our proud heritage as citizens of Texas.[33]

It is encouraging to hear such a statement from a state supreme court justice, and it is encouraging to see that there is some hope that those in foreign lands may have some recourse in our legal system. But it should be noted that the legal process in the United States is painfully slow. Further, this 1990 case only establishes the right to sue (in Texas). It does not guarantee that the complainants will be successful. Nor does it prevent such harms from occurring in the first place. Rather than depend on the court system, it can only be hoped that sooner rather than later the attitude of Judge Doggett will become forcefully present in corporate boardrooms.

Concluding Remarks

As we have seen, technological developments can put people at high risk at local, national, international, or even global levels. These risks can be incurred either voluntarily or without knowledge or consent. Those at highest risk, typically the poor or those in less technologically developed nations, have little say about their willingness to be exposed to these risks. There are some legal protections in more technologically advanced nations such as the United States. But these protections, although helpful, are inadequate. Corporate responsibility beyond what is required by law is needed.

We have provided examples of U.S. and multinational corporations undertaking ventures without careful regard for adverse affects on people and the environment. Ethical standards of responsible and effective communication need to be formulated and observed so that risks are known and understood by those who might be exposed to them. Wherever possible, informed choice should replace the practices of paternalism and withholding relevant information.

Mechanisms for change must be supported by governments, host country corporations and their executives and officials, multinational corporations, and international organizations. Given the high risks posed by our increasingly technological world, it is morally imperative that all parties play a proactive rather than merely reactive role in dealing with these problems.

Notes

1. The next two paragraphs are drawn from J. A. Jaksa and M. S. Pritchard, "Introduction," in *Responsible Communication: Ethical Issues in Business, Industry, and the Professions,* ed. J. A. Jaksa and M. S. Pritchard, p. 6 (Cresskill, N.J.: Hampton Press, 1996).

2. For a detailed discussion of the idea that knowledge implies responsibility, see J. G. Simon, C. W. Powers, and J. P. Gunnemann, "The Responsibilities of Corporations and Their Owners," in *Ethical Theory and Business,* 4th ed., ed. T. L. Beauchamp and N. E. Bowie, pp. 60–65 (Englewood Cliffs, N.J.: Prentice Hall, 1993). They even hold that ignorance may not excuse, citing Albert Speer's statement about his responsibilities in Nazi Germany: "For being in a position to know and nevertheless shunning knowledge creates direct responsibility for the consequences—from the very beginning" (A. Speer, *Inside the Third Reich* [New York: Macmillan, 1970], p. 19).

3. Again, this is discussed in some detail by Simon, Powers, and Gunneman, "The Responsibilities of Corporations." See also K. Alpern, "Moral Responsibility for Engineers," in *Ethical Issues in Engineering,* ed. D. Johnson, pp. 187–95 (Englewood Cliffs, N.J.: Prentice Hall, 1991); and C. E. Harris Jr., M. S. Pritchard, and M. J. Rabins, *Engineering Ethics: Concepts and Cases* (Belmont, Calif.: Wadsworth, 1994), chap. 3.

4. We discuss the idea of reversibility in more detail in J. A. Jaksa and M. S. Pritchard, *Communication Ethics: Methods of Analysis* (Belmont, Calif.: Wadsworth, 1994), p. 101.

5. The information on DBCP we discuss here is drawn from M. Velasquez, *Business Ethics* (Englewood Cliffs, N.J.: Prentice-Hall, 1992), pp. 421–25. For a more extended discussion of the history of DBCP, see C. Trost, *Elements of Risk* (New York: Times Books, 1984).

6. Statement of a Dow representative, quoted in U.S. Congress, Senate, *Worker Safety in Pesticide Production: Hearings before the Subcommittee on Agricultural Research and General Legislation of the Committee on Agriculture, Nutrition, and Forestry,* 95th Cong., 1st sess., December 13–14, 1977, p. 28.

7. Ibid., p. 24.

8. Velasquez, *Business Ethics,* p. 423.

9. *Worker Safety in Pesticide Production,* p. 26.

10. Ibid., p. 120.

11. One of the authors recently underwent (successful) surgery. Just prior to being administered an anesthetic that would render him unconscious, he was informed of possible risks from the anesthetic. The first piece of information offered was, "You could die." Forcing a smile, the author replied, "What are the odds?" "I don't know. I'm not very good with numbers." Obviously there is an art to providing patients with information that will help them make reasonable decisions!

12. For a discussion of this, as well as other troubling cases of women faced with the loss of jobs because of reproductive hazards, see R. Bayer, "Women, Work, and Reproductive Hazards," *Hastings Center Report,* October 1982, pp. 14–20.

13. H. Shue, "Exporting Hazards," in *Boundaries: National Autonomy and Its Limits,* ed. P. Brown and H. Shue, p. 134 (Totowa, N.J.: Rowman and Littlefield, 1981). Shue is citing the medical director's comments at an October 1978 hearing of the Subcommittee on Compensation, Health, and Safety of the House Committee on Education and Welfare, in San Francisco.

14. More recently, this kind of paternalism could commonly be found in medical practice in the former Soviet Union. See, for example, J. A. Jaksa and M. S. Pritchard, "Chernobyl Revisited," in *Responsible Communication,* ed. Jaksa and Pritchard, pp. 215–28.

15. K. Goodpaster, *Ethics in Management.* (Boston: Harvard Business School, 1984), p. 123.

16. Ibid.

17. *New York Times,* June 7, 1990, p. A-9.

18. "Congress Takes 'Poison' Out of Farm Bill," *Chemical Week,* October 24, 1990, p. 9.

19. As of this writing, the Clinton administration is proposing that the export of pesticides not approved in the U.S. be banned, unless the pesticides have been approved for use, or residues on food are permitted, in at least three countries with credible regulatory programs. See "Clinton Administration Unveils Tighter Pesticide Export Rule," *Chemical Marketing Reporter*

245, no. 5 (January 31, 1994):7. This proposal is opposed from two sides. Jay J. Vroom, president of National Agricultural Chemicals Association (NACA) holds that current laws are sufficient and that NACA has taken strong steps to improve the safety of its members' products. Greenpeace spokesperson Sandra Marquardt objects that the proposal does not go far enough. She claims that "it does next to nothing to curb exports of toxic pesticides." She adds, "Since when did the U.S. start relying on the registration programs of other countries?" (ibid., p. 19).

20. Portions of this program are available in segment 9 of *Ethics in Management,* Harvard Business School's videotape series.

21. P. Shenon, "Asia's Having One Huge Nicotine Fit," *New York Times,* May 15, 1994, sec. 4, pp. 1, 16.

22. Ibid., p. 16.

23. Ibid.

24. For detailed discussions of the ethical issues surrounding the exporting of infant formula, see Velasquez, *Business Ethics,* pp. 304–12.

25. T. Donaldson, "Fundamental Rights and Multinational Duties," in *Ethical Theory and Business,* ed. Beauchamp and Bowie, pp. 532–33.

26. Ibid.

27. Shue, "Exporting Hazards," p. 134.

28. Ibid.

29. For helpful materials on this see T. Cooper, ed., *Communication Ethics and Global Change* (White Plains, N.Y.: Longmans, 1989).

30. See Jaksa and Pritchard, "Chernobyl Revisited."

31. R. DeGeorge, *Business Ethics,* 2d ed. (New York: MacMillan, 1986), pp. 370, 372.

32. 786 S.W. 2d 674 (Tex. 1990). Concurring opinion by Judge Doggett is reprinted in *Ethical Theory and Business,* ed. Beauchamp and Bowie, pp. 576–81.

33. Ibid., p. 576.

11   Gendered Ethics on the Internet

Jana Kramer and Cheris Kramarae

The Internet is a medium said by many to be the solution to our social and educational problems, including racism and sexism. In the words of many reviewers, the Internet is presented as *the* most important, rapidly developing education tool in the world, eventually bringing information, knowledge, and equality to all, or almost all, people. These ethereal claims for the new electronic communication practices are not, however, concretely realized. We focus on what system of communication ethics might help critically improve the situation for girls and women on the Internet.

Women and girls should have integral roles "in the conception, design, content, use, implementation, economics, and legal polities of electronic communication networks on a local, national, and international level" (Women, Information Technology, and Scholarship 1995). We wish that others talking and writing on the Internet would make as explicit their ideas about girls' and women's involvement. While we do not review and propose actual, possible, and desirable Internet ethics for girls and women throughout the world, we do present and critique some principles of Internet ethics and ideology, and invite further discussion. We consider four popular themes used in conceptualizing the Internet in the United States. Our analysis of these themes indicates that myths and stereotypes form the basis of the developing ethics systems and imperatives for the Internet. What is needed is an open acknowledgment of the very important issues involving gender, ethics, and the future of the Internet.

We look at four ideological themes, and their conflicting values, that have dominated the early days of the Internet— anarchy, frontier, community, and democracy—and at the ways they have shaped the beliefs, ideology, and ethics of the Internet.[1] We consider the four models (all of which validate the dominant social structures), the place of women in the models, and the four corresponding systems of ethics. We contrast the latter with discussions of feminist ethics and aspects of moral experience that have been largely ignored by ethics theorists and by cyberspace practitioners.

Ethics and the Internet

A code of ethics is developed through experience, and therefore requires time to acquire and cultivate. For example, the ethical principles of a young child are quite different from those of an adult. Ethical principles are also contextual—what is ethical in one situation is not necessarily ethical in a different situation. It makes sense, then, that the Internet, which in essence constitutes a new form of communications, may have an ethical code that is not only different from previous communications ethics but is also not yet fully formed. For the Internet, as with other new technologies, "there is often a lack of cultural norms to guide people in ethical and appropriate ways of using a new medium of communication, and there is a corresponding need for consensus on a code of ethics for networkers" (Hiltz and Turoff 1993:504). But the lack of cultural norms specific to the Internet does not mean that a new communications medium is neutral. At the very least, general societal norms are imported into the medium by its users.

While there is a lot of discussion about the Internet being a new medium with lots of freedom for everyone to do their own thing, we all know that there have already been many Internet norms established, and without much involvement from women. Norms are those standards and "guidelines that shape human behavior in social situations[,] . . . subject to change[, but] . . . enforced stringently by the members of the social group" (Newby 1993:30). We would modify this by stating that norms are tailored and enforced by some people for some people; that is, not all members of "the social group" are equal makers and enforcers of norms. Now there are, for example, norms established primarily by teenage boys about how to write messages on the Internet. We can still *imagine* widespread discussions about what local and global electronic talk might be, about how individualism might be best expressed, about how community practices might best be represented—or even about how conversational dance might best be expressed. But that possible time of dreams and discussion about what signals we might wish to use seems to have passed. Even the Interactive Chat Relays seem fairly set in their ways. As Brenda Laurel says, we have now "a technology that is deeply gendered male as it currently exists" (quoted in *geekgirl*, 1995, issue 2, 12).

One critic, writing about the Internet, cautions: "many of the trends point toward a future that is far from ideal. . . . The Internet in its mature form conforms much more closely to the restrictions and norms of the dominant non-CMC [computer-mediated communication] society; therefore, it often solidifies preexisting boundaries. The Internet is not a panacea for creating ready communication channels among people for whom social barriers prevent access to communication media and information in general" (Newby 1993:30–31).

Unfortunately, the ethics of Internet *communication* is not the main focus of most people and groups writing about ethics and the Internet. Instead, they focus on such issues as an ethical code for computing professionals (regarding, for example, the duty to the client) and property issues (such as copyright protection). Ethical issues in communications are considered dealt with in "netiquette" guidelines. The term "netiquette," however, sounds more frivolous than "ethics," even though some of the netiquette rules approach what could be called ethical rules. For example, the Introduction to Florida Atlantic University's "The Net: User Guidelines and Netiquette" begins with the statement that "it is essential for each user on the network to recognize his/her responsibility in having access to vast services, sites, systems and people." However, the actual rules themselves seem a bit too simplistic to be considered ethical rules (e.g., "Keep paragraphs and messages short and to the point"). *Behind* the rules, however, one can perceive the ethical guidelines: responsibility to the Internet system, responsibility to other users of the Internet system, and responsibility to the larger context—general society with all its rules.

The fact remains, however, that the ethical rules lurking behind netiquette guidelines are not explicit. They also do not address the ethical systems of the four metaphors considered in this chapter. Rather, they merely emphasize personal responsibility and lawful behavior—without taking into account the different setting of the Internet, and the mythology and expectations that surround it. The name "netiquette" itself may weaken the impact of the communication guidelines, as users feel that etiquette is unimportant; after all, Miss Manners and finishing schools are generally not considered to be influential sources for shaping society.

Most written university or commercial policies on acceptable use and behavior on the Internet focus more on the commercial and legal values of intellectual property, privacy, security, and efficient use of resources than on the more human issue of communication. For example, the Internet Activities Board (now the Internet Architecture Board, or IAB, whose responsibilities include advice on Internet policy matters) failed to even mention, in its 1989 statement of policy concerning the proper use of the resources of the Internet, that harassment and personal attacks are unacceptable. The Computer Ethics Institute, which published "The Ten Commandments of Computer Ethics," similarly failed to discuss these communication issues. Universities generally do condemn harassing, obscene, or offensive messages, but often list this particular unacceptable behavior only after first discussing privacy concerns, intellectual property concerns, and prohibitions on using the e-mail capabilities to write to friends at other universities for nonacademic reasons.

Themes on the Internet

While the Internet is a new medium, out of necessity people talk about it mostly in terms related to what they know. Formulaic features associated with the old appear in the discussions of the wonders of the new.

Four themes prevalent in United States discussions of activities on the Internet are those using the terminology of anarchy, the frontier, democracy, and community. These four are not, of course, the only themes that have been used in discussing rights and responsibilities on the Internet. For example, other analysts have suggested the "superhighway" as a *functional* metaphor, and the print shop, broadcasting, the corner soapbox, and bookshops as *legal* metaphors for the Internet. (For example, Henry Perritt Jr. [1992], a law professor, has evaluated some of these metaphors for their use in legal decisions.) However, the four themes we discuss are those found most frequently in popular literature dealing with social settings on the Internet—and therefore with communication.

The four themes are not exclusive. For example, anarchy and frontier are often mentioned in the same cyberspace discussion as being closely related. (This is true as well in twentieth-century histories of the United States [Namias 1993:15].) We discuss these themes separately for purposes of clarity.

Anarchy

This social philosophy has a history of several hundred years and has meant different things in different times in Europe and the United States. Very generally, contemporary anarchists reject authoritarian government and accept only voluntary institutions. Anarchism aims at the utmost possible freedom compatible with social life. The term is sometimes used to define one who denies all law and promotes chaos by deliberately working outside politicam–practice. It has at times been used to define people who act for themselves in order to end social inequality. It has also been used to name a social disorder, a "male-inspired, competitive, acquisitive ethos," and "competitive opportunism" (Griswold 1988:22).

Timothy Leary, in an article on cyberpunks, writes about the people who pilot their own lives, mavericks who combine "bravery with high curiosity and super self-esteem" (Leary 1991:7). He writes that they have often been called "mavericks, roamers, free-lancers, kooks, visionaries, iconoclasts, insurgents . . . disloyal dissidents, traitors or worse" (7). They are the heroic, stubborn, creative, usually unauthorized, resourceful, and skillful individuals who access and steer "knowledge—communication technology" toward their own private goals. They do this, Leary writes, for "personal pleasure, profit, principal or growth"; they are, he suggests, the good people in the Cybernetic Society of the 21st Century (7).

Ethics of Anarchy

Hackers (a term associated with breaking security) are perhaps the best known anarchists on the Internet. Richard Stallman says that when he was at the MIT Artificial Intelligence Lab, the hacker's ethic was: "Rules did not matter—results matter. Rules, in the form of computer security or locks on doors, were held in total, absolute disrespect. We would be proud of how quickly we would sweep away whatever little piece of bureaucracy was getting in the way" (Stallman 1992:132). Steven Levy, in his 1984 book *Hackers: Heroes of the Computer Revolution,* included six tenets in his hacker ethic: "1) Access to computers should be unlimited and total. 2) All information should be free. 3) Mistrust authority—promote decentralization. 4) Hackers should be judged by their hacking, not bogus criteria such as degrees, age, race, or position. 5) You can create art and beauty on a computer. 6) Computers can change your life for the better" (cited in "Hackers" 1992:132). The computer game journals for teenage boys that carry ads and editorial material promoting video games also carry information on, for example, how to explode the plumbing system in schools and how to make a fake ID (*Flux* 1995[1]:1). Yet they also sometimes carry rules of arcade etiquette. As Jeff Yang states in "Laws of the Jungle," while many think of these "dens of electronic iniquity as lawless, dangerous places," the arcade "does have rules" such as "Thou shalt not abuse the machines" (Yang 1995:28, 30).

Women in Anarchy

In some discussions, men's anarchy appears to have use for women only to the extent that women are useful to men. (For example, women in the anarchist journal *Mondo 2000* appear more often as bodies than as minds.) However, some women also have an interest in anarchy. Kathy Acker talks of the value of living in such a large society that "anarchists go unnoticed. . . . A huge organization like AOL (America Online) with 200,000 [*sic*] members simply can not be controlled, even if they do throw a few people off" (quoted in Cross 1995:5).

Certainly there are many women on the Internet interested in playfully and seriously defying conventions and proprieties according to their own terms, interests, and pleasures. They are, however, more likely to be called "bad girls" than "anarchists." And even these "bad girls" often work collaboratively, as, for example, in the publishing of the "M@gic," and "M@yhem" of *geekgirl,* an outrageous journal by, about, and for witches on the Internet. The journal contains a "newbie" page to help Internet newcomers. Girls and witches, after all, are trained to prefer collaborative to individual work.

Frontier

The conquering of "unsettled" and "unknown" areas is, of course, a recurring theme in U.S. history. (Euro-Americans, like other "settlers," have called "unknown" and "unsettled" the lands they don't know and don't yet control.) While many women and men "pioneers" of many backgrounds were involved in the acquiring of "distant" territories, the prevailing story is that the frontier was conquered by strong white male heroes. They were the ones to go through hardships in order to "investigate the unknown, assert control over it, and appropriate its resources" (Stoeltje 1987:239). The frontier is the promise of new beginnings. It is male, adventure, boldness, daring, restless energy, independence, rough, violence, strength, heroic exploits, and danger. It is not female, intimacy, caring, vulnerability, meaning in daily customs, or artistic.

The wilderness and excitement of the archetypal West lives again—
in cyberspace. For example, William Gibson's influential novel *Neuro-*
mancer presented the protagonist, Case: "At twenty-two, he'd been a
cowboy, a rustler, one of the best in the Sprawl." Case is one of many
virile men in cyberspace who demand new design and a new morality
for their communication. Frank Connolly, associate professor of Information Systems at the American University, writes: "Cyberspace, the electronic frontier, is the realization of the American fantasy—the ultimate
in freedom and rugged individualism" (Connolly 1995:86). The western frontier metaphor is increasingly associated with the space frontier
as well (*Flux* calls one of the computer game genres "the adventure/space
shoot-'em-up" [East and Kitts 1995:5, 29]). For the past decade the frontier has been a primary model in men's discussions of the Internet. This
model has had important implications for the notion of ethics on the
Internet.

Ethics of the Frontier

Briefly, being ethical in this model means using one's own judgment and
accepting sole responsibility for decisions and actions. There are few laws
in this system, great flexibility and power, and a great deal of freedom.

The reviews of ethical approaches in Virginia Held's *Feminist Morality*
(1993) are especially useful. She points out, for example, how the conception of freedom as the absence of interference works better for many men
than for women who, in law and custom, have not been thought as able
to fend for themselves and have usually been considered as dependents
whose needs were provided by heads of households (162–63).

Women in the Frontier

While the popular image of the frontier is masculine and white, in
truth there were, for example, black cowboys, and many women "who
planted rose gardens from slips carefully transported across the prairie,"
and many women who branded cattle (Matsuda 1985:52). Black wom-
en were on all of the frontiers in what we now call the United States.
Native American women were of course very present in what writers call
the frontier. But historians have given us very partial, contradictory, and
stereotypical accounts of frontier women. We have the Madonnas of the
Prairies (as Spanish frontierswomen are often portrayed when they are
not described as seductive senoritas), the Brave Pioneer Mothers, the
Gentle Tamers, the Calamity Janes, and the Prostitutes. The women who
moved westward are now usually represented as negative, romanticized

stereotypes rather than women with real lives and multidimensional characters who helped to establish new societies (Myres 1982:3, 4).

Historians have noted the sexual subplots of frontier stories. We note the same "subplots" in the "art work" in many of the "frontier" computer/virtual reality journals. Look, for example, at issues of *Project X, Mondo 2000, Wired, Amiga Power, SW* (Shareware Magazine), *New Media, Virtual Reality World,* or whatever the most "path-breaking" journals are when you read this. There are relatively few women in the photos or drawings for articles or ads in these publications, and when women do appear they are usually presented as passive, sexy bodies rather than active, brainy bodies.

Democracy

The democracy model, along with the frontier and anarchy model, is overwhelmingly concerned with the individuals who are participating, rather than with the social whole. In cyberspace all are supposed to be equal—the essence of a democracy. Everyone has a "voice," but without visual or aural cues. Each person, in theory, is judged on the basis of opinions alone. In reality, however, the virtual persona is judged with whatever cues are available, just as the real person is judged in the real world. Those with obviously female sign-ons are given less credibility. The Internet is a true democracy only when all users are thought to be male.

Part of the "democratic" lure of computers, and of the Internet, comes from the fact that almost every person, conceivably, can own or get to use a computer that allows for publication via the Internet, unlike (for example) a print publisher or a television station. The debate over whether computers were democratizing or centralizing was going on ten years ago. Deborah Johnson noted at that time that "there are social and political forces in our society which tend to favor centralization of power" and that, therefore, computers would probably be used to centralize power (Johnson 1985:75). There is no doubt that computers have "democratization" advantages. But, as others have noted, "the question is who benefits most from computers in society?" (Mander 1991:68).

No one has claimed that cyberspace will lead to a new kind of democracy, just that it will somehow enable our democracy to be more democratic. And, as everyone knows, there are problems with our "real" democracy. Computer democracy leads to a democracy in which the wealthy and highly educated participate—those whom the system already serves. The poor cannot afford computers or Internet access and the uneducated do not have the necessary tools or skills.

Democratic Ethics

One person, one vote, is the rallying cry of democratic ethics. A democracy is the sum—and just the sum—of individuals. That is, in a traditional or true democracy where individuals vote in their own best interests and there are no checks on the power of the majority, the minorities are left out in the cold in protecting their interests. After all, if it were not for the protection of the United States Constitution (and state constitutions), women and minority men would be left even farther outside the democratic political process than they are now.

The ethic of liberal democracy, as a political theory, is that of freedom—freedom from interference (Held 1993:162). However, freedom from interference does surprisingly little good without the basic necessities of life: decent employment, clothing, medical care, and affordable housing. With this perspective, it is clear that the liberal democratic ethic supports those who are currently favored by existing social arrangements. The under-represented of the Internet will not be protected with the liberal democratic ethic. In discussing the democratic ideal of the Internet, there is no mention made of a corresponding constitutional protection of minorities.

Interestingly, a group called the Electronic Frontier Foundation (EFF), whose name implies that it would be most concerned with the "frontier" values of independence and "freedom," has issued a paper explicitly concerned with the democratic potential of the Internet and what is required to realize that potential. EFF has specifically recognized that in developing the potential for economic growth through the Internet "we must also be guided by core communications policy values." Key goals must include diversity of information sources, universal service, free speech, and common carriage. This new technology has given or can give individuals and small organizations "a degree of control over information that has never before been possible. However, if not implemented with core communications values in mind, the technology will do more harm than good" (EFF 1993:sec. 1). For example, the government has guaranteed universal service of the telephone network since 1934. EFF argues that we, as a society, must extend this guarantee to digital service. "Equity and the democratic imperative also demand that these services meet the needs of people with disabilities, the elderly, and other groups with special needs. Failure to do so is sure to create a society of 'information haves and have nots.'"

Similarly, the purpose of the April 1995 "Speak Truth to Power" call for an establishment of "The Cyberspace Society" (by Vigdor Schreibman, W. Curtiss Priest, and Richard K. Moor) was "to join together such people of good will, people who are concerned with the survival of humanity and the enrichment of the quality of life, and who agree that a genuine democratic process is the surest hope for a just and prosperous future" (CYBER-RIGHTS listserv, digest 12). The Cyberspace Ethic states that "The new institution should educate citizens of Cyberspace, pursuant to an enlightened democratic ethic for the future of the Information Age." The specifics of the ethical practices are left general; they can come from the "body of knowledge and experience that has been applied successfully in a large variety of academic and real-world situations." The goals include freedom of expression, privacy, security and copyright protection, equal access, and affordable service (CYBER-RIGHTS listserv, digest 12).

Women in Democracies

As in any democracy, the majority rules. This is of great concern where the Internet users are overwhelmingly—some estimate as much as 90 percent—male. It is difficult enough to have women heard and respected when they are half the population; what kind of hope for gender equality is there in the face of the odds on the Internet?

The central ethical value of democracy is "all people are created equal," or "one person, one vote." We may question whether this value works between women and men. It is unsurprising to note that men and women have different styles of communication, and that those styles of communicating are detectable through the screen of the virtual persona's assumed gender: "The existence of gendered styles has important implications, needless to say, for the claim that CMC is anonymous, 'gender-blind,' and hence inherently democratic. If our online communicative style reveals our gender, then gender differences, along with their social consequences, are likely to persist on computer-mediated networks" (Herring 1993:4).

It should be noted that the Internet *is* being used as a democratizing force. One new group, called the "Women's Leadership Network," plans to use the Internet to mobilize—or at least inform—women about upcoming legislative action. The organizers were "struck by the diversity of those responding" ("Women's Leadership Network" 1995). Although this will probably not affect cyberspace *as* a democracy, it does demonstrate the use and the possibility of the Internet as a democratizing *influence.*

But the fact that women can organize on the Internet does not take away from the criticism of the democratic model of the Internet that the unchecked majority rule will almost necessarily exclude women's interests.

Community

Many of those extolling the virtues of the Internet c d cyberspace discuss its potential for community. "Community," of course, has many different definitions, but in general it can be described as a group of people with emotional ties and shared experiences—people who support each other.

It is possible to have some community on-line—people with similar tastes and interests, and people who share experiences through the Internet (Rheingold 1995). But, as one writer notes, there is no "shared adversity" in cyberspace (Barlow 1995:55). Unlike a physical community in which one must tolerate (to one degree or another) *everyone* present, despite all their quirks, foibles, and irritating habits or ideas, on the Internet it is possible to associate exclusively with those just like yourself. A community without diversity is not a community; it's a club.

Finally, it is a poor community that knowingly allows whole segments of our real world to be excluded from the Internet. Poor people, illiterate people—those without easy access to computers and the written word are severely under-represented on the Internet. Most of sub–Saharan Africa, too, is not just invisible but absent on the Internet (Barlow 1995:54–55; Ohajah 1995).

Community Ethics

A true ethic of Internet community would include the charitable ethic—reaching out to help others, those not present, as well as those who are. This sense of concern for the welfare of the less advantaged on the Internet is not a part of cyberspace society. There is too much individualism, and not enough of a community structure, in the cyberspace community. The community model tends to lose sight of the special needs that some members of a community have. The community as a unit is the focus. But individuals, by definition, are not fungible. Each person has particular, unique needs that should not unthinkingly be sacrificed or ignored in order to make others comfortable or happy.

Another problematical issue for an Internet community is the practice of assuming a fictitious on-line persona. What kind of community can be forged when users are not honest about who they are, and cannot rely on what others say about themselves? Trust, an essential element for a cohesive community, is absent. Women in particular have the most to lose with fictitiously based and anonymous communities. Accountability and responsibility are lost. It is impossible to base a real community on only the benefits, with none of the responsibilities, of human interaction.

Women in Communities

One ethic of community is that the community comes first—the needs of the many come before the needs of the few. Often for women this means that their needs are put aside for the greater good. Women have had difficult roles to play in communities. They are the care givers, the ones to whom those in trouble turn. Initially, the communitarian philosophy appears congruent with feminist ethics. However, as Marilyn Friedman writes, philosophy is "a perilous ally for feminists": "Communitarians invoke a model of community focused particularly on families, neighborhoods, and nations. These sorts of communities harbor social roles and structures that have been highly oppressive for women" (1992:89). Where, she asks, are the trade unions and political action groups? Are lesbians and gays equal citizens in the communities? Are there political mothers as well as fathers?

Feminist Ethics and the Internet

There is no such thing as a single code of feminist ethics. As in all other areas of theory and practice, most feminists have encouraged a vigorous discussion of alternatives and a rejection of abstract universality. We can mention, however, several recommendations about ethics made especially by many people concerned about the traditional hierarchy of gender. These are revolutionary suggestions for changes that can come about not through violence but through mutual concern and work by women and men.

Feminist approaches to ethics often include attention to: the centrality of the well-being of children to the well-being of a people; rejection of gender and race hierarchies; entertainment that enriches and respects lives rather than entertainment that primarily serves commercial interests; connection with, rather than domination of, "nature"; the well-being of others in society as a whole; equal valuation and treatment of women and their work; policy making that enhances the equal treatment of people historically disadvantaged; and rethinking the ways that principles of equality, freedom, rights, and justice have been differentially applied to women and men.

Some of the customary principles of feminist ethics appear either to operate outside the four themes discussed above, or to point to problems with the themes. While, as noted above, there is no such thing as *the* feminist ethics, we can find some commonalities across discussions. Feminist ethics take account of women's lives, calling for alternative ways of knowing. Also, feminist ethics attend to values of cooperation, relationship, and interdependence. The variance with themes of anarchy and frontier are obvious. While the democracy and community themes are, on the surface, more compatible with feminist ethics, there are serious shortcomings in them as well.

We have offered brief critiques of the assumptions that seem to follow from some of the ideological themes used in North America to describe the Internet. There are other approaches implicitly or explicitly used in our culture that are likely to be involved in the plans the designers and users have for electronic communication.

For example, one of the ethical approaches claimed by many is that people should be guided and judged by the moral code of their society—those outside the society cannot pretend to know what is best for those inside. Feminists are among those who have pointed to problems with this "ethical relativism" approach. As Deborah Johnson asks, "How do we decide what group a person belongs to in order to know what code applies to him or her?" (Johnson 1985:11). The problems with "ethical relativism" seem particularly great if we are thinking about communication via computers. As we have noted above, recent surveys of the Internet indicate that men post much more than women. Does this mean that women are basically outsiders who should not presume to make recommendations about what kinds of behaviors are appropriate? We note this kind of reaction in the comments of the person responding to an article (about the Women, Information Technology, and Scholarship [WITS] group) that included discussion of sexual harassment on the Net: "They [the women] should learn how to grow up. . . . If they want to have men's jobs and be equal with them, then they'd better learn to be as strong as men. . . . No one is preventing them from setting up their own BBS systems [bulletin board systems] where they can play dictator . . . and enforce childish rules to clamp down on free speech . . ." (uiuc.general bulletin board, Sept. 1993). In other words, according to this critic, computer lists are basically men's, and women should either learn how to handle the harshness of the men's world or go organize their own with whatever silly rules they want. This same assumption, that the world of computer talk is basically men's, seems evident in the studies that show men becoming openly hostile when women talk as much or more than men in computer discussions. Susan Herring and her colleagues have demonstrated the ways in which men in several Internet discussion groups dominated the interaction: "men . . . first avoided addressing the women's expressed concerns, then, when women persisted, they turned on them with anger and accusations and finished off by co-opting key terms and definitions in the discussion, thereby reclaiming control of the discourse retrospectively" (Herring et al. 1995; see also Herring 1993).

"Ethical relativism" will not work well for many in a world wide web of electronic connections and communications involving both women and men. Yet it seems difficult or impossible to think in terms of everyone's codes and beliefs. How could we really begin to think about everyone?

Fortunately, many men as well as women in many countries are concerned that the Internet be a welcoming place for all. However, few of us have had much experience in actually thinking about the many, often enormous, problems that women have as women when we think about "humanity." Including women in this category will require us to think in ways for which our standard textbooks do not provide much guidance. One useful way of starting this thinking is to take the relation between parent and child[2] (rather than rational, economic, independent people in contractual relations) as the fundamental social relation and build our ideas about electronic communication from there. Not that this is necessarily where we would want to finish our analysis (see the caution by Held 1993:196), but it might help us to reconceptualize the ethics of the Internet in a useful way.

Let's see how this perspective helps us with thinking about codes for the Internet as we consider the child and the parenting as preceding the man and his contracts and freedoms (such as the "social contract," considered by many theorists, such as Hobbes, to be the essential justification of governmental authority). That is, instead of assuming that people's participation in society should be viewed as an agreement reached as a result of arms-length bargaining, we should look at participation as an extended "parent-child" relationship. This consideration is no easy task, since child and parenting come enmeshed in patriarchal practices and language. And we know that some children are abandoned, some are assaulted by their "caretakers," and others are dominated by those who would control them for as long as possible. Some parents are protective of their own but willing to ignore the plight of the children of strangers. We should not romanticize or universalize parenting. However, if we were to consider the child and the parent as the basic building block of human life, and created policies to enable children and those who parent the means and respect to take care of themselves, we would have a different plan for the world and for the Internet.

We would need to consider the importance and distinctiveness of parenting and caring in women's and men's experiences in many geographical areas. We would need to be concerned with establishing non-violent connections, and with various ways of showing respect for life and life-giving. Our concerns would not be as much about freedom of speech and the right to publish electronic pornography as about providing valuable communication tools to help children learn to be interdependent and caring of others. We would be concerned with how we could make parenting long distance more immediate and satisfactory for all. And rather than thinking about virtual reality as, primarily, "the emotional condom of the 21st century" for sex without responsibilities for others as some forecasters would have it, we could talk about developing new technologies for new ways of expressing intimacy and caring. Giving Birth rather than Mortal Kombat.

In *He, She, and It,* feminist author Marge Piercy speculates about the electronic interactions of the twenty-first century if current programming plans continue: "You watch or rent a stimmie and you enter that actor or actress. You feel what they feel. They're yours. But you don't belong to them. You are free from the demands of reciprocity" (1991:382). How different this is from developing programs built from an ethic of caring and sharing.

There is another, even more encompassing, approach we might consider. Ecofeminist theory and practice ask us to extend the ethical relationship not just to all humans but to living nature in its entirety (Gram-Hanssen 1994:63). We could consider a quantum ethics—the cosmic connectiveness that many scientists, ecofeminists, feminist spiritualists, and proponents of the Gaia hypothesis are talking about. While many of our communication classes and methodologies are still following the old science and thought patterns (including using strings of variables in precise, mathematical ways in order to try to be exact and to predict), contemporary scientists and many others have moved to new descriptions of reality and changing perceptions of the organizing principles of the universe, fluctuations that have deep implications for our understanding of communication practices. (Hypertext is one example of a new organizational form available on computers.)

As Margaret Wheatley (1994) writes about much past study of organization communication,

> Our training has been to look for big numbers, important trends, major variances. Yet it is the slight variations—soft-spoken, even whispered at first—that we need to encourage. . . . We've been so engaged in rounding things off, smoothing things over, keeping the

lid on (the metaphors are numerous), that our organizations have been dying, literally, for information they could feed on, information that was different, disconfirming, and filled with enough instability to knock the system into new life. (108)

If we are increasingly seeing new universal connections and a holism that comes from understanding the system as a system, our ethical beliefs can be expected to also undergo fluctuation, disorder, and change. In fact we can see that this is what is happening. While once a concern with ethical questions about communication systems would have been considered an aside, or a religious exercise outside discussions of the key concepts of our interactions, we are now finding that ethical concerns, under a number of names, are central to conversations about electronic networks. We have huge files, electronic and the old-fashioned kind, of memos and papers on electronic ethics—involving such issues as privacy, censorship, flaming, harassment, access, fees, and private/commercial/government relationships. And while most of these discussions are in the English language, we know that related discussions are taking place in many other languages and in many other geographical places.

We cannot, of course, even pretend to bring order to what some of us argue is valuable disorder. But paying attention to the ideological themes in our talk about electronic communication, and considering principles of feminist ethics, should help us to critique the ethics of the electronic communication patterns, develop new gender sensitivity, and offer fresh ideas about what more universal communication might become.

Notes

1. We have not included in our analysis the theme of the "information superhighway," which is perhaps the single most popular metaphor for the Internet. A highway is not an organizing principle of a society. That is, one can live on a frontier, or in an anarchy, community, or democracy—but one does not actually live on a highway. There is no particular ethical system (ethics being more than simple good manners) suited to a highway, and communication does not generally take place on the highway. Thus, while the highway metaphor works well in other situations, there simply is not much to say about ethics, communication, and highways. The very fact that the highway is the most prevalent metaphor for the Internet may, however, say something about the lack of attention focused upon interactions, as opposed to information-gathering, on the Internet.

2. We use the terms "to parent" and "parenting" in a manner synony-

mous with the usual use of the terms "to mother" and "mothering." We thus hope to participate, in a small way, in the reformulation of what it means to be a parent of either gender.

References Cited

Barlow, J. P. 1995. "Is There a There in Cyberspace?" *Utne Reader,* March–April, pp. 52–56.

Connolly, F. W. 1995. "Intellectual Honesty in the Era of Computing." *Technological Horizons in Education Journal* 22(9):86–88.

Cross, R. 1995. "Pussy and the Art of Motorcycle Maintenance." *geekgirl* 2:3–5.

East, M., and J. Kitts. 1995. "Essential CD-ROMS." *Flux* 5:28–29, 78.

Electronic Frontier Foundation. 1993. "Toward a New Public Interest Communications Policy Agenda for the Information Age: A Framework for Discussion." June 1. (Available on America Online, keyword: eff.)

Friedman, M. 1992. "Feminism and Modern Friendship: Dislocating the Community." In *Explorations in Feminist Ethics.* Ed. E. B. Cole and S. Coultrap-McQuin. Pp. 89–97. Bloomington: Indiana University Press.

Gibson, W. 1984. *Neuromancer.* New York: Ace Science Fiction Book.

Gram-Hanssen, K. 1994. "Toward an Expanded Concept of Ethics." In *Feminist Voices on Gender, Technology, and Ethics.* Ed. E. Gunnarsson and L. Troher. Pp. 55–65. Lulea, Sweden: Centre for Women's Studies, Lulea University of Technology.

Griswold, R. L. 1988. "Anglo Women and Domestic Ideology." In *Western Women: Their Land, Their Lives.* Ed. L. Schlissel, V. Ruiz, and J. Monk. Pp. 15–33. Albuquerque: University of New Mexico Press.

"Hackers." 1992. *Mondo 2000: A User's Guide to the New Edge* 1:132–35.

Held, V. 1993. *Feminist Morality: Transforming Culture, Society, and Politics.* Chicago: University of Chicago Press.

Herring, S. 1993. "Gender and Democracy in Computer-Mediated Communication." *Electronic Journal of Communication* 3(2):n.p.

Herring, S., D. Johnson, and T. DiBenedetto. 1995. "'This Discussion Is Going Too Far!': Male Resistance to Female Participation on the Internet." In *Gender Articulated: Language and the Socially-Constructed Self.* Ed. M. Bucholtz and K. Hall. Pp. 67–96. New York: Routledge.

Hiltz, S. R., and M. Turoff. 1993. *The Network Nation: Human Communication via Computer.* Rev. ed. Cambridge: MIT Press.

Internet Activities Board. 1989. Request for Comments: 1087. "Ethics and the Internet." January. (Available on the World Wide Web at http://ds.internic.net/rfc/rfc1087.txt.)

Johnson, D. G. 1985. *Computer Ethics.* Englewood Cliffs, N.J.: Prentice Hall.

Leary, T. 1991. "Cyberpunk." *Kagenna: The Ecology and Culture Frontier* [P.O. Box 15438, Vlaeburg 8018, Cape Town, South Africa] 6:7.

Mander, J. 1991. *In the Absence of the Sacred: The Failure of Technology and the Survival of the Indian Nations.* San Francisco: Sierra Club.

Matsuda, M. J. 1985. "The West and the Legal Status of Women: Explanations of Frontier Feminism." *Journal of the West* 24:47–56.

Myres, S. L. 1982. *Westering Women and the Frontier Experience, 1800–1915.* Albuquerque: University of New Mexico Press.

Namias, J. 1993. *White Captives: Gender and Ethnicity on the American Frontier.* Chapel Hill: University of North Carolina Press.

Newby, G. B. 1993. "The Maturation of Norms for Computer-Mediated Communication." *Internet Research* 3(4):30–38.

Ohajah, E. 1995. "Africa Is Being Cut Out of the Net (and No One Cares to Stop Its Freefall through Cyberspace)" [editorial]. *Minneapolis Star-Tribune,* April 14, p. 16A.

Perritt, H. H., Jr. 1992. *Metaphors for Understanding Rights and Responsibilities in Network Communities.* Villanova: School of Law, Villanova University.

Piercy, M. 1991. *He, She, and It.* New York: Fawcett Crest.

Rheingold, H. 1995. "The Virtual Community." *Utne Reader,* March–April, pp. 60–64.

Stallman, R. 1992. "The Hackers." *Mondo 2000: A User's Guide to the New Edge* 1:132.

Stoeltje, B. J. 1987. "Making the Frontier Myth: Folklore Process in a Modern Nation." *Western Folklore* 46 (October):235–53.

Wheatley, M. J. (1994). *Leadership and the New Science: Learning about Organization from an Orderly Universe.* San Francisco: Berrett-Koehler.

Women, Information Technology, and Scholarship (WITS). 1995. *Gender Equity in Global Communication Networks: A Global Alert.* [Brochure available from WITS, Graduate School of Library and Information Science, University of Illinois at Urbana-Champaign, 112 LIS, Champaign, IL 61820.]

"Women's Leadership Network Uses Internet to Fight Conservatives." 1995. *focusPOINT,* April 19, p. 5.

Yang, Jeff. 1995. "Laws of the Jungle: How to Avoid Getting Your Ass Kicked at the Arcade." *Flux* 1(1):28–31.

Contributors

Ronald C. Arnett, chair and professor in the Department of Communication at Duquesne University, is a past editor of the *Journal of Communication and Religion* and has been on a number of editorial boards of communication and business ethics journals. He is the author of *Dwell in Peace: Applying Nonviolence to Everyday Relationships* (1980), *Communication and Community* (1986), for which he won the Religious Speech Communication Association Book Award, and *Dialogic Education: Conversation about Ideas and between Persons* (1992), and the coeditor of *The Reach of Dialogue: Confirmation, Voice, and Community* (with Rob Anderson and Kenneth Cissna, 1994). His teaching and research interests include the philosophy of communication, ethics, and interpersonal/organization conflict.

James W. Chesebro, professor in the Department of Communication at Indiana State University, was the 1996 president of the Speech Communication Assocation and is a past editor of *Communication Quarterly* and a past director of education services for the Speech Communication Association. The recipient of distinguished service awards from the Eastern Communication Association and the Kenneth Burke Society, he is the editor of *Extensions of the Burkeian System* (1993), coeditor of *Methods of Rhetorical Criticism: A Twentieth-Century Perspective* (1990), coauthor of *Computer-Mediated Communication* (1989), and author of "The Media Reality: Epistemological Functions of Media in Cultural Systems" (SCA's 1985 Golden Anniversary Award monograph). His teaching and research interests include media criticism, Burkeian rhetorical theory and criticism, rhetorical theory and criticism, interpersonal communication, and audience analysis and prediction.

Clifford G. Christians is a professor of journalism and media ethics and a research professor of communications at the University of Illinois at Urbana-Champaign, where he also directs the doctoral program in communications. A past editor of *Critical Studies in Mass Communication,* he has published over seventy articles and book chapters and is the author or coauthor of four books, among them *Media Ethics: Cases and Moral Reasoning* (with Mark Faceler and Kim Rotzoll, 4th ed., 1995) and *Good News: Social Ethics and the Press* (with Mark Faceler and John Ferre, 1993). His teaching and research interests include the philosophy of technology, the philosophy of social science, communication theory, and professional ethics.

James A. Jaksa is a professor of communication and codirector of the Center for the Study of Ethics at Western Michigan University. He has published numerous articles in the areas of communication ethics, moral development, and pedagogy and is the coauthor of *Communication Ethics: Methods of Analysis* (with Michael S. Pritchard, 2d ed., 1994) and *Voices from Silence: The Trappists Speak* (with Ernest Stech, 1980) and the coeditor of *Responsible Communication: Ethical Issues in Business, Industry, and the Professions* (with Michael S. Pritchard, forthcoming). He also directed and served as editor of the *Proceedings* of the 1990, 1992, and 1994 National Communication Ethics Conferences and is directing the 1996 conference.

Richard L. Johannesen is a professor in and former chair of the Department of Communication at Northern Illinois University. He has published numerous articles and book chapters and is the author of *Ethics in Human Communication* (4th ed., 1996), the editor of *Ethics and Persuasion: Selected Readings* (1967), and the coeditor of *Contemporary American Speeches: A Sourcebook of Speech Forms and Principles* (with R. R. Allen and Wil A. Linkugel, 7th ed., 1992). His teaching and research interests include virtue ethics, character, and political communication.

Cheris Kramarae is a professor of speech communication and the director of women's studies at the University of Illinois at Urbana-Champaign. Her coedited books include *Amazons, Bluestockings, and Crones* (with Paula Treichler and Ann Russo, 1992), *Women, Information Technology, and Scholarship (WITS)* (with H. Jeanie Taylor and Maureen Ebben, 1993), and *The Knowledge Explosion: Generations of Feminist Scholarship* (with Dale Spender, 1992). She is the editor of *Technology and Women's Voices: Keeping in Touch* (1988) and also general editor, with Dale Spender, of a forthcoming international women's studies encyclopedia. Her teaching and research interests include gender and language, language and power, and women's involvement with the Internet.

Jana Kramer is an attorney in practice in Minneapolis, Minnesota. The author of articles on legal and feminist issues regarding the Internet and on feminist utopias, she has enduring interests in feminism, the law, and the social impact of emerging technologies.

Josina M. Makau is an academic planner and interim dean of arts, human communication, and creative technologies at California State University, Monterey Bay. An associate editor of several journals, including the *Quarterly Journal of Speech Research, Communication Monographs, Free Speech Yearbook,* and the *Journal of Applied Communication Research,* she has published essays on practical reasoning, pedagogy, and communication ethics. She is the author of *Reasoning and Communication: Thinking Critically about Arguments* (1990). Her teaching and research interests include moral development, communication ethics and argumentation theory, practice, and pedagogy.

Barbara Paige Pointer, a professor of ethnic studies and folklore at California State University, Hayward, was a corecipient of the CSU Woman of the Year Award in 1990. She has published numerous articles and book chapters on slave narrative tradition, the black legendary hero tradition, and educational equity and social policy. Her current project is an interpretive study of American female humor, entitled *American Funny Women: The Female Comic Persona as an Index of Changing Role Status.* During 1994–96 she was a visiting professor at Oregon State University, where she also served as acting director of the Difference, Power, and Discrimination Program.

Michael S. Pritchard is chair of the Department of Philosophy at Western Michigan University, director of the Center for the Study of Ethics in Society, and codirector of the Center for Philosophy and Critical Thinking in Schools. He has published more than thirty articles and book chapters and is the author or coauthor of seven books, among them *On Becoming Responsible* (1991), *Communication and Ethics: Methods of Analysis* (with James A. Jaksa, 2d ed., 1994), and *Engineering Ethics: Concepts and Cases* (with C. E. Harris and Michael J. Rabins, 1995). His teaching and research interests include moral theory, moral development, and applied and practical ethics.

Lea P. Stewart, a professor in the Department of Communication and director of the Ph.D. program in communication, information, and library studies at Rutgers University, is an associate editor of the *Howard Journal of Communication* and the *Journal of Applied Communication Research* and a past president of the Organization for the Study of Communciation Language and Gender. A widely pursued workshop leader on issues of conflict and diversity, she has published over thirty-five articles and book chapters and is the coauthor of four books, among them *Communication and Gender* (with P. J. Cooper, A. D. Stewart, and S. Friedley, 3d ed., 1996) and *Building Bridges: Interpersonal Skills for a Changing World* (with W. B. Gudykunst, S. Ting-Toomey, and S. Sudweeks, 1995). Her teaching and research interests include communication and gender, cultural diversity in organizations, and whistle blowing.

Dolores V. Tanno is an associate professor in the Department of Communication Studies at California State University, San Bernardino, and a member-at-large of the Speech Communication Association's legislative council. An associate editor of *Women's Studies in Communication* and a member of the *Howard Journal of Communications* editorial board, she is also coeditor of the *International and Intercultural Communication Annual* (with Alberto Gonzalez, 1995-97) and *La Raza: Exploring Latinographic y Latinagraphic Criticism* (with Alberto Gonzalez, 1996). Her teaching and research interests include intercultural communication, rhetorical theory and criticism, and communication ethics.

Julia T. Wood, the Nelson R. Hariston Distinguished Professor of Communication Studies at the University of North Carolina at Chapel Hill, is cofounder of the National Conference on Gender and Communication Research and editor of the *Journal of Applied Communication Research.* She has published more than fifty articles and book chapters and has authored eighteen books, among them *Toward the 21st Century: The Future of Communication* (1995), and *Gendered Lives: Communication, Gender, and Culture* (1996). She is also the coeditor of *Who Cares: Wom-*

en, Care, and Culture (with Richard Gregg, 1994). Her teaching and re-search interests include the intersections among communication, gender, culture, and personal relationships.

Gale Auletta Young is a professor of speech communication and codi-rector of the Center for the Study of Intercultural Relations at Califor-nia State University, Hayward. A nationally recognized consultant on issues of race and diversity, she was a corecipient of the CSU Woman of the Year Award in 1990. She has published numerous articles and book chapters on race relations, diversity, and education policy and practices. She is the coauthor of *Unmasking the Myths of Racism in the Classroom* (with Terry Jones, 1994) and *Confronting Diversity Issues on Campus* (with Benjamin Bowser and Terry Jones, 1993) and the coeditor of *The Inclu-sive University: Multicultural Perspectives in Higher Education* (with Ben-jamin Bowser and Terry Jones, 1995).

Index

Girls: communication cultures and, 10;
  Internet and, 226–29, 231–33, 235,
  236–41
Glazer, N., 75
Global ecological problems, 221
Global order: ethnicity and media and,
  187–203. *See also* High-risk technolo-
  gies; Technology
Gobineau, A. de, 76
Goffman, E., 147n.9
Goleman, D., 101, 146n.5
Goodness: of community, 29–31, 44. *See
  also* Common good
Gore, T., 163, 164, 165
Government: high-risk technologies and,
  218, 220–21; tobacco industry and,
  218. *See also* First Amendment; Four-
  teenth Amendment; Law
Graber, M. A., 159
Grady, W., 198
Gram-Hanssen, K., 240
Grassroots media production, 194–201,
  202n.4
Great White, 163
Greenwalt, K., 175
Gregoria Apaza Center for the Advance-
  ment of Women (CPMGA), 195
Griffin, C., 59, 60, 64n.6
Griswold, R. L., 230
Gross, L., 143–44
Growth. *See* Personal growth
Gudykunst, W. B., 99, 122
Guerilla warfare: in media production,
  194–97
Guinier, L., 106n.6
Gunnemann, J. P., 223nn.2–3
Guns 'N' Roses, 163
Gunther, G., 172
Gutmann, A., 181

Habermas, J., 203n.8
Hackers, 230–31
Haddon, A. C., 77
Haiman, F. S., 103, 171–73, 174, 175,
  176–77
Hamer, D. H., 132
Hand, L., 177

Haraway, D., 8
Harding, S., 8, 9, 118
Hare, R. M., 203n.9
Hariman, R., 75
Harlan, J. M., 172
Harm: from words, 102. *See also* High-
  risk technologies
Harmonic discourse, 119
Harriman, A., 111
Harris, C. E., 223n.3
Hartsock, N. C. M., 8
Hate speech, 102–4, 169–78, 180–81
Hauerwas, S., 44
Hayes, J. J., 128
Heathenism: ethnicity and, 75–76, 91
Hecht, M., 80
Hedonics: same-sex relationships and,
  139–40, 147n.8
Heidegger, M., 192
Held, V., 232, 234, 239
Hennessy, R., 8
Hentoff, N., 172, 173, 174
Herdt, G., 128
Herrick, J. A., 64n.6
Herring, S., 235, 238–39
Hierarchy: community and, 199; ethnic-
  ity and, 76–77; gender and, 114, 115,
  122–23; hate speech and, 176, 178–
  79; judgment of differences and, 15;
  multicultural communication and, 75;
  pornography and, 167, 169. *See also*
  Paternalism
Higher education: dialogue and, 82; hate
  speech and, 102–3; Internet policies
  and, 229; language and equity and,
  89–107; political structure of, 96. *See
  also* Pedagogy; Professorate
High-risk sexual behaviors: same-sex
  relationships and, 142, 147n.10
High-risk technologies, 206–25; "circle
  of poison" debate and, 214–15, 219–
  20; communication ethics and, 207–
  8, 209–23; ecological problems and,
  221; exporting, 206, 207, 214–15,
  216, 217–18, 220, 224–25n.19;
  government and, 218, 220–21; infant
  formula, 218, 225n.24; informed